The Art of Jewish Living

A Time to
Mourn,
a Time to
Comfort
2nd Edition

A Guide to Jewish Bereavement

Dr. Ron Wolfson
with a Foreword by Rabbi David J. Wolpe

JEWISH LIGHTS Publishing

A *Time to Mourn, a Time to Comfort,* 2nd Edition:
A *Guide to Jewish Bereavement*

2011 Quality Paperback Edition

Requests to the Publisher for permission should be addressed to Turner Publishing Company, 4507 Charlotte Avenue, Suite 100, Nashville, Tennessee, (615) 255-2665, fax (615) 255-5081, E-mail: submissions@turnerpublishing.com.

The University of Judaism is an academic institution dedicated to the study and enhancement of Jewish life.

The Federation of Jewish Men's Clubs gratefully acknowledges the kindness of the following for permission to quote from these copyrighted works:

"A Time to Be Born and a Time to Die," by Elliot N. Dorff, University of Judaism, Los Angeles, California, 1992. "How to Watch a Brother Die," from *Decade Dance* by Michael LaSalle, Alyson Publications, Boston, Massachusetts, 1990. "Ethical Wills," from *So That Your Values Live On: Ethical Wills and How to Prepare Them* by Jack Riemer and Nathaniel Stampfer, Jewish Lights Publishing, Woodstock, Vermont, 1991. "It Is Never Too Late," from *Passages in Poetry* by Harold M. Schulweis, Valley Beth Shalom, Los Angeles, California, 1990. "Talking to My Grandfather," from *A Hearing Heart* by Danny Siegel, Town House Press, Pittsboro, North Carolina, 1992. *The World is a Narrow Bridge: Stories that Celebrate Hope and Healing,* edited by Diane Arieff, Sweet Louise Productions, Los Angeles, California, 2004.

Library of Congress Cataloging-in-Publication Data
Wolfson, Ron.
A time to mourn, a time to comfort : a guide to Jewish bereavement by Ron Wolfson ; with a foreword by David J. Wolpe.— 2nd ed.
p. cm. — (The art of Jewish living series)
Includes bibliographical references.
ISBN: 978-1-58023-253-1 (quality pb)
ISBN: 978-1-68162-967-4 (hc)
1. Jewish mourning customs. 2. Consolation (Judaism) I. Title. II. Series.
BM712.W65 2005
296.4'45—dc22
2004029855

Manufactured in the United States of America
Published by Jewish Lights Publishing
An imprint of Turner Publishing Company
Nashville, Tennessee 37209
www.jewishlights.com

Books in the Art of Jewish Living Series
by Dr. Ron Wolfson

Hanukkah, 2nd Edition:
The Family Guide to Spiritual Celebration

Passover, 2nd Edition:
The Family Guide to Spiritual Celebration

Shabbat, 2nd Edition:
The Family Guide to Preparing for and Celebrating the Sabbath

Other Books by Dr. Ron Wolfson

God's To-Do List:
103 Ways to Be an Angel and Do God's Work on Earth

The Spirituality of Welcoming:
How to Transform Your Congregation into a Sacred Community

The Seven Questions You're Asked in Heaven:
Reviewing & Renewing Your Life on Earth

For

Jules Porter—

leader, friend, mensch—

who has brought the Art of Jewish Living

to so many

Contents

Foreword by Rabbi David J. Wolpe ix

Introduction x

Acknowledgments for the Second Edition xvii

Acknowledgments for the First Edition xviii

How to Read This Book xx

Biographies of the Voices in This Book xxi

The Art of Jewish Mourning and Comforting xxvii

PART 1: FACING DEATH 1

The Process of Dying 5

Visiting the Dying 8

Talking with the Dying 11

Caregiving 14

PART 2: A DEATH IN THE FAMILY 17

Medical Issues and Jewish Law 22

Advance Directives for Health Care 24

The *Vidui* Confessional 25

What Happens When a Person Dies? 29

Special Cases 31

Neonatal Death 33

Miscarriage 40

The Death of a Child 43

AIDS-Related Deaths 46

PART 3: THE ART OF JEWISH MOURNING 51

Grief-Work and the Experience of Jewish Mourning 54

The Phases of Jewish Bereavement 62

PART 4: FROM THE DEATH TO THE FUNERAL   65

For Mourners   70

    "What Do I Do Now?"   70

    Making Funeral Arrangements   72

    Helping Grieving Children   93

    Preparing for *Shiva*   103

For Comforters   106

    When a Friend Experiences a Death—
      The Art of Jewish Comforting   106

    What Can You Do?   107

    Close Friends   109

    Friends   114

PART 5: THE FUNERAL   117

For Mourners   119

    The Service   122

    How to Write and Deliver a Eulogy   128

    The Kaddish   130

    The Mourner's Kaddish   131

    Questions about the Funeral   137

    Sephardic Burial Customs   144

    Special Cases   146

For Comforters   149

    How to Attend a Funeral   151

PART 6: *SHIVA*   155

For Mourners   157

    Shiva   160

    How Long Is *Shiva?*   161

    The Observance of *Shiva*   165

    The Open House—or—Who's the Host? Who's the Guest?   172

    Seudat Ha-havra'ah—The Meal of Condolence   174

Prayer Services during *Shiva*   179

Questions about *Shiva* Services   185

Sephardic Customs during *Shiva*   187

Children during *Shiva*   188

Dealing with the Aftermath   190

"Getting Up" from *Shiva*   191

"Sitting *Shiva*" out of Town   193

For Comforters   195

How to Make a *Shiva* Call   197

"What Do I Say?"   201

"Don't Take My Grief Away"   205

Hearing with a Heart   209

What You Can Say   212

Sharing Memories   218

Additional Reflections for Mourners   221

How to Talk to Comforters   222

Family Time   224

Planning for the Future   226

PART 7: "WHAT CAN I WRITE?"   229

For Comforters   231

How to Write a Condolence Letter   232

For Mourners   237

How to Respond to Comforters' Letters   237

PART 8: *SHLOSHIM* TO *YIZKOR*   239

For Mourners   241

Shloshim   244

Questions about *Shloshim*   245

Saying Kaddish   247

Gravestones and Unveilings   251

Visiting the Grave   254

Memorial Tablets	257
Yahrtzeit	258
Yizkor	263
Naming Children	267
Excessive Grief	268
Exhumation	269
Remembering the Deceased	270
Starting Over	272
Being Single Again	274
For Comforters	276
Remembering the Living	276
The Community and the Bereaved	280

PART 9: HOW TO PREPARE FOR YOUR OWN DEATH — 285

Before Funeral Arrangements	287
An Ethical Will	291
A Living Will	296
Estate Instructions	310
Distribution of Personal Items	313

PART 10: AFTERLIFE — 315

What Happens after We Die?	320

Epilogue	324

APPENDICES — 327

Estate Instructions	329
Estate Planning Checklist	332
Glossary	333
Selected Bibliography	335

Foreword

When someone dies, we are faced with two sorts of questions: specific questions about what to do in the moment of grief and general questions about the meaning of life and death. It is easy to be overwhelmed and lose ourselves in all the issues raised by death: How do we care for ourselves, and for those close to us who are grieving? How do we think about death, and explain it? How do we reestablish a relationship with the world and with God?

These questions lie at the heart of the Jewish approach toward death. Judaism is honest without brutality, compassionate without evasion. It helps us cope with death, and equally important, it guides us in helping others when they are bereaved. Like every great religious tradition, Judaism shows its deepest wisdom in times of loss.

Judaism offers guidance in matters both of action and of attitude. It gives us specifics about how to behave in the face of death. And it urges general explanations about how death fits into the scheme of life and of faith.

Ron Wolfson's book captures the best in Judaism's approach. It is honest, tender, and wise. *A Time to Mourn, a Time to Comfort* speaks in many voices: the voices of those who have endured grief, the voices of rabbis who deal daily with tragedy, the voices of those who are spiritually searching, and the voices of those who have found their own path through dark times.

Throughout this book, the reader will learn how people today seek traditional answers to cope with life and loss. How do I arrange for a funeral, and why did God do this to me? Both questions are part of encountering the end of life. In these pages we hear answers, ancient and modern, that speak to our hearts.

Judaism finds healing in God, in the community, and in the resources of each individual soul. It illuminates a path by which we can, step by step, be led to the affirmation of the biblical Job: "The Lord has given, and the Lord has taken away; Blessed be the name of the Lord."

Rabbi David J. Wolpe

Introduction

The first funeral I ever attended was at the Beth El Cemetery on a tranquil hillside among the cornfields on the outskirts of Omaha, Nebraska. I was twenty-two years old. My Bubbe, Ida Paperny, had died after a long illness, and I had returned from college to attend her funeral. Having grown up in a family that shielded children from the reality of death, I now stood at her gravesite, quietly sobbing, as much at the sight of my bereaved parents and relatives as for my beloved grandmother. It was at that moment that I first realized that the wise and powerful Jewish rituals surrounding death are as much for the survivors as for the deceased.

Two years later, my Zayde, Louis Paperny, lay on his deathbed in Clarkson Hospital. My wife, Susie, and I were summoned to Omaha to his bedside, where he lay surrounded by his family. Since Bubbe died, I had studied Jewish mourning practices in college and was intellectually more aware of what was about to happen. But I was totally unprepared emotionally to witness my Zayde's death.

My grandfather Louis was a larger-than-life figure. Well known throughout the region as a generous and colorful businessman and philanthropist, Zayde Louie was the patriarch of our family who lavished love on everyone, particularly his grandchildren. Whether playing gin rummy, or taking us to his box behind home plate at the Triple A ballpark, or locking us in his patented powerful leg scissors, each of us nine grandchildren were known to him as "the best boy/girl in the United States of America." Coming to America as a humble fruit peddler at the beginning of the century, he built Louis Market into the largest grocery store in three states. Short, stocky, and tough, he possessed an unbelievable strength developed over many years of hauling heavy sacks of potatoes and other produce by hand. Yet, he was one of the most gentle and emotional men I have ever met; his eyes quickly filled with tears at the simple sight of a grandchild crawling into his lap.

I loved Zayde for all that he stood for: his strength, his independence, his caring for those less fortunate, his popularity as a public figure, his devotion to Jewish life. He lay in the hospital bed, weakened by many years of illness and totally dependent on the doctors and technologies of modern medicine. The end was near. Zayde had slipped into a coma, a deep and peaceful sleep. The physicians had done all they could; the machines had been removed. Surrounded by his devoted daughters, sons-in-law, and grandchildren, Louis Paperny was about to leave this world. As he drew his last breath, an incredible calm came over his body, and I whispered the words he could not: *"Shma Yisrael, Adonai Eloheinu, Adonai Eḥad*: Hear O Israel, *Adonai* is our God, *Adonai* is One."

I had no idea what would happen next, but what did occur was certainly nothing like the movies. No nurse came into the room to cover the body with a sheet. No doctor came in to pronounce him dead. Rather, we, his family, sat close to him, sobbing and weeping, letting the reality of the finality sink in. Zayde was gone, and now we had to embark upon the ancient rites of coping with death in the Jewish tradition, rites designed both to honor the dead and empower the living.

In stark contrast to the weeks and months of waiting as Zayde "slipped away," his burial would be completed in less than twenty-four hours. Within minutes of his death, the rabbi and funeral home had been contacted, a time set, an obituary written, and a lightning-fast series of phone calls made to alert the community to the news. Since all the arrangements were handled by my mother and her sisters, I felt lost and frustrated at not being able to do something to express my grief—or my love of Zayde. Then I remembered something I had learned in my studies that enabled me to act.

I announced to my parents that I wanted to be a *shomer*, an attendant, to my grandfather's body. I wanted to go to the mortuary and stay with Zayde throughout the night. Traditionally, people from the community are asked or hired to fulfill this act of *kevod ha-meit*, honoring the deceased. Frankly, my parents had never heard of such a thing, but they quickly gave their blessing. The next thing I knew, I was at the door of the Jewish Funeral Home, ready to fulfill the *mitzvah* (commandment) of *shmirah*.

It was the first time I had ever stepped foot in a mortuary, and to be quite honest, it gave me the shivers. The thought of spending the night in a place with a dead body was at best disconcerting. Yet, the wonderful old man who greeted me at the door quickly dispelled any feelings of doubt. He thanked me for coming and praised me for my decision. When I expressed curiosity about the other rituals of preparing the body for burial, he took me into the room where *taharah,* the ritual preparation of the body, was performed. I saw what looked like an operating room, a clean and sterile environment in which the body is lovingly washed and shrouded according to the ancient rites. The members of the *ḥevra kadisha,* the group of volunteer laypeople who prepare the body for burial, had already been to the funeral home to do this *mitzvah* for my grandfather. The funeral home director explained why the body is not to be left alone and suggested that I read Psalms or study the Bible to pass the time. Usually, a stranger from the community is asked to be the *shomer.* "What a wonderful *mitzvah* you are doing for your Zayde," he said to me as he left the home.

Suddenly, I was there by myself, except of course for Zayde in the next room. It was an eerie feeling, but I did not feel like I was alone. I picked up a book of Psalms and began reading the Hebrew to myself. Thankfully, my brothers Bobby and Doug and a couple of cousins decided to join me throughout the night. We reminisced about Zayde and the truly wonderful times we spent with him.

The time flew by, and before we knew it, morning had broken. The hearse arrived to bring the body to the synagogue for the funeral. I didn't want to leave Zayde for a minute, so my mother had sent my suit to the funeral home and I changed there.

It is said that participating in the rituals surrounding death is the most selfless act of love in all of Jewish tradition because the deceased cannot thank you or repay your kindness. That is true, although the love and thanks I saw in my mother's eyes when we met at the synagogue for Zayde's funeral was indeed a gift to me.

Perhaps because I was so tired, or perhaps because my task had been completed, I cannot remember much about the funeral. Nor do I remember much about the seven-day *shiva* period of mourning that followed, except that for the first time I began to appreciate in depth the great wisdom in the Jewish approach to grief. As the week progressed, the intense emotions of the first days gave way to reflections on Zayde's life and achievements. Bubbe and Zayde's house, the center of our extended family, became a hub of never-ending activity. There were daily prayer services attended by family and friends. There were lots of people dropping by to offer their condolences. There was a steady stream of food. There were hundreds of condolence cards and donations in memory of Zayde, many from his loyal customers over the years, mostly Christian neighbors who adored and admired the man they knew simply as "Louie." By the time *shiva* ended, the grieving process had progressed, and most of us were ready to move on to the next stage and resume life and work, filled with the memories of this incredible man. *Zikhrono livrakhah*—may his memory be for a blessing.

I have been bereaved, but I have not yet been a mourner. As contradictory as that sounds, it is true. I have lost a child, but I have not mourned her.

Susie and I were married for three years before "we" got pregnant. I say "we" because throughout the uneventful pregnancy, I felt as close to the baby-to-be as a father could. I marvelled at every stage of development during the nine months, especially when the baby moved. What an amazing feeling it is to touch a human being *in potentia* within the womb! A leg or an arm would push out from Susie's belly, seemingly anxious to come out and play.

Pregnancy is a time of great excitement and wonderful dreams about what will be. Will it be a girl or boy? Will she look like Susie or me? What will we name him or her? How will having a child change our lives? We had taken Lamaze childbirth classes and awaited the due date. Despite the superstitions about setting up a nursery, we had ordered the basic furniture and bought a few toys. We hadn't thought for even an instant about the possibility that something could go wrong, terribly wrong.

Our first child was born full term on the afternoon of May 6, 1974, and died thirteen hours later. The baby had become stressed during a prolonged labor, and Susie was rushed into an emergency Caesarean section. Due to the stress, the baby had ingested contaminated embryonic fluid, a medical condition known as meconium aspiration. Despite the valiant efforts of a team of neonatal specialists throughout the night, there was no way to save her. The baby had been rushed from the delivery room to the neonatal intensive care unit of Children's Hospital, across the street from Barnes Hospital where Susie remained.

Susie's parents stayed with her, and I waited through the night at Children's with my parents. The doctors and nurses were superb, bringing us updates on the baby's condition, but holding out little hope. At one point, a social worker suggested I see the baby. It was a heart-wrenching moment. I spent most of the night crying, thinking about Susie and how devastating this loss would be for her.

Susie had spent the night recovering from the operation in the last room at the end of the hall on the maternity floor. The first inkling she had that something was wrong came when a nurse walked into the room and took down several decorative pictures of smiling mothers holding their newborns. I talked to her by phone, admitting that there was a problem, suggesting that she try to rest from the ordeal of the labor and operation. Early in the morning, an intern, a terrific young man who had worked all night on the case, came into the waiting room to give me the news, but his crying eliminated the need for words. The shock overwhelmed me, even though I knew it was coming. I literally ran across the street to the hospital wing where Susie had been taken. "She died" were the only words I could get out before collapsing into her arms. We cried together for a long time at this most unhappy ending. Little did I know that the ordeal had just begun.

No one knew how to handle this tragedy—no one. The nurses moved Susie from the maternity floor to the urology ward to "save her" the pain of hearing the sounds of babies. The obstetrician came to say he was sorry and then warned us that, because he had had to do a C-section, he would have to add $350 to his fee. Our parents, expecting their first grandchild, were devastated. Our friends rushed to the hospital to offer comfort, but most only exacerbated the hurt with comments like: "You're young. You'll have other children." "It'll be okay." Well, it was definitely not okay.

Jewish tradition failed us, too. What should have been a moment of supreme joy had become the ultimate nightmare. Instead of rejoicing as new parents, we were plunged into intense grief as mourners. Except, according to Jewish law, there was no mourning for our baby.

As incredible as it seems to the modern mind, traditional Jewish practice stipulates that there is to be no official mourning for an infant who dies before reaching thirty days of maturity. There are historical reasons for this. In the Middle Ages, large numbers of infants did not survive birth. To the legal authorities of the time, relieving parents of the obligation to mourn a stillborn or an infant less than a month old was viewed as lifting a great burden from them. But to us, it was a great robbery—stealing the traditional forms of bereavement at the precise moment we needed them most. There was no funeral—the cantor arranged for the mortuary to take the baby to the cemetery for burial. There was no *shiva*—even though many friends and family came to our home to offer their condolences and support. There was no gravestone—she was buried in a tiny unmarked grave in a special section of the cemetery. There was no *yahrtzeit*, no *Yizkor*, no memorials. It's as if the tradition wanted the memory of the experience to be wiped out completely, as if it never happened.

I bought it. My reaction was not to mourn. "Let's forget about this and look ahead to the future," I reasoned. "We'll get pregnant again. We're moving to Los Angeles. We'll make a fresh start." For Susie, the loss was overwhelming. She was plunged into enormous grief, anger, and pain. Despite the assurances of doctors, social workers, and me that we would recover, Susie felt unheard and abandoned. And Judaism offered her no vehicle for her grief, no status as a mourner. Ironically, for a tradition that is so wise in most matters of loss, its answer for the death of an infant was hollow and unhelpful.

We moved to Los Angeles and came under the care of a wonderful doctor specializing in high-risk pregnancies. It took two years for us to get pregnant again—two years of unresolved mourning for Susie and two years of denial for me. After a very carefully monitored pregnancy, we celebrated the birth of Havi Michele. Two years later, Michael Louis was born. Seven years after the death of our first baby, Susie joined the first support group for mothers experiencing neonatal death ever held in Los Angeles and finally began to resolve her grief. To this day, I feel I have never truly mourned the loss of our first baby. Perhaps, just perhaps, if the tradition had offered me some way to mourn, I might have been able to cope with this loss in a healthier way.

It was a Sunday night about 10:30 p.m. I had just fallen asleep when the phone rang. Susie took the call and then hurriedly awakened me. "Jerry Weber's been shot!" she exclaimed. I couldn't believe my ears, yet, in an instant, we were on our way to UCLA Medical Center. We didn't say a word during the fifteen-minute drive, fearing the worst, hoping it was all a mistake.

We found our dear friend Sally collapsed on the floor of a waiting room in the emergency department in the throes of uncontrollable sobbing. When she saw us, she began to yell, "They killed him, they killed him!" as she fell into our arms. The shock was overwhelming. "What happened?" we asked the stranger who had been with Sally from the moment the incident occurred and had called us to the hospital. "They were at a drive-up automatic teller machine and two guys robbed them in the car. Jerry gave them the money and then tried to drive away, but they shot him," she explained. Sally cried, "He gave them the money, his wallet ... forty dollars. For forty lousy dollars, they killed him!"

That terrible night plunged the Weber family and their many, many friends into a nightmare of grief and loss. Jerry's violent death hit the community like a sledgehammer. A beloved communal worker, eulogized by his rabbi, Harold Schulweis, as the *shadḫan* (matchmaker) of the community, Jerry was well known and admired for his work as the founding director of the Council on Jewish Life of the Los Angeles Jewish Federation. His funeral was attended by more than a thousand people representing virtually every movement and organization in Los Angeles Jewry.

Even with the enormous shock of Jerry's sudden death, Sally wanted the *shiva* for Jerry to be an experience that would honor the Jewish tradition he loved so much and offer those who visited warm memories of this unique man. Thus, each prayer service was supplemented by a brief study session offered by one of Jerry's coterie of rabbinic friends. Each visitor was given a sheet of paper on which to write memories of Jerry that were shared with the family and anyone who wished to read them. Even the usual petty conversations were discouraged in favor of reflections on Jerry's life. In an extraordinary week that saw hundreds of visitors come through the Weber home, Sally and her family were comforted by the many expressions of concern and shared grief, but also by the warm memories of Jerry and his impact on all of us. *Zikhrono livrakhah*—may his memory be for a blessing.

These experiences with death, loss, and grief have had a major impact on my life, as a human being and as an educator. The inevitability of death means that each of us will at one time or another be mourner and comforter. How to mourn? How to comfort? These are the subjects of this book.

Acknowledgments for the Second Edition

When the original edition of *A Time to Mourn, a Time to Comfort* was first published as a volume in the Art of Jewish Living series, a project of the Federation of Jewish Men's Clubs and the University of Judaism, it was intended to be a text used in seminars and courses about the Jewish bereavement process. Much to our surprise, many rabbis began distributing copies of the book to mourners at the time of loss, despite the depth and breadth of the material. It appears that, for many, the appetite to know the hows, whats, and whys of Jewish mourning is considerable.

In this volume, *A Time to Mourn, a Time to Comfort, Second Edition,* we have retained much of the text of the first edition and updated the references and resources. We have added a story about those unsung heroes in our midst—the caregivers who attend the dying with compassion and love. It is also good to report that the community is far more sensitive today to the needs of those parents experiencing miscarriage and neonatal loss.

Thanks to the talented and caring staff of Jewish Lights Publishing, beginning with its visionary leader, Stuart M. Matlins. Stuart recognized the value and impact of the Art of Jewish Living books and has brought them to the attention of a wide audience. Amanda Dupuis, senior project editor, is a superb editor. She and her colleagues have brought an accessible and warm style to the book.

Inevitably, death claims us all. The voices of several of those interviewed for the first edition have been physically silenced, but their wisdom lives through these pages. May the memories of Herman Feifel and Richard Lopata be a blessing.

May God continue to comfort all those who are among the mourners of Zion and Jerusalem and sustain those who love them.

Ron Wolfson
University of Judaism
Los Angeles, California

Acknowledgments for the First Edition

This volume is the fifth in the Art of Jewish Living series, a project of the Federation of Jewish Men's Clubs and the University of Judaism. The other publications—*Shabbat, Passover,* and *Hanukkah*—have been welcomed by those seeking to infuse new meaning and creativity into age-old Jewish celebrations.

The acknowledgments begin with the creator of the Art of Jewish Living series, Jules Porter. An extraordinary man and Jew, Jules epitomizes the best in Jewish lay leadership. His commitment to renewing Jewish practice in our generation is unwavering. In addition to his responsibilities as a past president of the FJMC and board member of the University of Judaism, Jules is serving as president of Sinai Temple, a major Conservative congregation in the West. The Art of Jewish Living is his labor of love, and anyone touched by any one of these books is indebted to Jules Porter.

The Federation of Jewish Men's Clubs is led by outstanding lay and professional leadership. The current president, J. Harold Nissen, and the Art of Jewish Living chairman, Ken Bravo, both deserve recognition for their efforts to bring quality programming and materials to the Conservative movement. Rabbi Charles Simon, executive director of the FJMC, was very helpful in shaping this text.

My colleagues at the University of Judaism continue to support my work in Jewish family education. Thanks to Dr. David Lieber, president emeritus, and new president Rabbi Robert Wexler for their encouragement. The manuscript was enriched by the comments of Rabbi Elliot Dorff and Rabbi Joel Roth, both members of the Committee on Jewish Law and Standards of the Rabbinical Assembly of America. The suggestions of Rabbi James Michaels and Ann Smith, who field-tested the text in a course on Jewish bereavement at Temple Israel in Wilkes-Barre, Pennsylvania, were very helpful. A special word of gratitude is due Bruce and Shelley Whizin for their enormous trust and faith in my work. Thanks to my colleague David J. Wolpe, for his meaningful words in the Foreword.

On the technical side, the book has been skillfully constructed by an outstanding creative team. Linda Watson and Gail Minkow lent their organizational talents, Jane Golub, Alan Rowe and their colleagues at Alef Type & Design provided the design, and Jules Porter and his staff did the beautiful photography. My good friend Joel Lurie Grishaver applied his outstanding editorial skills to the project. Thanks to them all for producing an appealing volume.

The individuals and families interviewed for the book provide its warmth and humanity. They graciously offered their experiences, insights, pains, and triumphs so that others facing the task of mourning and comforting can do so in a healthy and healing way. Thanks to Rabbi Harold Schulweis, Rabbi Bernard Lipnick, Rabbi Jack Riemer, Rabbi Moshe Rothblum, Rabbi Ben Zion Bergman, Rabbi Sam Joseph, Rabbi Sharon Kleinbaum, Dr. Herman Fiefel, David Techner, Lois Rothblum, Tamara Greenebaum, Benjamin Dwoskin, Richard Lopata, Sandy Goodglick, Alan Shulman, Allen Brown, Saralei Foote, David Novak, Carol Starin, Dennis Gura, Ann Metnick, Abram Kukawka, Susan Knightly, Leonard Yakir, Bruce Whizin, and Danny Siegel for their contributions. The staff of Mount Sinai Memorial Park and Mortuary, particularly Arnold Saltzman, Martha White, and Morley Helfand, were very helpful in sharing their sensitivity and expertise.

We would like to acknowledge the gracious support of the following individuals, families, and foundations: The Milken Family Foundation, Encino, California; Dr. Sidney Kobernick, Sarasota, Florida; Mr. Robert Belfer, New York, New York; Dr. Alan Phillips and Family, New York, New York; The Morris and Betty Kaplun foundation, New York, New York; and the estate of Harry Pick.

I am blessed with an extraordinary family. To my children Havi and Michael, I hope that in a way these Art of Jewish Living books are my ethical will to you, revealing the deep love I have for our Jewish tradition and my prayer that you will choose to take your place in the chain of Jewish continuity. To my wife, Susie, my affection and unending gratitude for being my partner, my guide, my love.

Ron Wolfson

How to Read This Book

This book attempts to reach two audiences simultaneously: mourners and comforters.

You may be reading this book because you have recently sustained the death of a loved one. We join with your family and friends in wishing you the traditional Jewish words of condolence: "May God comfort you among the other mourners of Zion and Jerusalem."

Mourners will find that the book follows the chronological events associated with bereavement, beginning with dying and ending with *yahrtzeit*. Each chapter contains a section written especially for you.

You may be reading this book because you are preparing to comfort a family member or friend who has recently been bereaved. Your role as a comforter is absolutely crucial in assisting the mourner during the grieving process. Jewish tradition places a high value on offering deeds and words of comfort to the mourner. Comforters will find that Parts 4 through 8 contain sections detailing your role during the bereavement process.

You may be reading this book as part of a course on Jewish bereavement. You are to be congratulated for having the courage to take the steps necessary to learn about and prepare for the eventuality of your own bereavement and, ultimately, your own death. As shocking as that sounds, this book is designed to help you do both, before the need arises. You will want to read about what mourners face and how to be a helpful comforter.

The chapter entitled "How to Prepare for Your Own Death" provides detailed information on advance planning for health-care directives, ethical wills, estate planning, and other concerns.

Biographies of the Voices in This Book

Richard Lopata

Richard Lopata is a real estate developer in Los Angeles. His wife, Caryl, died in 1984 of breast cancer after a long struggle with the disease. Caryl was an elementary school teacher and bilingual specialist. The Lopatas raised two children, Laurie and Robert. When Laurie was five, she was diagnosed as having cystic fibrosis, an inherited disease that destroys the lungs. Caryl Lopata founded the Valley Guild for Cystic Fibrosis, raising many millions of dollars for research to find a cure for the usually fatal condition. Laurie Lopata was preparing for a career in medicine when she died of cystic fibrosis in December, 1991. She was twenety-eight years old.

Tamara Greenebaum

Tamara Greenebaum's experience with death in a rural community, within a small, but dedicated, Jewish community, illustrates how challenging it is to cope with loss from a distance. It also vividly illustrates how responsive a small Jewish community is to a family facing death. Tamara is the dean of admissions at the University of Judaism.

David Novak

David Novak grew up in and has been a member of the Conservative movement throughout his life: Temple Israel in Manchester, New Hampshire; Kol Shofar in Marin County, California; Beth Shalom in Spokane, Washington; Herzl-Ner Tamid in Seattle, Washington; and Beth Chayim Chadashim, the gay and lesbian synagogue in Los Angeles. No stranger to bereavement, David experienced the deaths of seven close relatives before the age of thirteen.

Today, as a leader in the Jewish gay community of Los Angeles, he is witnessing the inexorable, slow, tragic deaths of many friends to the AIDS epidemic.

Carol Starin

Carol is the executive director of the Jewish Education Council in Seattle, Washington. She met her husband, Joel Starin, in the first grade of religious school. A partner in a major law firm in Seattle, Joel was a very active member of the Jewish community. He was diagnosed with brain cancer fifteen years before he died at the age of forty-three. Carol and their two teenage sons, Rob and Geoffrey, are coping with the aftermath of Joel's death three years later.

Herman Feifel

Herman Feifel is a prime force in the academic study of death and dying. Chief psychologist at the Veterans Administration Outpatient Clinic in Los Angeles and clinical professor of psychiatry and the behavioral sciences at the University of Southern California School of Medicine, he published the groundbreaking book *The Meaning of Death* in 1959. Steeped in Jewish tradition and learning, Dr. Feifel is uniquely qualified to comment on the Jewish approach to dying and bereavement.

Allen Brown

Allen Brown is a former executive of Eastman Kodak Company in Rochester, New York. He has served as president of his Conservative synagogue and is currently an international vice president of the Federation of Jewish Men's Clubs. Allen's father, Harold, died of renal failure in 1992.

Saralie Foote

Saralie Foote, a friend of the Brown family, stepped forward to organize the *shiva* after the death of Allen's father. Saralie herself has suffered the deaths of a brother in his twenties and her father.

Benjamin Dwoskin

Ben Dwoskin was the founding general manager and CEO of the Mount Sinai Memorial Park and Mortuary in Los Angeles, the largest synagogue-owned cemetery and mortuary in the country. Recently retired after thirty-eight years in the post, Ben is an active leader in the Los Angeles Jewish community.

Arnold Saltzman

Arnold Saltzman is the current executive director of the Mount Sinai Memorial Park and Mortuary in Los Angeles. A Jewish communal worker by training, Arnold is the former director of the Jewish Family Service in Los Angeles.

Martha White

Martha White is a preneed counselor at Mount Sinai Memorial Park and Mortuary in Los Angeles. She has directed the Community College of Jewish Studies and taught in a number of adult education programs in the community.

Moshe And Lois Rothblum

Moshe Rothblum is rabbi of Adat Ari El, a Conservative congregation in North Hollywood, California. He has served as president of the Southern California Board of Rabbis. Lois Rothblum is director of the Educational Resources Center and instructor in education at the University of Judaism in Los Angeles. We interviewed Moshe and Lois on the final day of *shiva* for his mother, Ruth Zahava.

Gail Dorph

Gail Dorph is the director of the Fingerhut School of Education at the University of Judaism in Los Angeles. Good friend to the Rothblums, Gail was interviewed during a *shiva* visit to their home.

Jack Riemer

Jack Riemer is rabbi of Congregation Beth David in Miami, Florida. A well-known speaker and author, he is the editor of *Jewish Reflections on Death* and coauthor of *So That Your Values Live On: Ethical Wills and How to Prepare Them.*

Bernard Lipnick

Bernard Lipnick is rabbi emeritus of Congregation B'nai Amoona in St. Louis, Missouri, where he served as rabbi for forty years. Rabbi Lipnick earned a Ph.D. in education from Washington University.

Susan Knightly

Susan Knightly, an author, and her husband Leonard, Yakir, a filmmaker, live in Brooklyn, New York. Married only fifteen months, they experienced two miscarriages during the first year of their marriage. Their third pregnancy ended with the birth and death of their son Joshua. Susan, a Jew by choice, and Leonard decided that the most appropriate way for them to deal with their grief was to engage in the ritual of Jewish bereavement.

Sandy Goodglick

Sandy Goodglick is a leading layperson in the Los Angeles Jewish community, serving on the board of directors of the University of Judaism and the Brandeis-Bardin Institute. She is the principal behind SIM-PLEX, a service firm that assists people in organizing their financial affairs.

Harold M. Schulweis

Harold Schulweis is rabbi of Valley Beth Shalom in Encino, California. A highly influential rabbi, his innovations in synagogue programming include the *havurah*, pararabbinic and paraprofessional counseling programs, and a family empowerment center. He is founding chairman of the Jewish

Foundation for the Righteous, an organization devoted to supporting non-Jews who rescued Jews during the Holocaust.

Bruce Whizin

Bruce Whizin is a member of the board of directors of the Shirley and Arthur Whizin Center and the University of Judaism. He is a marriage and family therapist in Los Angeles.

Ben Zion Bergman

Ben Zion Bergman is chairman of the Bet Din of the Pacific Southwest Region of the Rabbinical Assembly and professor of rabbinic literature at the University of Judaism. He serves as a member of the Committee on Jewish Law and Standards for the Rabbinical Assembly of America and is a member of the National Bet Din of the Conservative movement.

Abram Kukawka

Abram Kukawka was born in Slovotich, Poland, eighty-three years ago. He immigrated to the United States in 1951, settling in Omaha, Nebraska, with his wife, Hildegarde, and daughter Susan. In 1975, upon his retirement, his children gave him a membership in the Omaha Jewish Community Center where he became part of a group of senior men called "The Round Table" who meet daily in the Men's Health Club. Abe's wife died in 1989. Now he is coping with the steady march of death claiming his friends in the Health Club.

Dennis Gura

Dennis Gura and his wife, Kathy, are active members of the Jewish community in Venice, California. Dennis has served as president of Mishkon Tephilo, a Conservative synagogue. In 1991, their daughter Rebecca died of leukemia at the age of six. Defying the statistics, Dennis, Kathy, and their four-year-old son, Ethan, have kept their family intact and strong in the face of this tragic loss.

Ann Mitnick

Ann Mitnick, her husband, and another couple decided to make preneed arrangements for their funerals. To take the edge off the situation, they went "plot-shopping" together.

Sam Joseph

Rabbi Sam Joseph is a professor of education at Hebrew Union College–Jewish Institute of Religion in Cincinnati, Ohio. He is a cofounder of the Fernside Center, a counseling center for children coping with death and bereavement.

David Techner

David Techner is a funeral director at the Ira Kaufman Chapel, a large Jewish funeral home primarily serving the Conservative and Reform Jewish communities in Detroit, Michigan. He has appeared on numerous television programs discussing issues of grief, particularly male bereavement. David and his wife, Ilene, suffered the death of their eight-month-old daughter Alicia on January 19, 1978.

Sharon Kleinbaum

Sharon Kleinbaum grew up in a family that belonged to the Conservative movement, attended an Orthodox yeshiva high school, received her ordination from the Reconstructionist Rabbinical College, and worked in the Religious Action Center of Reform Judaism. Today, she is the rabbi of Congregation Beth Simchat Torah in New York City, the world's largest gay and lesbian synagogue. With a membership of 1,200 people, Rabbi Kleinbaum must comfort a congregation that loses one of its members to AIDS almost every two weeks. She has become a forceful advocate for full acceptance of homosexuals into the mainstream of Jewish life.

The Art of Jewish Mourning and Comforting

We are not alone.

This is the fundamental message of Judaism about death and bereavement.

Every law and every custom you will read about in this book has at its core the overwhelming motivation to surround those who are dying and those who will grieve for the dead with a supportive community. While some may argue that facing death heightens one's feeling of aloneness, the Jewish approach seeks to place loss and grief in the context of family and friends.

We will all die.

No matter how hard we try to cheat death, the inevitable conclusion of living is dying. When this realization finally hits us, there can be any number of reactions. Some will be saddened. Some will drift into melancholy. Some will be depressed. Some will live in denial. The Jewish approach is reality-based. There is a time to be born—and a time to die. From dust we are fashioned—to dust we return. No denial. No avoidance. The art of Jewish dying is a fundamental factor in the art of Jewish living.

We will all mourn.

Sooner or later, we are all bereaved. Death takes a parent, a child, a sibling, a spouse—and we become mourners. Thousands of years before modern psychoanalysis, the rabbis who fashioned these practices understood grief and how to heal it. These practices are not easy to take. The thud of the earth thrown on the casket by the mourner brings us face-to-face with the reality of our loss and the inevitablity of our own mortality. But, at the very same moment, we take the first step on the path to healing, the long road back to life renewed. The Jewish approach shows us the way to mourn, the way to grieve, the way to recover, the way to remember.

We must all comfort the mourner.

Judaism asks us to honor the dead and comfort the mourner. These are two of the most important imperatives in Jewish life. How do we honor the dead? By respectful care of the body, by accompanying the deceased to the burial place, by honoring the memory of the person's lifetime of achievement. How do we comfort the mourner? By being there, in body and spirit, by enabling the mourner to grieve and to pray, by surrounding the mourner with community, by easing the mourner's way to a new life after death, by remembering the deceased and not forgetting the mourner.

In these pages, you will find the stories of mourners and of comforters. You will learn how the Jewish tradition wants us to approach death and mourning. You will learn how to comfort the mourner. And you will even learn how to prepare for the inevitability of your own death—may you live to be one hundred and twenty!

May you be empowered to face the reality of death by learning this aspect of the *Art of Jewish Living*.

PART 1

Facing Death

HERMAN FEIFEL: In the old days, when you got seriously ill, you didn't tarry long. The _hevra kadisha_ (burial society) was dealing with you within hours. Now, with the new ability to extend and elongate life, medical technology has created a situation of dependency and dehumanization for many of the dying.

Remember that wonderful classic picture of a doctor sitting at the bedside of a child through the night? He was there, he was witness. Unfortunately, today we have tended to forfeit the "laying on of hands" with the dying and exchanged it for oxygen tents, respirators, and impersonal intravenous tubes—a doubtful bargain psychologically. We die in big, technological hospitals with their superior facilities for providing medical care and alleviating pain. But it tends to transform a person's death into a public event, something that befalls everyone, yet no one in particular.

In terms of the Jewish tradition, there is now a reawakening in health circles to appreciating not only the ethical problems of dying, but also its spiritual dimension. The human being is mind and soul as well as body.

RON WOLFSON: Hasn't there been a backlash to the use of medical technology to extend life through extraordinary means?

HERMAN FEIFEL: Definitely. The hospice movement, living wills, current propositions being offered on state ballots dealing with terminally ill patients all attest to the discomfort people feel about this. They reflect a growing demand by individuals to possess greater governance over their dying and burial.

Dying is part of the business of living. Yet, for most of us, dying is isolated from our daily lives. We rarely see death—real death. Our elderly don't die at home; they meet their end in the cold, clinical environment of the hospital. Our society places a value on youth, on health, on living; death has been called "the new obscenity." Despite the latest efforts to bring "spirituality" into our consciousnesses, there clearly continues to be a huge gap between human beings and ultimate issues like the meaning of life ... or of death.

Yet, when we confront someone who is about to die, we are brought face-to-face with our own mortality. This shadow of a person lying on the bed could be me, will be me. I seek my refuge in the comfort of denial. "Denial," as the T-shirt says, "is more than a river in Egypt." Denial of death separates the dying from the living. The dying are sent to old-age homes and convalescent hospitals. Out of sight, out of mind. No need for reminders that someday it will be my turn.

Judaism rejects the denial of death. It asserts boldly and truthfully that we are formed from dust and to dust we shall return, as clearly expressed in a Jewish source often cited by the Rabbis:

> Fear not death; we are destined to die. We share this with all other mortals, with all who ever lived, with all who ever will be. Bewail the dead, hide not your grief, do not restrain your mourning. But remember that continuing sorrow is worse than death ... be consoled when the soul departs.
>
> Seek not to understand what is too difficult for you, search not for what is hidden from you. Be not over-occupied with what is beyond you, for you have been shown more than you can understand.
>
> As a drop of water in the sea, as a grain of sand on the shore are a person's few days in eternity. The good things in life last for limited days, but a good name endures forever.
>
> Adapted from *Ben Sira*

The Process of Dying

During the past twenty years, much work has been done to help people face death—their own and others'. Beginning with the pioneering work *The Meaning of Death,* edited by Dr. Herman Feifel, continued in the well-known *On Death and Dying* by Elisabeth Kübler-Ross, and reflected in the many self-help books including M. Robert Buckman's *I Don't Know What to Say ... How to Help and Support Someone Who Is Dying,* this literature concludes in a unanimous voice: "Don't ignore the dying." Every expert agrees that, in virtually all cases, a terminally ill person wants, indeed needs, to talk about what is happening. Family and friends are the crucial factor in the effort to enhance the quality of living for the dying.

Kübler-Ross popularized the idea of stages of dying. The five stages she identifies are: denial, anger, bargaining, depression, and acceptance. As a result of the work done in the twenty-two years since her book, most experts now understand that these categories more accurately describe reactions to dying rather than discrete stages that all go through. In fact, any stage theory is subject to the vagaries of individual differences. Most people evidence a variety of emotional reactions at every step along the way to death, and it is highly likely that several different emotions may be expressed simultaneously. Even so, for those attempting to comfort the dying patient, recognizing these factors can lead to better communication and support.

When someone gets the news that he or she is dying, an avalanche of feelings is unleashed: shock, disbelief, denial, anger, guilt, hope, despair, fear, depression. You, who are trying to comfort and support, may experience the same feelings as you identify with the patient (she feels despair—

you feel despair), or you may feel opposite feelings (she feels hope—you feel fear), or you may be reacting to the emotions sent your way (he feels anger and directs it toward you—you are angry in return).

Offering emotional support depends on how you fit into the sometimes complicated picture of the relationships between the patient and significant others. You should expect variability of emotions and repetitive discussions of feelings and situations.

Be careful when offering advice; the patient and his or her medical team are already planning a course of treatment. Learn enough about the disease to be informed, but be alert not to be a source of conflicting opinion. Although the condition may be incurable, there are realistic hopes that can be supported: hope that pain can be relieved, hope that dignity can be maintained and, most importantly, hope that you will not abandon the patient. Perhaps the greatest support of all to a terminally ill person is the assurance that she or he will not die alone.

Being ill brings with it a variety of physical symptoms and emotional responses. With some diseases, deterioration of the body does not happen immediately, but eventually the disease begins to take its toll. Then, the daily regimen of fighting the illness becomes the central factor in the patient's life. There is an awful uncertainty that begins to develop. As the physical symptoms manifest themselves, certain things will bother the patient more than others. For cancer patients, it is often the loss of hair. For others, it may be the need for a catheter or oxygen or a wheelchair. Eventually, the patient may express the feeling that the treatments and machines are a waste of time and money: "What difference does it make? I'm going to die anyway."

There are no simple answers to combat strong feelings of despair. In fact, for some of those seeking to comfort the patient, the same feelings of frustration and hopelessness can easily creep into the mind. Your life significantly changes when caring for a dying person. There is no doubt that you feel some resentment at the loss of independence and the weight of the demands made on you. These are normal reactions. One of the best ways to overcome feelings of malaise is to act. Find ways to help the patient make choices—choices about treatments, care, the quality of life. By discussing available options and ongoing feelings, the comforter will help to keep the patient on track and focused on what can be done, rather than wallowing in despair or self-pity.

Finally, a sense of acceptance emerges in the last stages of a terminal illness. The emotional climate moves from anger, denial, and uncertainty to a soft, tender sadness—a sadness at leaving family and friends, a sadness that the joys of life are about to end, a sadness for the sadness experienced by the loved ones surrounding the patient.

It is a cliché, but also a likely truth, that people die as they have lived. If a person is generally cheerful, then once acceptance sets in, death is approached in an easy, unafraid manner. If a person is generally difficult, the death is unlikely to be easy. Supporters of the dying are advised to help let the person die in his or her own way. This is the time to consider writing a living will and a durable power of attorney to make known the patient's desires with regard to extraordinary life-sustaining measures.

Medical experts point out that most people experience a kind of emotional calm as the moment of death approaches. If goodbyes have not been exchanged yet, this is the time. Observant Jews may wish to recite the last confessional, the *Vidui,* with the help of family, friends, or a rabbi. Often, the person will slip into a state of unconsciousness in the hours or minutes before death. The struggle finally over, it is a time of peace.

Visiting the Dying

While the patient may have accepted fate, often we feel we cannot. But we must. There are important ways that supporters can help to enable the patient to let go. Among them are helping with last wishes, arranging wills, contacting long lost relatives or friends, funeral arrangements. Sometimes the patient would prefer to die outside the hospital. The hospice, a home-like environment for the terminally ill, has proven to be a tremendous comfort to the dying and his or her loved ones. Most have medical staff and social workers specially trained to care for those near the end of life. There is usually a very high level of support for the patient and the family and a special camaraderie among all who are in residence.

Finally, for the family and friends, the most important message to the dying at the end of life may be to say, "You will not be forgotten." Everyone wants to feel that his or her life has had meaning to someone. Everyone wants to feel that a contribution has been made to this life that will be remembered. It is important for the dying person to hear from loved ones that he is loved, that she has changed your life, and that he will be remembered.

With the advances in modern medical technology, the time between the onset of serious illness and death is often days, months, or even years. Jewish tradition values life above all else; virtually anything is permissible within Jewish law to save a life, except for adultery, murder, and idolatry. Thus, when a loved one is sick, we are asked to visit them as often as possible, attend to their needs, and cheer them up. The *mitzvah* of *bikkur ḥolim,* visiting the sick, is one of the most important obligations in Jewish tradition.

Various suggestions have been made by Jewish commentators and authorities throughout the centuries about how to fulfill the *mitzvah* of *bikkur ḥolim.* For example, close relatives should visit the sick immediately, but friends are to wait until the third day of the illness so as not to unduly scare the patient. However, if the illness is quite serious, even friends should not delay their visit. Since the ultimate goal of a visit is to comfort and cheer the ill, it is important to take into consideration the time of one's visit.

One source suggests that a visitor should not come in the early hours of the morning when the doctors and nurses are busy with the patient nor late in the evening when the patient is most likely to be tired. Although this advice sounds like the rationale of a modern hospital's visitation protocol, it is actually found in the Babylonian Talmud (*Niddah* 40a), written nearly two thousand years ago!

Other advice includes additional points that could be taken right off a statement of visitor's policies:

- One should not visit when the patient's needs are being attended to (Maimonides *Hilḥot Avelut* 14:5);
- One should not bring sad news to a patient nor weep for the dead in his or her presence (*Yoreh De'ah* 337);
- One should not stay too long during a visit (Abrahams, *Hebrew Ethical Wills,* p. 40).

What should visitors do? Make the patient comfortable, try to cheer him or her up and pray for his or her recovery. In Jewish tradition, it is common practice to ask a rabbi or other official of a congregation to offer a *Mi Sh'beirakh* prayer during the synagogue service, usually at the time of the reading of the Torah. The prayer for the sick reads:

May the One who blessed our ancestors, Abraham, Isaac, and Jacob, Sarah, Rebecca, Rachel, and Leah, bless and heal _____. May the Holy One in mercy strengthen him [her] and heal him [her] soon, body and soul, together with others who suffer illness. And let us say: Amen.

In some congregations, advance notice of the person who is sick should be given to the rabbi or another official of the community, while in others, anyone who wishes to call out the name of the one who is ill can do so on the spot. It is helpful to know the Hebrew name of the patient, or if it is not known, most congregations will say the English name.

Another important, yet often neglected, act of kindness toward those who are ill is to belong to a *bikkur ḥolim* committee at a congregation. In most congregations, the obligation to visit the sick falls upon the rabbi or cantor. Most rabbis and cantors make hospital rounds weekly. These visits are a wonderful comfort. Yet the obligation to visit the sick is for everyone.

When death is imminent, the value of being with a loved one is so great that it is even permitted to violate the rules of Shabbat in order to visit the critically ill near relative (*Kol Bo'al Aveilut,* p. 22). According to Rabbi Isaac Klein, a great modern commentator on Jewish law within the Conservative movement, "Human life is so precious that its preservation takes precedence over nearly every other consideration. Therefore, we may even violate the rules of behavior on Shabbat, if necessary, in order to visit the critically sick and help a person afflicted with a dangerous illness" (Klein, *A Guide to Jewish Religious Practice,* p. 272, quoting the *Orekh Ḥayim* 328:2).

Finally, although according to Jewish law one may not do anything to diminish the hope of the dying, there is one exception specified in the law: One should help the dying person arrange for the disposition of her or his property, if this has not already been done. See the chapter on "How to Prepare for Your Own Death" for advice on this sensitive issue.

Talking with the Dying

RON WOLFSON: Do you find that dying patients are willing or even anxious to talk about their death?

HERMAN FEIFEL: The problem is more with the living. A goodly number of dying patients prefer honest and plain talk about the seriousness of their illness. They evince a sense of being understood and helped, rather than becoming frightened or panicky, when they can talk about their feelings concerning death. There is truth in the idea that the unknown can be feared more than the most dreaded reality. There is almost nothing as crushing to a dying patient than to feel that she or he has been abandoned or rejected. It seems that in many circumstances it's not *what* the patient is told, but rather *how* it is done that counts. Patients can accept and integrate information that they are to die in the near future, but want a gradual leading-up to this, rather than, as one patient put it to me many years ago: "Don't give me a cold-shower technique."

Incidentally, in this case, let's say you tell the dying patient something he or she doesn't want to hear—denial is an amazing thing. He or she won't hear it fully, it won't register. So, even if we misjudge, it shouldn't stop us from talking. Obviously, if the patient does not want to talk about this, his or her view should be respected. But the topic should certainly be on the agenda.

Overall, most dying patients don't expect "miracles" concerning their biological situation. Their essential communication is the need for confirmation of care and concern.

SANDY GOODGLICK: I've learned that the most important thing you can do is to let the person who is dying know how you feel about them, how much you love them. A couple of days before my father died, he and I had a little argument. He wouldn't see a cardiologist. It took me two days to get him there. After this tough time, he finally said to me, "I know you love me very much." I said, "Yes, I do. I probably love you too much because I care so very much about you." He said, "Yes, I worry about that sometimes." So, he certainly knew how I felt about him. We need to let people know how we feel about them all the time. Let people know at the moment. If you wait, you may not have the opportunity.

BRUCE WHIZIN: The most important thing is not to leave any unfinished business. Don't leave anything undone. The week before my mom died, I had a talk with her. She always felt strongly that when it's over, it's over. I said, "Mom, when you get to the other side, I want you to promise to keep an eye out for me." She said, "You know how I feel about that." I said, "Well, when you get to the other side, if you find it's different, just promise you'll keep an eye out for me." She kind of softened for a minute and then said: "If I get to the other side, and if I find it's different, I'll keep an eye out for you."

Now, my dad is facing his death and he wants to talk about it. He's talked about the kind of funeral he wants. And he's even said some funny things. We were talking about his various assets and what to do with them and he looked at me straight-faced and said, "You know, it's hard to run a business from the grave!"

DAVID TECHNER: I recently talked with a teenager who had been diagnosed with terminal cancer. People had been visiting with him just a few days after the diagnosis and finding it very difficult. He said to me, "I'm not even sick yet, and they're sitting *shiva*!" We have to be very careful to always keep in mind that terminally ill people are still sensitive, living human beings.

It is never easy to talk with a dying patient, yet communication is the lifeline to personal dignity. Rather than abandoning and ignoring the terminally ill, it is critically important to engage the person in a sharing of emotions and information. Dr. Robert Buckman suggests the following guidelines to encourage good conversations with the dying:

- **Sit down.** When a visitor stands over a patient in a hospital bed, it is very difficult to engage in a conversation that feels comfortable. Sit in a chair or, if appropriate, on the side of the bed. Try to be eye-level with the patient.
- **Be sure the person wants to talk.** Remember, the patient is undergoing a treatment regimen that can be exhausting. Or the person may not be in the mood to talk. If you're not sure, ask: "Do you feel like talking?"
- **Be a sensitive listener.** Good listeners really listen. Don't interrupt and don't anticipate what you think the patient will say. Just listen.
- **Encourage the patient to talk.** Use verbal prods: "Tell me more" or "I see ..." Use nonverbal prods: nod in agreement, maintain eye contact. Reflect back to the speaker what you think you've heard by paraphrasing his or her words.
- **Respect silence.** If the person stops talking, it is often to collect emotions. Offer your hand. Don't be afraid of the silence; sometimes there really is nothing to say.
- **Describe your feelings.** It is helpful for the patient to know that you too find it difficult to speak about these matters.
- **Don't change the subject.** The patient may get into areas that are troubling to hear. As tough as it may be for you, try to hear her or him out.
- **Be careful with advice.** We all have ideas on how to fix things. But, if you give advice early in a conversation, you may find it stops the exchange.
- **Reminisce.** As people approach the end of life, they often want to tell stories about their lives. As bittersweet as this may be, it is a wonderful way for the patient and the listener to reach a sense of fulfillment and completion.
- **Don't be afraid of humor.** Funny stories, jokes, and incidents help people ventilate. A whole literature now exists (see Norman Cousins's body of work) on the therapeutic value of laughing.

Additional information and local resources on comforting the dying can be acquired by contacting The National Center for Jewish Healing, www.jewishhealing.org, 850 Seventh Avenue, Suite 1201, New York, New York 10019, (212) 399-2320.

Caregiving

Joe Rothkop had broken his leg in a major car accident. While recuperating at a Los Angeles area rehabilitation facility, he met Boysie Sarmiento, a young nurse assistant working in the physical therapy clinic. The two men bonded instantly, sharing a story of caring and healing, giving and receiving, learning, and love.

No two people could have been more dissimilar. Joe, a tall, handsome, nearly ninety-year-old man who hailed from Omaha, Nebraska, and Boysie, a diminutive, wispy twenty-year-old immigrant from the Philippines, were patient and caregiver brought together by the need for healing. Having to provide care in the often stifling rehab center was challenging and frustrating for Boysie. But Joe, his wife, and their daughters noticed that Boysie never seemed fazed by anything. If he was embarrassed or sickened by the tasks he was asked to do, he never let on. He approached each interaction with a smile and an attitude that came from some deep reservoir of human compassion. Joe responded to this with his own wonderful warmth.

When Joe was finally ready to return home, his family asked Boysie if he was interested in becoming Joe's full time care giver. Boysie had only recently graduated his nurse assistant's program, and had never taken on this kind of responsibility. However, out of a fondness for Joe nurtured through the months of rehabilitation, he agreed to take the job. My family has been close to the Rothkops for more than seventy years, so, when Joe and Harriet moved to California from Omaha a dozen years ago, Susie and I included them in many of our family functions and, of course, the Rothkops reciprocated. When Joe's health made it difficult for him to go out, we would visit and witness first-hand the extraordinary relationship between Joe and Boysie. Most of the time, they would giggle. Two men giggling—over inside jokes, funny situations, and Joe's attempts at humor. Joe loved good stories and loved repeating them even more; Boysie laughed and laughed, no matter how many times he'd heard them. Proud of Boysie's steadily improving English, Joe would sometimes ask him to tell these stories himself. Boysie's English wasn't the only language that was improving. Joe set about teaching him Yiddish. Joe wasn't very religious, but he loved being Jewish. One day, while Boysie wheeled him out the front door, Joe noticed a five-pound box of matzah on the hallway table. "What's that?" Joe asked Boysie. "Oh, that's our matzahs, Joe," Boysie matter-of-factly responded. We once visited Joe on a Friday evening, and Boysie welcomed us at the front door. "Shabbat Shalom!" he exclaimed.

The affection between Joe and Boysie was palpable. Joe was like a father to him, encouraging his studies and his dreams, the strongest of which was his desire to become an American citizen. When Boysie passed his exam and got his papers, Joe was back at another rehab center, but he and his family still arranged a huge party to celebrate Boysie's accomplishment, complete with Uncle Sam hats for the nurses, Sousa marches, and an enormous cake. Joe's wife, Harriet, recalls that no matter how difficult it was to take care of Joe, Boysie always had a smile and a warm word. Caring for more than just Joe's physical condition, Boysie listened and learned as Joe taught him life lessons, enabling Joe to be a teacher, a mentor, a guide. In a way, they were care givers for each other.

As the end came, Joe was surrounded by his family, his friends, and Boysie. We were each privileged to say our goodbyes to him, to hold his hand, to kiss his forehead, to let him go. When it was Boysie's turn, he caressed Joe's face and his eyes filled with tears. He said simply: "*Gay shlofen,* Joe." At Joe's funeral, his wife, daughters, and son-in-law shared expressions of love and warmth with all those who knew him, but perhaps the most heartfelt thanks were offered to Boysie, for giving care and dignity, laughter and love to their beloved husband and father.

Toward those unusual human beings who are the true healers in our midst, we can feel nothing except the deepest and most profound gratitude for the gifts they give us.

Danny Siegel, friend and poet, writes about the view from the bed of a dying person in his poem entitled "The Chances."

When we were children, we had no sense of odds.
In Monopoly, we never thought it would happen to us,
"Go Directly to Jail,"
and even when it did,
by the next day we had forgotten all about it,
even if, strange as it was when it happened,
our piece fell on the wrong square two or three times in a row.
And we could play cards days on end,
and one of us lose almost every time,
but, as we saw it,
there was nothing about the cards that seemed of themselves unfair.
The next afternoon we could take up where we had left off
as if nothing unusual or wrong or bad had happened.
You lie in bed, a human image of your diagnosis.
The machine and charts
and the operators of machines and the interpreters of charts
have pronounced their solemn odds—not good—
in the ninety-something to single digit range,
and you put on your best face for me and the rest of your friends
who have come by to say more than hello.
We shift from one leg to another,
stumbling over each other to recite
as if from some Biblical text,
"What a great season the Redskins are having!"
and all chime in about how they stomped Atlanta yesterday,
and, not wanting to hurt us, you ask gently,
"What are the chances the Rabbi was right
back when we were in Hebrew School,
You know, about there being a Next World after This One,
all peace and light?"

—*A Hearing Heart*

PART 2

A Death in the Family

ALLEN BROWN: A few weeks before he died, I got a call from the hospital saying that my father refused dialysis. He had been on the machine for four and a half years, and he wanted to stop it. The doctors wanted me to come down right away and talk some sense into him. He agreed to continue it, but they had to put another shunt in. When they did the procedure, his heart stopped. The pounding on his chest broke a tumor on his lungs. He was in bad shape.

The doctors asked me to sign a document to give them permission to let him go if his heart stopped again. I called Rabbi Skopitz. He said that Jewish law allowed the machines to be turned off if there was no hope of recovery. He said, "The decision has to be yours, but if you make the decision, you have to feel that you're doing the right thing ..."

My two sisters begged me to sign the document, but my mother and I were against it. We didn't know what Dad wanted—he was out of it. Finally, I signed it, but to this day I don't think I did the right thing ...

The doctors held back the dialysis and expected Dad to die. Amazingly, he came out of it. When he woke up, he asked the doctor, "When am I going to have dialysis?" So, the doctor called me up and said, "You better get down here; your father wants dialysis." I said, "You've got to be putting me on!"

I talked with Dad and told him what the doctors said and what the rabbi said. As I talked, Dad would not look at me. He was crying. I was crying. But he couldn't make a decision. My two brothers-in-law went in to talk to him alone, and my Dad said to them, "Allen won't let me go off dialysis, but I want it stopped. I can't do this anymore." So it was his request that gave the final permission. He died two days later.

The last few days we were able to talk. All the children and their spouses and the grandchildren came to see him. He recognized everybody. Dianne and I were with him the morning he died. Dianne would say: "C'mon Dad, give me a big smile," and, all of a sudden, he would get a big wide grin you wouldn't believe a person so sick could do. It's something I'll remember the rest of my life. He would hold our hands, he was emotional … He cried, we cried, he laughed, we laughed. He was always trying to kiss us through the oxygen mask. At the end, I reached out to grab his hand and he grabbed tight onto my hand, and then he went.

The doctors let us stay in as long as we wanted. A little later, the rabbi came and went in to say something. The week before when we thought he was going, the rabbi said a prayer—the *Vidui*.

TAMARA GREENEBAUM: Well, my mother was diagnosed with cancer about seven months before she died. I live six hundred miles away from my parents, who live in a community north of San Francisco. As soon as we knew, I started going up there a lot.

There is a very small but wonderful Jewish community there. Even though the rabbi and others would call and ask if they could cook or do things for my parents, they characteristically wanted to handle things themselves. This extended to me and my sister too.

My mother went to a holistic health retreat when she got really very sick. Then she went to a hospital near San Francisco. The people in Mendocino were very helpful. But, it was clear things were not getting any better. Finally, my father called me at work, something that is absolutely verboten in our family, and told me he had just talked to the doctor who said there had been some test results that were very bad. He wanted me and my husband and my sister to convene at the hospital immediately. The next day we did.

My parents have had living wills for a long time so there would be no extraordinary means used to keep them alive if they were very sick. Even though that was the case we were faced with, my father just had trouble making the decision by himself and wanted the family there to help him. My husband is a rabbi and he wanted his *hekhsher* (approval) as well.

We met with the doctor and agreed that no extraordinary means should be taken. My mother was so sick and failing so fast and in so much pain that it was decided to keep her just on the pain medication and discontinue everything else.

We wanted to tell her about it. The doctor had told her that the results had been very bad. So we went into her room and told her that we would make her as comfortable as possible and that we were not abandoning her. But she couldn't communicate by then.

The new medical technologies have posed tremendous dilemmas for the dying person and her or his family. Shall we allow the doctors to perform extraordinary measures to maintain life or shall we let nature take its course? How do we define "extraordinary measures"? Feeding tubes, respirators, dialysis machines—who is to say whether these modern miracles of medical technology are saving lives or sustaining a vegetative organism? Who is to decide when a person is "too far gone" to come back?

Then there are the financial considerations. The costs of dying are horrendous. Hospitalization, expensive drugs, nursing care, home care, special procedures; it is hardly unusual for a lengthy terminal illness to strain the limits of health insurance programs. When the insurance runs out, a very long illness can easily destroy a family economically.

Who will be the primary caregiver for the family? Someone usually steps forward to take on this responsibility, but what if no one does? And what of the siblings who live in another city? When difficult decisions need to made, what shall their input be? What if family members disagree? A brother feels guilty over his real or imagined slighting of the dying parent and insists on keeping him or her alive, no matter what the cost in money and personal strain. A sister is reconciled to the fact that the parent will die and feels that it would be a relief to the dying person and to the family if heroic means were not used to prolong the agony. Meanwhile, the parent is in a coma, unable to express a preference.

Medical Issues and Jewish Law

My colleague and friend Dr. Elliot Dorff, a leading authority on Jewish law and medical ethics, has written extensively on the difficult questions facing dying patients and the Jewish responses to them. In a spirited exchange of views within the Committee on Jewish Law and Standards, Rabbi Dorff and Rabbi Avram Israel Reisner both presented views on how Jews should decide the awesome questions concerning the end of life. Although their legal reasoning differs (see *Conservative Judaism*, Vol. 43 [3], Spring 1991, for both papers), their conclusions concerning treatment options have much in common. Here, then, are their major points:

- The patient should hold a large area of autonomy with regard to his or her treatment where risk and prognostic uncertainty exist, as they almost always do.
- This would allow patients to declare certain treatment options off limits, to choose hospice care if desired, and to draft advance directives for medical care, but only within the parameters established to be in accord with Jewish law.
- Jewish law seeks to remove all impediments from the death of a *goses*, literally, one who is ready to die. Thus, a Jewish patient and/or her or his family is permitted to withdraw mechanical life support where unsupported life has been shown to be impossible. If the attending physician and any rabbi advising the family determine that the patient is unlikely to be restored to unsupported meaningful life, then Do Not Resuscitate (DNR) orders may be issued.

- On withholding medication, nutrition or hydration to a terminally ill patient, Rabbis Dorff and Reisner disagree. Rabbi Dorff
  would permit withholding or withdrawing medication, nutrition,
  or hydration (which he considers to be the equivalent of medication in such a case). Rabbi Reisner would prohibit withholding
  medication, nutrition, or hydration, as long as they are believed
  to be beneficial and as long as the patient has not ruled out these
  treatments in a valid advance directive.
- When a patient is in a persistive vegetative state, Rabbi Dorff
  would permit withholding or withdrawing artificial nutrition and
  hydration since he views the person as a *terefah* (an "impaired"
  life). Rabbi Reisner finds no grounds for denying even this *hayyei
  sha'ah* (limited life) and would require full maintenance.
- Both rabbis agree that treatment for pain should be pursued.

Since both positions have been accepted by the Conservative movement's Committee on Jewish Law and Standards, a patient or the family of
a patient facing these wrenching decisions can choose from these alternatives: As we will see, perhaps the best choice is to have the patient prepare
an advance directive for medical care that reflects personal preferences
within the parameters of Jewish tradition.

Advance Directives for Health Care

These complications of dying have led to the development of a document known as an "advance directive for health care" or a "living will." It is a legal instrument used to record the instructions of a patient regarding her or his life should the medical condition become life-threatening. Specifically, the living will outlines the conditions under which a patient would not want medical procedures that would prolong life in a vegetative state. Many states have established legal forms for patients to declare this desire. In addition, a document known as a "durable power of attorney" gives someone appointed by you the right to fulfill your instructions concerning medical care in the event you become incapacitated. A living will drafted in accordance with Jewish law by Rabbi Elliot Dorff can be found in the chapter "How to Prepare for Your Own Death."

Contact your attorney to prepare a living will and a durable power of attorney. He or she will know the requirements for these documents in your state. Once the documents are prepared, review them on a regular basis. It is most important for people in their twenties and thirties to prepare these documents because that's when most of the complicated cases arise, usually from near-fatal accidents. Then again, what you write down when you're thirty may not reflect how you are going to feel when you're eighty! As with any other type of will, don't procrastinate. Write it, then review it often.

The Vidui *Confessional*

BEN ZION BERGMAN: People call me when death is imminent. I've explained to people what the *Vidui* says and what it's supposed to do.

RON WOLFSON: Do people feel comforted by it?

BEN ZION BERGMAN: Yes. They do. For some people, it's a superstitious kind of thing. For others, they think it will ensure some kind of entrance into heaven or whatever. For others, it's a way of making some kind of religious affirmation. It's also a moment of passage and the *Vidui* is an act of religious meaning. Either the person who is dying reads it or a member of the family. These are few and far-between experiences, but it can be very comforting when explained and done with meaning.

Although many laypeople associate "confession" with the Roman Catholic church, the truth is that Judaism has within it an important place for personal confessions. The most widely observed "confessional" is the public pronouncement of "sins" during the High Holy Day season. The *Al Het* prayer details the collective ways we "missed the mark" during the year just past.

The deathbed confessional, known as the *Vidui* (confession), is less well known, except to rabbis who may or may not ask the terminally ill to recite it or, if the patient is too sick, may offer to say it themselves on the person's behalf:

אֱלֹהַי וֵאלֹהֵי אֲבוֹתַי, תָּבֹא לְפָנֶיךָ תְּפִלָּתִי וְאַל תִּתְעַלַּם
מִתְּחִנָּתִי . אָנָּא, כַּפֶּר לִי עַל כָּל־חַטֹאתַי שֶׁחָטָאתִי לְפָנֶיךָ
מֵעוֹדִי עַד הַיּוֹם הַזֶּה בּוֹשְׁתִּי וְגַם נִכְלַמְתִּי כִּי הִסְכַּלְתִּי
לַעֲשׂוֹת מַעֲשִׂים רָעִים וַחַטָּאִים וְעַתָּה, קַח נָא עָנְיִי
וּמְרוּדִי לְכַפָּרָתִי, וּמְחַל לִמְשׁוּבָתִי, כִּי לְךָ לְבַד חָטָאתִי .

יְהִי רָצוֹן מִלְּפָנֶיךָ יהוה אֱלֹהַי וֵאלֹהֵי אֲבוֹתַי, שֶׁלֹּא אֶחֱטָא
עוֹד, וּמַה שֶּׁחָטָאתִי לְפָנֶיךָ, מָרֵק בְּרַחֲמֶיךָ הָרַבִּים, אֲבָל
לֹא עַל יְדֵי יִסּוּרִים וַחֲלָיִם רָעִים וּשְׁלַח לִי רְפוּאָה שְׁלֵמָה
עִם כָּל־חוֹלֵי עַמְּךָ יִשְׂרָאֵל.

מוֹדֶה (מוֹדָה) אֲנִי לְפָנֶיךָ, יהוה אֱלֹהַי וֵאלֹהֵי אֲבוֹתַי,
שֶׁרְפוּאָתִי וּמִיתָתִי בְּיָדֶךָ. יְהִי רָצוֹן מִלְּפָנֶיךָ, שֶׁתִּרְפָּאֵנִי
רְפוּאָה שְׁלֵמָה וְאִם גָּזַרְתָּ שֶׁאָמוּת מֵחוֹלִי זֶה, תְּהִי מִיתָתִי
כַּפָּרָה עַל כָּל־חֲטָאִים וַעֲוֹנוֹת וּפְשָׁעִים שֶׁחָטָאתִי וְשֶׁעָוִיתִי
וְשֶׁפָּשַׁעְתִּי לְפָנֶיךָ וְתַסְתִּירֵנִי בְּצֵל כְּנָפֶיךָ, וְאֶזְכֶּה לְחַיֵּי
הָעוֹלָם הַבָּא

אֲבִי יְתוֹמִים וְדַיַּן אַלְמָנוֹת, הָגֵל בְּעַד קְרוֹבַי הַיְּקָרִים אֲשֶׁר
נַפְשִׁי קְשׁוּרָה בְנַפְשָׁם

בְּיָדְךָ אַפְקִיד רוּחִי, פָּדִיתָה אוֹתִי יהוה, אֵל אֱמֶת

שְׁמַע יִשְׂרָאֵל, יהוה אֱלֹהֵינוּ יהוה אֶחָד.

יהוה הוּא הָאֱלֹהִים יהוה הוּא הָאֱלֹהִים

My God, and God of my ancestors, accept my prayer. Do not ignore
my supplication. Forgive me for all the sins that I have committed in
my lifetime. I am abashed and ashamed of these deeds I have committed. Please accept my pain and suffering as atonement and forgive my
wrongdoing, for against You alone have I sinned.

May it be Your will, *Adonai* my God and God of my ancestors, that I sin no more. With Your great mercy, cleanse me of my sins, but not through suffering and disease. Send a perfect healing to me and to all who are stricken.

I acknowledge to You, *Adonai* my God and God of my ancestors, that my life and recovery depend upon You. May it be Your will to heal me. Yet, if You have decreed that I shall die of this affliction, may my death atone for all sins and transgressions which I have committed before you. Shelter me in the shadow of Your wings. Grant me a share in the world to come.

Parent of orphans and Guardian of spouses left behind, protect my beloved family, with whose soul my own soul is bound.

Into Your hand I commit my soul. You have redeemed me, *Adonai*, God of truth.

Hear, O Israel: *Adonai* is Our God, *Adonai* is One.
Adonai is Our God. *Adonai* is Our God.

Short version:

I acknowledge before You, my God and God of my ancestors, that my recovery and my death are in Your hands. May it be Your will to heal me completely, but if I should die, may my death be an atonement for all sins that I have committed.

Hear O Israel: *Adonai* is Our God, *Adonai* is One.

Version to be read should the patient be unable:

Adonai our God and God of our ancestors, we acknowledge that our life is in Your hands. May it be Your will that You send perfect healing to _____. Yet, if it is Your final decree that she [he] be taken by death, let it be in love. May her [his] death atone for the sins and transgressions which she [he] committed before You. Grant her [him] a portion of the abundant good which is held in store for the righteous, and give her [him] life replete with joy in Your presence, at Your right hand forever. Protector of orphans and Guardian of spouses left behind, protect her [his] beloved family, with whose soul her [his] own soul is bound. Into Your hand s/he commits her [his] soul. You have redeemed her [him], *Adonai,* God of truth.

Hear O Israel: *Adonai* is Our God, *Adonai* is One.

Praised be God's glory for ever and ever.

Adonai is Our God. *Adonai* is Our God.

What Happens When a Person Dies?

The initial care of the deceased has one major purpose: to respect the God-created vessel in which the soul resided. The human being is sacred in Jewish tradition and the manner in which it is brought to its final resting place has been shaped by the ultimate value *kevod ha-meit,* honoring the dead. The Talmud (*Sanhedrin* 47a) establishes this principle when commenting on the biblical requirement of speedy burial (Deuteronomy 21:22–23) as a way to avoid *nivul ha-meit,* disgracing the dead.

Jewish tradition is an amalgam of law and custom. Sometimes it is difficult to distinguish between the two, yet the distinction is important to make. Jewish law holds within it the authority of a long legal tradition. Jewish custom varies from community to community and over time. When it comes to the practices suggested by the tradition to be done immediately upon the death of a person, the lines between law and custom are blurry indeed. Through the centuries, a number of practices developed that, to a large degree, reflect the superstitions of the folk religion. To the modern mind, these customs may seem primitive, yet each practice reveals a deep respect for the body and the soul:

1. **Open the windows in the room.**
   Clearly, this tradition stems from a belief that the soul leaves the body upon death. Lest it be trapped in a physical space, the windows are opened to allow the soul to begin its journey.
2. **Light a candle and place it at the head of the deceased.**
   The candle symbolizes the soul. Some follow the custom of surrounding the body with candles.

3. **Close the eyes and mouth and straighten the limbs of the deceased.**
Despite the movies you've seen, people do not necessarily die
with their eyes closed. This seems to be a gesture of respect, establishing a "normal" or dignified appearance of the body.

4. **Lay the body on the floor, feet pointed toward the door, covered
with a sheet.**
A very old tradition required this act of *hashkavah,* "laying out."

5. **Cover all mirrors.**
It was thought that the soul could see the reflection of loved ones
and might try to snatch them across to the other side. The custom
of covering mirrors is still followed in many traditional *shiva*
homes, although the rabbis reinterpreted the practice as an attempt to reduce our vanity at a time of despair.

6. **Pour out any drawn water.**
The folk religion believed that spirits used water as a medium.

7. **Do not leave the body unattended.**
While there may have been other reasons for this custom in ancient days, the idea of "guarding" the body from the moment of
death until burial is rooted in respect for the deceased (*kevod
ha-meit*).

8. **It is traditional for those witnessing the death of a person or hearing about it for the first time to recite the following words:**

בָּרוּךְ אַתָּה, יהוה אֱלֹהֵינוּ, מֶלֶךְ הָעוֹלָם, דַּיַּן הָאֱמֶת

Barukh ata, Adonai Eloheinu, Melekh ha-Olam, Dayan ha-emet.

Praised are You, *Adonai,* Our God, Ruler of the Universe,
the true Judge.

Special Cases

Issues with regard to the body

The principle of *kevod ha-meit* underlies several other important issues with regard to the disposition of the body.

Autopsies

In general, Jewish tradition forbids autopsies on the grounds that the body is sacred and should not be violated after death. However, autopsies are permitted in two specific cases:

1. When the physician claims that it could provide new knowledge that would help cure others suffering from the same disease
2. When the law of the land requires it

However, in all cases, the entire body is to be buried following the autopsy.

When our friend Jerry Weber was killed, an Orthodox member of the family desperately tried to prevent an autopsy. Although his wife, Sally, was at first inclined to agree, two factors made an autopsy mandatory: In a criminal investigation, an autopsy must be performed, and the cause of death had to be established for insurance purposes. The issue then became how quickly the autopsy could be performed in order to proceed to a timely burial. With the help of a friendly city official, the autopsy was performed immediately, and the funeral was not delayed.

Donating tissue

With the tremendous advances in medical science, it is now possible to donate organs and tissue upon death to the living who require transplants. On the surface, this would seem to be mutilation of the body, regarded as *nivul ha-meit,* disgrace to the dead. Indeed, some authorities hold that such donations should not be offered. However, many modern commentators have interpreted the donation of organs as the ultimate *kevod ha-meit* by bringing healing to the living. Therefore, it is permissible and, according to many, even a *mitzvah* for a person to will organs or tissues of the body for transplantation into other bodies for healing purposes. What about the requirement that the entire body be buried? Ultimately, the transplanted tissue will receive burial when the beneficiary of the transplant dies.

Cremation

The requirement to bury the body in the ground can be traced to the earliest chapters of the Bible. In the Garden of Eden story, God tells Adam: "By the sweat of your face, you will eat bread, until you return to the ground; for out of it were you taken; you are dust, and unto dust you shall return" (Genesis 3:19). The idea is expanded further in Ecclesiastes 12:7: "The dust shall return to the earth as it was, and the spirit shall return to God who gave it." According to some authorities, cremation is absolutely forbidden, so much so that no funeral rites are offered and the survivors are not allowed to observe any of the rites of mourning, including the recitation of the Kaddish!

My colleague and friend Rabbi Bradley Shavit Artson points out that to voluntarily cremate a body after millions of Jewish bodies were cremated in the Nazi death camps is simply unthinkable. Moreover, the burial site itself becomes a place of comfort for the survivors, a place that would not exist if the body is cremated.

Nevertheless, in cases where the family decides to cremate the body in disregard of Jewish practice, the Committee on Jewish Law and Standards has ruled that a rabbi may officiate only at the service in the funeral home, but not at the burial of ashes, lest her or his participation be interpreted as approval (*Rabbinical Assembly Proceedings,* 1939, p. 156).

Neonatal Death

SUSAN KNIGHTLY: I had been diagnosed with cervical cancer. One day, during my fifth month of pregnancy, I was taking a short walk and sneezed. Immediately, I knew the baby was in trouble. I got back to the apartment and called 911. When we got to the hospital, I went into labor. Fifteen hours later, I gave birth to Joshua, ten inches long and one pound, who died during the descent through the birth canal.

This was our third miscarriage in thirteen months. It's amazing how much bonding occurs in those first months. We had been feeling the baby kicking for about four weeks. Leonard would come home and "kiss" the baby. Of course, from the minute you hear you're pregnant, you endow the baby with a personality. We already imagined the baby playing the cello and finger painting! What people really don't realize is that very early on you have this kind of bonding with the baby. From the moment we conceived, I felt I was inviting a soul into my body.

"Please, can I hold the baby?" After I gave birth, I wanted to hold Joshua. We had a wonderful nurse who was so empathetic. She brought the baby to us, dressed in a diaper, a shirt, and a blanket, and I got to hold him. He was a beautiful little boy; he had my husband's features. The doctors were just blown away by this; they couldn't cope with it. They were completely unavailable to me emotionally. Fortunately, the nurse stayed five hours past the end of her shift to be with us.

When I held the baby, the reality of this loss hit Leonard. For him, it had been very exciting to anticipate the baby, but obviously it wasn't the same as it was for me. But when he saw me holding the baby, it became clear that this was a real person, this was his son, this was a life. It gave him license to grieve.

The hospital gave us two choices concerning what to do with the baby; we could leave the baby there for research purposes or bury him in a mass grave. We wanted neither. I'm a convert to Judaism, and Leonard grew up in a traditional Jewish home. So we called our rabbi to ask about the protocol. "There is no protocol," he replied. We decided to have a Jewish burial. We made several midnight calls to Jewish funeral homes and found one that was very understanding. In fact, they offered their services for no charge at all. They recommended a cemetery near us in Brooklyn that had a section for premature babies and small children.

Just before the funeral home came for the baby, we decided to say Kaddish in the hospital. We prepared the body ourselves. Leonard wanted the baby buried in his bar mitzvah *tallis,* so we wrapped him in it, along with some baby's breath and a small rose. Then we said Kaddish.

We arranged a time for a graveside service, alerted our close friends and synagogue community, and two days later we held a funeral service for Joshua. The rabbi said a few of the traditional prayers, and Leonard and I each read eulogies we had prepared that let our friends hear what this process was like for us and described our hopes and feelings about Joshua. We had asked our friends to bring readings they felt would speak to the moment, and several of them read poems and shared a few words. We each shoveled earth into the grave until it was completely filled. It was quite beautiful and an important moment of closure for us.

Then we sat *shiva.* Friends arranged meals for us, each night we had a *minyan* service, and we were surrounded by community. It was so crucial for us not to be alone. We had to give ourselves permission to grieve. We knew if we did not experience our feelings now, we would later, and it wouldn't be healthy. The ritual allowed us to cry, and saying Kaddish enabled us to focus on our grief.

There were friends of ours who had grown up in traditional Jewish homes who were skeptical of our sitting *shiva.* But, once they saw how this was allowing us to deal with our grief, they really understood how important it was to have the community around us. There is a real emphasis in our community, particularly among women, on re-creating the ritual to speak to us. We had conversations about what we were doing throughout the *shiva*, and I think that helped people understand.

Every step along the way has been hard. Leaving the hospital was very hard, burying the baby was very hard, the end of *shiva* was very hard. But each step has been a bit of closure for us. For several weeks, someone from the *bikkur holim* committee of the synagogue made sure that someone came to the house at lunch. I also got a call almost daily from the National Jewish Women's Organization Pregnancy Loss Peer Support Network. Every day, I got to tell the story. The telling of the story allowed us to talk our way out of the shock.

Today, our grief continues, but we feel very whole, very healed. I can't help but compare how I feel now compared to how I felt after my two earlier miscarriages, when I had no permission to grieve over my loss. I was very ill for weeks afterwards. After this experience of expressing my feelings, rather than feeling ravaged and destroyed, I feel cleansed. I've even recovered physically very well.

I'll tell you something even more amazing. My mother had suffered from depression for many, many years, and I never knew why as a child. When this happened to me, she said, "You know, when you were three years old, you had to leave me for six weeks. I lost a baby. It was a premature baby who lived only two days. My greatest regret is I never got to hold that baby. Every time you graduated, every time you had a date, every step you took of initiation into anything, I thought about that baby." Of course, I knew she was sad about something, but I never knew why. She was so thankful that I had so much support. She said to me, "Thank God you're Jewish, and you have something to get you through this."

It's every parent's worst nightmare. A stillborn, a premature infant who can't make it, a baby born without a chance to live. No one ever talks about the possible complications of birth that can threaten the life of a baby. Not in childbirth classes. Not in the doctor's office. Not in the excited conversation of expectant parents. So when the unimaginable happens and a baby dies at or shortly after birth, the parents, their families, and the community are totally unprepared.

One reason we are so shocked by a neonatal death is that the medical technology to monitor pregnancy is so advanced. We know so much about the baby, even *in utero*, that the failure to prevent this loss seems nearly unbelievable. It didn't used to be that way at all. Until quite recently, the rate of neonatal death was quite high. In the Middle Ages, parents anticipated many pregnancies, fully aware that a high percentage of the babies would not survive. As sad as miscarriages and stillbirths were, the family and the community knew of the risks and expected a certain amount of loss.

The rabbis were aware of this as well. Although there are some dissenting opinions that allow mourning even a one-day-old newborn, the predominant position of Jewish law was that if a baby did not survive for thirty days, it was as if the baby had not lived. The two major *halakhic* (legal) statements on which this custom is based are these:

> We do not mourn for fetuses (*nefalim*), and anything which does not live for thirty days, we do not mourn for it.
> Maimonides, *Mishneh Torah, Hilkhot Aveilut* 1:6

> The infant, for thirty days, even including the full thirtieth day (if it dies), we do not mourn for it.
> *Shulḥan Arukh, Yoreh De'ah* 374:8

The reason for the limit of thirty days appears to derive from the fact that thirty days is the age at which we are commanded to redeem the firstborn (*pidyon ha-ben*). For the rabbis, this marked the point at which a fetus became fully viable.

The result of this ruling was that none of the practices of mourning was to take place if the infant was born dead or did not survive to the thirty-first day. Although the child was buried, there was no funeral per se, the grave was left unmarked, and the parents might never know where the grave was located. It was undoubtedly considered an act of kindness to the parents and the community, for without the restriction, families would have been in mourning almost continuously.

Today the opposite is true. The tremendous sense of loss and the overwhelming need to grieve felt by the parents of an infant who dies before the thirty-day benchmark does not go away just because the *halakhah* prevents the mourning rituals from taking place. The medical profession has now recognized that parents experiencing a baby's death must face the loss, and protocols to enable them to mourn have been developed within recent years. Parents are encouraged to see and touch the baby, pictures may be taken, mementos kept. It is recommended that the parents name the baby; it will be much easier in the future to talk about "Daniel" than "Baby Boy." Social workers routinely recommend funerals, and support groups for bereaved parents experiencing neonatal death can be found in many communities. Yet, most rabbis and most Jewish laypeople presented with this type of loss would be hard-pressed to know what to say, except to repeat the painful words, "There is no mourning for this child."

Jewish law has remained viable and relevant because each generation of interpreters applied the *halakhah* to its own time. The Committee on Jewish Law and Standards of the Rabbinical Assembly of the Conservative movement adopted a new position vis-à-vis neonatal death in 1992 by accepting the *t'shuvah* (rabbinic responsum) of Rabbi Stephanie Dickstein to the question, *"What should be Jewish practice following the death of an infant who lives less than thirty-one days?"*

Rabbi Dickstein points out that the commonly held belief that there is no mourning for a child who does not survive to thirty-one days is not the only position found in Jewish legal literature. In Mishnah *Niddah* 5:3, we find this statement: "A one-day-old infant, if he dies, is considered to his father and mother like a full bridegroom," and therefore the child would be mourned. In the Babylonian Talmud, tractate *Shabbat* 136a, we read that the sons of Rav Dimi and Rav Kahana mourned for their newborns who died. Even Maimonides states: "If a man knows for certain that the child was born after a full nine months, even if it dies on the day it is born, we mourn it" (*Aveilut* 1:7). The *Shulḥan Arukh* concurs (*Yoreh De'ah* 374:8).

Rabbi Dickstein also points to the universally accepted requirement to bury a newborn infant, stillborn, or fetus miscarried after the fifth month.

Rabbi Dickstein has led the Conservative movement to establish new legal responses that carry with them the full authority of Jewish law. Here are the major points of this new practice:

- In the case of a full-term pregnancy, when an infant dies for any reason, at any time after birth, its parents and other family members should be obligated for full bereavement practices, just as for any other child. The parents should recite Kaddish for thirty days and should observe *yahrtzeit*. Young siblings have no obligation to say Kaddish and post–bar/bat mitzvah siblings should be encouraged to use the traditional rituals to work through the many feelings they have.

- The body should be buried in accordance with Jewish practice. The funeral should follow standard practice with appropriate readings of comfort in place of a eulogy. Parents should be encouraged to attend the funeral, as should family and close friends. The funeral should be held as soon as possible, although if the mother wants to attend, burial may be delayed until she recovers enough physical strength following the delivery to attend.

- If the infant was not named prior to death, it is usually given a name at the grave. The name may be the one the parents intended to use for their child (although this might be difficult for the surviving grandparents whose own parents may have been remembered with this name), or they might choose a Hebrew name like Mena*h*em or Ne*h*amah, names that in translation indicate a desire for "comfort." There are two reasons for the naming: According to Jewish folk tradition, giving a name will enable parents to "find" their child in the world to come, and psychologists consider the practice of naming to be an important help in healing the parents' grief.

- If the information gathered from an autopsy can help determine the advisability of future pregnancies for the couple or of treatment of diseases to which other children of the couple might be susceptible, it should be allowed, even encouraged.

- A complete *shiva* should be observed, beginning with the meal of consolation and including daily prayer services for the mourners.

Communal participation in the *shiva* makes real this loss and overcomes the tremendous isolation the parents feel. If things had turned out differently, the community would have been there for visiting the baby and welcoming it with Jewish birth rituals. The family whose newborn dies should not be denied its community. It is also extremely important, especially for the father, to allow permission to do nothing else but mourn during the *shiva* period.

- The father and the mother should be treated equally as mourners. Both parents will react differently to the loss, but as pointed out in the Introduction, it is particularly important for the father to recognize his loss, for it is no less real than the mother's. When the father is treated as a mourner, he is relieved of the burden of "being strong" for his wife. He has a specific set of ritual tasks to do that encourage him to confront the magnitude of his loss in all its dimensions.

- In the case of infants born prematurely, there is still debate within the Law Committee on how to define "viability." Some, including Rabbi Dickstein, argue that between five months and thirty weeks the decision concerning mourning might be made by the local rabbi and the parents.

Certainly, there may be those who feel the centuries-old practice of not mourning a neonatal death could be more comforting than engaging in the whole ritual of Jewish bereavement. But for those who desperately need a vehicle for grief, this recent ruling allowing for the mourning of newborns is indeed a welcome development.

Miscarriage

Rabbi Debra Reed Blank, a 1989 graduate of The Jewish Theological Seminary, writes that there are three tragedies involved in a miscarriage:

> The most obvious is the loss of the potential child and the ensuing grief of the couple ... the less obvious is the community's abandonment of this couple during their time of grief ... the third facet of this tragedy is the lack of guidance from Jewish tradition.

In response to her own miscarriage, Rabbi Blank developed an approach to how Jewish practice might help a couple channel and express their emotions and a guide for communal response. She bases her recommendations on the concept of *bikkur ḥolim*, the universal requirement to visit the sick.

The mother who has miscarried is certainly a *ḥolah* ("ill"), for any woman who miscarries is considered ill based on her physical condition alone. The father is also a *ḥoleh*, for he has undoubtedly experienced psychological trauma. Therefore, Rabbi Blank offers the following ritual possibilities:

- A *Mi Sh'beirakh*, a prayer said during the Torah service requesting God's blessing for one who is sick, may be recited in the synagogue;
- After the woman has physically recovered, she may recite *Birkat Ha-gomel*, a prayer said by one who has recovered from illness and is called to the Torah;

- A visit to the *mikvah,* the ritual bath, can be a symbol of a new beginning;
- *Bikkur holim* visits from close friends upon news of the miscarriage and others later on can demonstrate communal support and can help in meeting the needs of those who are ill. Make a specific offer of help during this visit and don't stay too long. The traditional prayer for physical and emotional recovery can be said by the visitor:

הַמָּקוֹם יְרַחֵם אֲלֵיכֶם בְּתוֹךְ חוֹלֵי יִשְׂרָאֵל.

Ha-Makom y'rahem aleikhem b'tokh holei Yisrael

May the Omnipresent show compassion to you among the
other *holei* of Israel.

The Committee on Jewish Law and Standards has accepted Rabbi Blank's suggestions as appropriate responses to miscarriage within the scope of *halakhah.* The former chairman of the committee, Rabbi Joel Roth, points out the complication of "the linkage between abortion and fetal mourning.... Those two, on a certain level, are somewhat inconsistent, one positing that we consider the fetus virtually as alive and the other positing that we consider the fetus as virtually not living, thereby allowing abortions on the one hand and strict mourning practices on the other" (Speech to 1990 Women's League Biennial Convention). Nevertheless, it is likely that those whose responsibility it is to interpret Jewish law will continue to hear the pleas of those couples and families who experience the tragedy of miscarriage and stillbirth for appropriate Jewish ritual responses.

I have a confession to make. Our baby died in May of 1974. That fall, for the first time in my life, I stayed in the synagogue during the *Yizkor* service, even though my parents, thank God, are still alive. I was always very much aware of the superstition that led children with living parents to step out of the service when the memorial prayers were said. That fall, I remained in my place and recited the prayer for a deceased child. I had no name to announce, but I had the need to remember the loss of potential. I had the need to express my grief and sadness. I had the need to reaffirm my faith in God that the future would be brighter and that the incredible pain inflicted on Susie and me would be healed. To this day, I remember our first child during *Yizkor* and on the anniversary of her death.

Until June 3, 1992, this practice was not *k'halakhah,* according Jewish law. Now, it is, and it will be a comfort to know that we can remember our first child without reservation within the Jewish tradition we love so much.

My good friend Rabbi Marvin Goodman, and his wife, Deborah, experienced the loss of a stillborn child in 1981. They, too, struggled with the grief, intellectually rationalizing and accepting the *halakhah,* but desperately searching for a way to mourn the baby through Jewish ritual. Their solution was to buy a single unopened rose every Friday and to read something about or by children before the Erev Shabbat meal. Marv poignantly writes: "I had very much looked forward to blessing our child at this time. Instead, this simple ritual was a public reminder of our loss and provided me a process through which to work out my grief."

"Focus on *Halakhah," Women's League Outlook,*
Spring 1992, p. 16.

The Death of a Child

DENNIS GURA: Rebecca was seventeen months old when diagnosed with leukemia. She was six when she died. She was determined to make it to her sixth birthday.

When we learned Rebecca had cancer, the first thing out of the mouth of the social worker was, "You know, 80 percent of the parents who go through this end up divorced." Kathy and I were determined that wouldn't happen to us, for Rebecca's sake at least.

Oh, we had our fights. You can't imagine how intense it is to fight cancer for four years. Counseling helped. But, really, our commitment to Rebecca, to each other and to keeping our family together was most important.

Lots of friends who had kids the same age dropped out of our lives when they learned that Rebecca had cancer. I guess it was just too scary for them. And I'm sure our anger drove away others. Those friends who stayed close to us tended to be those with a religious commitment. Of course, our synagogue community was fantastic. People would offer to do things for us, little things, but they meant a lot. The first Shabbat we were in the hospital friends brought us candles, wine, _ḥallot, bensh-ers_—so we could make Shabbat there—in the protective isolation unit.

RON WOLFSON: What happens when a child dies before a parent?

HERMAN FEIFEL: Rough business. The way of life is for the old to die before the young, for parents to die before children. In Jewish tradition, for children to die before parents puts you onto quicksand. Who will say Kaddish for you?

DENNIS GURA: Sometimes Kathy and I feel like we haven't grown one day older since the day Rebecca died. Somehow, a part of us died that day, too. On the other hand, I'm reminded of the Hasidic story of the woman whose child died; she is in incredible grief. She goes to the *rebbe* and asks him what to do. He says: "Bake a cake." "What?" she asks. "Bake a cake, but use only flour you borrow from those whose pain is less than yours. Bring it to me next *Shabbes*." Shabbat comes and the lady returns to the *rebbe* empty-handed. "Where is the cake?" he asks. She says: "I couldn't get the flour, for there was no one with less pain in their lives than me."

When a child is diagnosed as terminally ill, parents often have different reactions. Some parents, armed with available information about causes, complications, and expectations about the course of the illness, rally together to support the child, the family, and each other. Other parents respond with a tortured, frenzied search for unproven treatments and cures. Specialists dealing in terminal illnesses among children report that strong families often become stronger in the face of the crisis, while families with preexisting stresses and tensions often find these aggravated, sometimes to the point of dissolution. Unfortunately, there is a higher than average incidence of separation and divorce in families that experience the death of a child. The medical and spiritual communities have begun to address this problem by offering a variety of supports for families with terminally ill children, including specially trained counselors and social workers. There has also developed a heightened awareness of how the child him- or herself comes to cope with the illness—from the initial inference that the illness is "serious" to the ultimate realization that death is coming.

DAVID TECHNER: My wife and I had a tough time after the death of our child. I used to come home on pins and needles. "How was your day?"

I would ask her, knowing it had been terrible. I had befriended the psychologist Sonya Friedman, and she gave us such a gift. She met with us and said: "Look, I know you're in trouble. You're afraid of each other. You're afraid you're going to say something that will hurt the other. You can't talk to each other. I want to give you a homework assignment. For the next six days, you're going to sit across from each other, look each other straight in the eye, and talk about Alicia for fifteen minutes." You know what happened? The weight of the world went off our shoulders. Because we had to, we talked about Alicia. We cried. We laughed. It's so important to communicate with each other. We became better people because ot it.

During the months after our daughter's death, it was nearly impossible to be around other babies. To this day, it's an issue. Our daughter would have been fifteen years old this year, and I still have problems being around fifteen-year-old kids. I wonder to myself: "Would Alicia have been as cute? Would she be wearing braces? Would she be as popular?"

How can parents help each other in coping with the death of a child? Experts suggest that each parent understand that emotional reactions may very well differ, and each partner should offer respectful "space" for the grief of the other. At the same time, it is critical to maintain open lines of communication. Often, a counselor's help is necessary to achieve this, for the pain is so deep and intense, it is difficult to keep the relationship open and healthy. Seeking such help is a sign of strength, not of weakness.

Most rabbis consider the death of a child to be one of the most difficult and challenging moments of their careers as pastoral counselors. The tragedy is nearly unspeakable. The inevitable "why" questions, the anger and rage toward just about everything and everyone, including God, are particularly penetrating, testing one's faith in a profound way. Somehow the tradition seeks to comfort a bereaved parent, a bereaved sibling, a bereaved community. Yet the scars left by the death of a child seem never to fully heal.

AIDS-Related Deaths

DAVID NOVAK: We just put up the third huge memorial wall in our synagogue. Imagine every year going through *Yontif* seeing faces in the
crowd that you know will not be there next year? And these are not
Aunt Sadie or Uncle Max who are eighty, ninety years old. These are
third generation American Jews in their twenties and thirties—doctors,
lawyers, teachers. It haunts you. We've been through a lot of public
mourning in our synagogue. Our president died recently. At the funeral,
the whole congregation was in grief. It was impossible to comfort anybody. We sat *shiva* with his surviving life partner.

RON WOLFSON: How is your community dealing with the AIDS crisis?

DAVID NOVAK: Every Friday night at our synagogue, we greet mourners—new mourners. There is no question that we need to do this. Every
week, we read not only the list of *yahrtzeits,* but the list of those members who have died in the last year. It's long—probably twenty-five,
thirty names. There is such pain.

At Kol Nidre, I met a young man who looked the picture of perfect
health who told me he just tested positive for HIV. He had only come
out to his parents two years ago. His parents are survivors of the
camps. Can you imagine? Year 1—"Hi, I'm gay." Year 2—"I'm HIV-
positive." To be a survivor and to survive your child—this plague has
turned the normal life cycle upside-down. It's unbelievable.

There is a whole new ritual developing around AIDS. One of our
members wrote a series of new prayers she calls "The Liturgy of Defi-

ance." There is a feeling that we, like Reb Levi Yitzhak of Berditchev, have to argue and challenge God.

RON WOLFSON: What should be the response of the straight community to the death of a homosexual from AIDS?

DAVID NOVAK: It's very important to acknowledge what the person died from. You can't ignore what it was, what the parents, or family, or life partner went through. The life partner is mourning the death of a spouse. It is not a time for moral judgments. It's a time for compassion.

SHARON KLEINBAUM: AIDS is similar to many chronic illnesses, with its own ugly twists. People with AIDS go up and down radically. The dying process starts once someone is diagnosed HIV-positive. In my community, people talk about their latest T-cell counts the way other people talk about their latest diet. They can live asymptomatic for a number of years, but they are living with a death sentence. It creates a severe anxiety that affects them and everyone around them. It can be a long, drawn-out process.

For parents of AIDS victims who are coming in from out-of-town and confront their son who was once a healthy 225-pound man and is now an emaciated, infection-ridden skeleton, it is very hard to deal with.

One of the most important facts for people to realize is that there are people in my community who fall between "close friend" and the seven recognized categories of mourners. Many gay people have lifetime companions or spouses, and when a death occurs, the surviving same-sex spouse is in mourning as much as any other spouse.

Quite often, very painful conflicts arise between the family of origin and the family of choice when a gay person dies. Unfortunately, the family of origin has all the legal rights with regard to the funeral. My job as a rabbi is to reach out and comfort both groups.

RON WOLFSON: How can the family of origin be sensitive to the family of choice?

SHARON KLEINBAUM: The family of origin has to recognize that a life companion is a spouse and needs to be treated as such. Just as a heterosexual spouse would be treated in certain ways when making funeral and *shiva* arrangements, that spouse should be included in these decisions.

When things get ugly, it is usually because the family of origin has not resolved themselves to the fact that their child is gay. Often, they will take their anger out on the life partner: "My child is not gay; this person was the evil influence." They will attempt to cut the gay partner and the community out of the mourning process. Another way this denial works is when the family of origin does not want any mention of AIDS in the obituary or at the funeral.

The major problem is that while the gay person may be "out," the family of origin is often still "in the closet." They are terrified of what their community would do to them if this got out. But what this fear really does is deny them the support of their friends and families at the very time they need it most.

This illness and death affects every member of the family. To the extent that the Jewish community does not allow homosexuality to be an open issue, it forces everyone into the closet.

The major reason so many gay people don't turn to the synagogue during their illness and death is that they have felt rejected in their life. How can I see religion as a place of comfort when it has shut me out?

I think our community will respond to courageous rabbis like Harold Schulweis and Marshall Myers who have said to gay and lesbian people: "You are welcome in our synagogue while you are alive, not just when you are dying."

We have a wide variety of backgrounds among our membership, but our funeral and mourning practices are actually quite traditional.

RON WOLFSON: Are partners buying plots together?

SHARON KLEINBAUM: Yes, but because so many of our members are so young, the likelihood of being buried together is slim. The surviving spouse may eventually find another partner.

The gay community as a whole has dealt incredibly well with death and dying. What our synagogue provides is a place that is completely destigmatized. We have a *shiva minyan*. We have seventy-five people who serve on a *bikkur ḥolim* committee and who are a bereavement group for those past *shloshim*.

We have had about 115 deaths from AIDS in the congregation, all people under the age of fifty, and there is no end in sight.

RON WOLFSON: How does a community cope with such overwhelming death? How do you cope as a rabbi?

SHARON KLEINBAUM: As a rabbi, I feel personally blessed. I feel I'm doing God's work, and I'm right where I need to be. I'm filling needs that are unfortunately not being filled by the rest of the Jewish community. I feel grateful.

As a community, we've learned to live with it. When a person dies, someone will stand up on Friday night in *shul* and say something about the deceased. Then we read the very beautiful *Agnon Kaddish*. At *Yizkor,* we read the entire list. It's quite emotional.

Although the AIDS virus does not discriminate between heterosexuals and homosexuals, it has brought disproportionate death and grief to the gay community. As more homosexual Jewish men and women come out publicly to family and friends, many of them members and children of members of synagogues, the straight community will be further challenged to deal with their presence, their needs, and their attempts to cope with the inordinate loss.

According to Jewish law, absolutely no discrimination is made with regard to the burial of someone of homosexual orientation. Abner Weiss, an Orthodox rabbi, states in his book, *Death and Bereavement: A Halakhic Guide,* that victims of AIDS "are entitled to a full ritual cleansing." Moreover, as homosexuals continue to develop forms of partnership commitments, it is entirely possible that couples may wish to be buried side by side, even with shared gravestones.

PART 3

The Art of Jewish Mourning

DAVID TECHNER: When I was on *Donahue,* he asked me, "How did you get over Alicia's death?" I said, "You're making a big assumption. You assume I've gotten over her death. I'm not. I never will. I never want to get over it. I'm used to it, but I'll never get over it. Every year when May 18 comes around, it's a birthday I can't share with Alicia. I'm used to that day, but I'm not over it. Every year at Hanukkah time, I think of Alicia. I'm used to it, but I'm not over it."

The big problem is that people need permission to feel terrible fifteen years after the loss, and we don't allow it. We give people a few days, a week, a month, and then we think they should be "over it." We want our bereaved friends to be over it, because then we don't have to deal with the other's grief anymore. You're never over it.

The term *phases of grief* should be banned from the English language. The great disservice of the idea of "phases" is that mourners think something's wrong with them if they don't experience the phases in exactly the right order and exactly the way the experts describe how it should feel. Take acceptance. When the grief subsides, we "accept" it. And everyone reaches that point of acceptance. Nonsense. I prefer the term *adjustment.* I get used to my grief, but I never accept it.

Grief-Work and the Experience of Jewish Mourning

Grieving is the way we mend broken hearts. When we sustain a bad wound, the body heals in stages: Initially, we feel shock and numbness, then the sharp pain of the injury, and slowly the hurt subsides. Even so, we are often left with a scar, reminding us of the seriousness of the trauma. "Grief-work," the process of mourning, is the way the psyche, bruised and battered by the pain of loss, heals itself.

Responses to loss cannot be accurately predicted nor explained in neatly defined phases. Just as in the process of dying, bereavement involves a number of responses that come in and out of the mind and body at different times. In unexpected moments, just when we think the acute pain is over, a wave of sorrow or a deep ache of loss can overcome us.

Moreover, there is no timeline for the healing of grief. For some, the intensity of pain subsides within months; for others, it is years before the adjustment to the loss is in place. It is critically important for mourners to realize that there is no "right" way to grieve, nor is there any "limit" on how long the "phases" of grief will last. Each of us will experience bereavement in a unique way.

Yet most experts on grief-work identify three broad experiences in this healing process: (1) shock, (2) experiencing the pain, and (3) resolution and adjustment.

Shock

The first response to news of a loss is profound shock. It feels as if you've been hit by a truck. You cry out and, just as with a serious physical injury, the body and mind go into shock.

With the shock comes a feeling of numbness. You cannot even feel yourself physically. This numbness is a protective device, a way to allow the harsh reality to sink in gradually. It enables you to cope with the feelings bit by bit, raising the pain threshold and initially muting the full emotional impact of the loss.

This numbness, this shield against the emotions, allows you to do what must be done in the immediate moments after a death occurs. How else could you get through the tasks of making burial arrangements, planning a funeral, setting up a *shiva* home without the shield of numbness? For some, the numbness is so effective that these things are accomplished with stunning efficiency. This type of bereaved individual seems relatively unaffected and accepting of the loss. But, often, the roller coaster of emotions that is the singular characteristic of grief replaces this initial feeling of numbness, sometimes very suddenly.

Of course, Jewish tradition recognized this experience of grief. *Aninut*, the time between the moment of death and the funeral, is defined by the numbness brought on by the initial shock of loss. The rabbis knew through vast experience that it is nearly impossible to comfort the bereaved during this time. The shock and numbness will simply not allow it. Even when we try, the words fall empty, unheard.

Instead, the rabbis instruct the *onen/onennet* to keep occupied with the details of burying the dead, while consolers bide their time or attend to the preparations for the *shiva* period to come. With amazing psychological insight, the tradition teaches that those who wish to comfort must wait until the bereaved are ready to be comforted. Even though our first inclination is to try to comfort, the shock and numbness experienced by the bereaved prevents our most sincere efforts.

Experiencing the pain

The second experience of mourning is the most difficult to endure. When the numbness and shock wear off, the reality of the loss hits. Intense emotions often boil over in fits of sadness, anger, melancholy, and anguish. When grief reaches the heart, the real pain begins.

In the Jewish tradition, grief reaches the heart at the funeral. Everything about the funeral is designed to confront the bereaved with the reality of death. The eulogy stimulates our memories and our emotions, the prayers talk not just of the demise of the deceased, but of the mortality of all human beings and the confrontation with the grave. The thud of the earth on the casket shakes the bereaved out of shock and disbelief, clearing the way for the difficult work of mourning.

Aveilut, mourning, begins at this moment of raw emotion. The *shiva* time that lies ahead will be filled with the symptoms of grief-work. Among them are:

- **Sadness.** The sadness that the bereaved experience is overwhelming. It is an ache felt in the deepest part of the soul. It is a feeling of complete emptiness, hollowness. Its most predominant expression is tears—tears of sadness, tears of loss. While there are predictable times when the tears flow, there are also unexpected moments that trigger them. Suddenly, a memory pops into your head, and you begin sobbing. Seeing someone with whom you and the deceased shared wonderful times will bring on uncontrollable weeping. You open a closet door after the funeral, and at the first glance of a row of suits, you break down. Eventually, you cry yourself out, exhausted. Of course, it is impossible to enjoy yourself with amusements, parties, television. It is even difficult to enjoy the company of those who give you the most pleasure—children, grandchildren, friends. Sometimes a feeling of despair comes with the tears. But, often, the tears ultimately bring a kind of comfort, the lubricating fluid of the healing process.

    The Bible is filled with accounts of the wailing that accompanies loss. Jewish tradition allows for the sadness of bereavement, encouraging its expression throughout the funeral and *shiva* period.

- **Anger.** A natural response to loss is anger—anger born of frustration and helplessness. This anger is directed at many—doctors, hospitals, drunken drivers, rabbis, employers, family, friends— even God. It is not uncommon to find yourself lashing out at those you love the most.

   Why my son? Why my wife? Why has this bad thing happened to this good person? From Abraham to Job to Wiesel to Kushner, the questioning of God is well within the mainstream of the Jewish response to loss.

- **Guilt.** Guilt is one of the most common responses to loss. It appears in a variety of ways:

   Guilt born of survival. "I should have gone first."

   Guilt born of anger. "Why did you die and leave me?"

   Guilt born of the inability to cope with loss. "I shouldn't be so distraught. Why can't I get ahold of myself?"

   Guilt born of feeling relief that the deceased is gone. "How dare I feel happy again!"

   Guilt born of regret. "If only I had taken her to another doctor ..." "I should never have driven him so hard ..." "I'll never forgive myself for the fight we had ..."

Pangs of guilt are natural and, according to some experts, necessary. In a twist of irony, guilt feelings, when overcome, enable the mourner to consider the positive ways he or she acted. "Yes, I could have done more for Mom, but now that I think about it, I really was a pretty good son." Of course, overwhelming guilt can be disabling and should be dealt with appropriately. Ultimately, whatever guilt feelings exist should be forgiven. Forgiving oneself is an important step on the road to healing grief.

Jewish tradition knew this. In a practice that unfortunately is no longer in vogue, it suggested that each person at a funeral ask the deceased for forgiveness. Surely the rabbis knew that it was unlikely the deceased would hear this plea (although many of them had a vivid imagination of the afterlife). Rather, the psychological wisdom of asking forgiveness lies in the expiation of guilt that accompanies the plea. We ask not that the deceased forgive

us; we ask ourselves for forgiveness—a task that is far more difficult. Judaism wants us not to be too hard on ourselves.

- **Physical complaints.** Mourners often complain of physical ailments, including shortness of breath, tightness in the throat, feelings of emptiness in the stomach, overwhelming weakness,
headaches. Most bereaved have very little appetite, experience
difficulty sleeping, and feel totally exhausted.

  Judaism insists that the bereaved eat immediately after the funeral as a sign of the slow return to normalcy, yet most mourners
report difficulty in consuming this meal. During the course of the
shiva, this feeling subsides and appetite returns. However, the intensity of the *shiva* often leads to a lack of sleep and a profound
sense of exhaustion. In fact, the feeling of exhaustion is the most
frequently cited response to the *shiva* experience.

- **Fear.** Having stared death in the face, the bereaved often express
their own fear of dying or of other loved ones dying. Or, widows
fear being alone, children fear losing the other parent, and adult
children fear the future once both parents are gone.

  Jewish tradition attempts to smother these fears by surrounding the bereaved with community. The message is clear: "You are
not alone." That is why the community comes to the mourner for
the *shiva,* that is why the community welcomes the bereaved back
to its fold on the Shabbat during *shiva,* that is why each experience of Jewish mourning is celebrated not alone, but within the
context of a supportive community.

- **Pining and searching.** Pining is the soulful longing for the deceased that leads to searching, the powerful urge to find a "lost"
love. Often, this phenomenon is uncanny and disconcerting. You
begin to "see" your loved one in the faces of others. You "hear"
his or her voice. You sense the presence of the deceased in a
room, at a table, during a prayer.

  Judaism wants us never to forget the memory of the departed.
The *shiva* is not the end of mourning—it is just the beginning. We
mourn the loss of loved ones four times a year during the *Yizkor* memorial service and on every anniversary of a death for the rest of our
lives. Jewish tradition teaches us that we can never get them back
physically, but we can have them with us in our memories forever.

- **Lapses in clear thinking.** The bereaved may experience enormous emotional swings that sometimes result in such a mental tumult that normally clear-thinking people can become confused, use poor judgment, and even experience temporary memory loss. The days immediately following the funeral are not a good time to make important decisions and choices.

  Again, the wisdom of the seven-day *shiva* period allows the bereaved time to gather themselves for the inevitable decision making that follows a loss. "Where shall Mom live?" "What about the will?" "How do we divide up the personal items in the household?" When a family sits *shiva* for seven days, there is time for the initial grief to subside so these decisions can be made.

- **Falling apart.** Mourners often evidence changes of behavior in both relationships with others and in daily activities. For those who grieve, the simplest of chores—paying bills, shopping for groceries—often feel like major burdens. Sometimes, the mourner wanders around the house, aimlessly picking up things, putting them down, rearranging photos on mantles, or simply staring into space. The mourner loses control of his eating or drinking, takes foolish risks, gives away precious possessions. The mourner feels like she's falling apart.

  Judaism suggests the mourner spend thirty days slowly returning to regular routines, to work and to the daily challenges of living. For thirty days after the funeral, the bereaved's activities are restricted somewhat, allowing a gradual return to the complexities of living. During this time, friends and family can provide tremendous comfort in reassuring the bereaved that these feelings of being out of control are perfectly normal for those who have experienced profound loss. For some, a support group can be helpful in smoothing the transition back to normalcy. The important message is that these feelings will subside in time. Grief-work is not over quickly.

Resolution and adjustment

Many mourners and comforters expect that the process of grief will be over in a matter of days or weeks. But there is no timetable for the healing of the human heart. Each person is unique; each person heals differently and at different rates. Even when the healing process seems to be well on its way, something as routine as finding a much-loved photo, a birthday, an anniversary, or a favorite shared ritual can throw the timetable off track.

Part of the problem inherent in any grief timeline is the issue of expectations: "By this time, you should [fill in the blank]": ... have control of yourself;" "... be able to get back to work;" or "... be dating again."

Mourners have expectations for themselves about when grief will subside and these expectations are fueled by others' expectations. If these expectations are not met, if the timeline is not followed, somehow we think something is wrong.

This is simply not true. Grief has no clock. In fact, there will be ups and downs, even when it appears that an adjustment has been made and the most intense grief seems resolved. Especially when the deceased is remembered at birthdays, anniversaries, the *Yizkor* and *yahrtzeit* memorials, there will likely be some pain involved. This is normal and healthy.

Most experts believe that the bereaved can return to relatively normal functioning within a few months, yet life may be strongly influenced by the loss for up to a year or even as long as three years later. These experts point out that the duration of the bereavement depends in large measure on how successfully the bereaved has done the "grief-work" itself, how well the person has allowed the suffering and pain to happen and work itself out.

The resolution of grief is characterized by five achievements on the part of the bereaved:

1. **Adjusting to the pain that comes with mourning.** Allowing the suffering, giving expression to the pain, enduring the waves of sadness all hasten the healing.
2. **Adjusting to the finality of the loss.** J. William Worden explains in his book *Grief Counseling and Grief Therapy:* "Part of the acceptance of reality is to come to the belief that reunion is impossible, at least in this life."
3. **Crystallizing memories of the deceased.** The bereaved experience what can only be called a "life review" as they recall the memories of life with the deceased loved one. Gradually, a mental

"photo album" of the person emerges. Eventually, the most meaningful memories become integrated into the bereaved one's own life, reuniting with the loved one in death in a way rarely possible in life.

4. **Letting go.** Judith Viorst, in her popular book *Necessary Losses*, argues that, ironically, one way to let go of the dead is to take them in. We can establish internally a presence of the deceased, by identifying with some aspect of his or her life, by creating within our hearts and minds a small corner for the fond memories.

The ultimate test of whether or not the bereaved have "let go" is their ability to establish new relationships, even feel affection for someone new. The greatest honor to themselves and to their loved ones is when the bereaved can live life fully once again.

5. **Fully, but never the same.** For many bereavements, particularly the death of a child, it is nearly impossible to accept the loss. Adjust to the loss, get "used to" the loss, yes, but never accept.

Excellent resources that further explore grief-work include *Mourning and Mitzvah: A Guided Journal for Walking the Mourner's Path through Grief to Healing* by Anne Brener; *After Great Pain: A New Life Emerges* by Diane Cole; *Grieving: How to Go On Living When Someone You Love Dies* by Theresa Rando; and *How to Survive the Loss of a Love* by Melba Colgrove, Harold H. Bloomfield, and Peter McWilliams.

The Phases of Jewish Bereavement

HAROLD SCHULWEIS: One of my earliest memories in the rabbinate was a call from a professor at Berkeley whose father had died. He asked me, in his words, "How do I mourn?" A sophisticated intellectual, he was totally lost. He sought a way to express his pain within the context of his inherited tradition. He wanted the Jewish wisdom for holding on and letting go. He wanted, as well, the ritual ways to identify his values with his father's.

Two thousand years before modern psychology discovered "grief-work," the rabbis of the Talmud had established a staged series of steps to manage mourning.

There are six basic phases of the Jewish bereavement cycle. Each has a specific time period and a set of major practices and common emotional states that assist the mourner through the grieving process. Remember: Although these phases are time-bound, the emotions of a mourner's grief may or may not correspond to these times. The experience of bereavement is highly individualistic, and while the time may move quickly, the resolution of grief often takes months or years.

We will spell out each of these phases in detail below, but first, let's look at a general overview of the Jewish approach to mourning:

Phase one: *aninut*

Time:	From the moment of death until the conclusion of the funeral.
Major Practices:	Making funeral arrangements, preparing for the funeral, no mourning, no prayer services, no "official" condolence calls.
Common Emotions:	Shock, numbness, anger, denial, disbelief.

Phase two: *aveilut* (for seven relatives: mother, father, spouse, sister, brother, son, daughter)

Time:	Seven days of *shiva,* beginning at the conclusion of the funeral (Day One) through the next six days, unless cancelled by a festival. The first three days are for intense mourning, followed by four days of mourning and reflection.
Major Practices:	"Sit" at home, say Kaddish at prayer services conducted in the home (or synagogue), receive consolers; no work or shaving.
Common Emotions:	Sadness, relief, melancholy, comfort, happiness when recalling fond memories of the deceased.

Phase three: *shloshim*—thirty days (for seven relatives)

Time:	From the end of *shiva* (Day Seven) through thirty days from the day of burial.
Major Practices:	Return to work, say Kaddish at prayer services in the synagogue; no entertainment; men do not shave.
Common Emotions:	Loneliness, busyness, waves of sadness.

Phase four: *shanah*—eleven months (for parents)

Time:	From the day of burial through eleven months.
Major Practices:	Saying Kaddish at prayer services in the synagogue,

some restrictions on behavior (including attendance at genuinely happy events) until a full year has passed, unveiling of gravestone.

Common Emotions: Gradual return to normal feelings, occasional twinges of sadness, recovering from grief, return of humor.

Phase five: *yahrtzeit*

Time: Anniversary of the day of death.

Major Practices: Say Kaddish at prayer services in the synagogue, light a memorial candle, give *tzedakah*.

Common Emotions: Sadness at memory of loss.

Phase six: *yizkor* (for seven relatives)

Time: Yom Kippur, Shemini Atzeret, last day of Passover, second day of Shavuot

Major Practices: Recite special memorial services in the synagogue, light memorial candle (although some light a candle only on Yom Kippur), give *tzedakah*.

Common Emotions: Sadness, memories.

PART 4

From the Death
to the Funeral

ALLEN BROWN: Dad died at 12:30 p.m. All the doctors and nurses who worked with him came into the solarium to pay their respects. By 1:30, I called our Jewish funeral home. A meeting was set for 3:00. My son took me to the funeral home, just the two of us. My sisters took my mother home and Dianne started to make *shiva* arrangements, although I later found out that her friend, Saralie Foote, already had everything under control. When I got to the funeral home, I ran into a problem. My parents didn't have plots. I was able to get two plots for them, and then I bought two plots for us because I realized we didn't have plots either. You don't think about this until it happens.

Since I am traditional, I had to make arrangements through the funeral home for the <u>h</u>evra kadisha to come down to bathe him, dress him, watch him, until the next morning of the funeral.

I guess the part that hit me the worst was not at the funeral home. By the time I got home that afternoon, the funeral director had already delivered the items for the *shiva*—the *shiva* chairs, the wax candle, the prayer books. The men from the funeral home had to pass my house on the way to pick up Dad, so they dropped it off. It really brought it home that this was happening.

The next morning, Rabbi Skopitz came over to talk to us. He's known Dad for years, but he wanted more information for the eulogy. He took us through the funeral service, some of the dos and don'ts. He told us we had the option of putting dirt into the grave. He suggested that I should definitely do it. My sisters asked if they could too, and he said definitely, yes.

I remember we were sitting in my mother's apartment in a high-rise. Just as the rabbi was talking, a bird flew onto the balcony. We all looked at it, and my mother said she had never seen a bird do that before. It stayed there until the rabbi finished everything he was supposed to say and then it flew away. It was really weird.

TAMARA GREENEBAUM: My father did not want to have a funeral for my mother. My husband had to talk him into it.

He just doesn't like them. He avoids them like crazy. Maybe he's been to half a dozen in his whole life. It turns out they had filled out questionnaires at the holistic health clinic that asked about their view of their life and afterlife. My mother's answers were clear: She was happy with her life, she was completely unspiritual, she had no doubt that we had nothing in this life but what we have now ... My dad was so comforted by this ... He feels the same way, so I think that's why he doesn't believe in funerals.

There is no Jewish mortuary in the community in which they live. Just in the last year they have set up a _hevra kadisha_. They had just begun to deal with the non-Jewish mortuary on how to conduct a Jewish funeral in the community. The congregation had just acquired a portion of an old cemetery and had built a fence around it. So my mother was going to be the first person buried there. No one—not the mortuary, not the congregation, and certainly not my family—had had any experience with this. There was not even a Jewish casket in town.

Gary, my husband, finally convinced my dad that it would be good for him if there were a funeral, and really good for the community. He also convinced him that if he didn't want to sit _shiva_, it was his choice, of course, but that at least a community _minyan_ the night of the funeral would be a really great source of comfort to him.

When my mother died, he called the rabbi and the mortician. When we found out that there was no casket, the rabbi suggested that maybe some of the congregants would build a casket, which we thought was a wonderful idea. But it would have held up the funeral by at least a day, and my father was adamant about doing things as quickly as possible, so we were able to locate a casket in San Francisco.

We made one call to a member of the board of the synagogue who arranged everything for the _shiva_ meal at home after the funeral. Three phone calls and everything was arranged. I commented to my dad that if this had happened in Los Angeles, it would have taken the family a whole day on the phone to do what we did with three phone calls. The close-knittedness of the community made it so much easier for the family.

I mean, my father called the rabbi and said: "Margaret, this is Lou. Get me two plots," and that was that.

CAROL STARIN: When Joel died, I made one phone call, and all the arrangements for the funeral and *shiva* were done. By choosing the traditional way of Jewish burial, there were no other choices to be made. When my father buried my mother, he had to choose a casket. He even had to choose which dress she should wear to her grave. Then, when he was sitting in the chapel before the service, a guy brought him a bill to sign! When Joel died, I didn't see a bill until after the thirty days. The important point is that it was so comforting, so hassle-free, to make one phone call.

FOR MOURNERS

"What Do I Do Now?"

Despite the shock, the first reaction of mourners to the death of a loved one is "What do I do now?" If the death has occurred in a hospital, a social worker, nurse, or doctor will be with you to discuss the disposition of the body. Generally speaking, all you have to do is ask them or one of your family or friends to contact a Jewish funeral director, a rabbi or a synagogue executive director. Once informed, these professionals will take all steps necessary to arrange for transportation of the body to the funeral home. They will also set an appointment with members of the family to select a plot (if not prearranged), a casket, and to make other arrangements for the funeral. Normally, the rabbi and the funeral director will determine what times are available and then will discuss the options with you when he or she visits the family.

One of the first decisions to be made is to decide where the family will "sit *shiva*," where the mourners will be staying during the time after the funeral. There are several factors to consider in this decision. If one member of a couple dies, often the surviving spouse wants the *shiva* in his or her home. The initial days of mourning are already difficult enough to handle; displacing the bereaved from the home is usually not advisable. On the other hand, if the surviving spouse lives in an apartment or other space not suitable for having *shiva* visitors, a child or other relative with a larger home may be called upon to host the *shiva*. In this case, be sure to have relatives or friends available to take turns staying with a surviving spouse so he or she does not have to be alone. Wherever you decide to center the *shiva*, be aware that it is likely to disrupt the routine of the host family for up to a week. If you are not already home at the time of death, someone should take you there so that other preparatory steps can be taken.

Who are the mourners?

Jewish tradition specifies seven relatives for whom we are obligated to mourn: mother, father, spouse, sister, brother, and son and daughter. As we shall see, the laws of mourning are substantially the same for all seven relatives, except that, for a parent, Kaddish is recited for eleven months rather than the thirty days specified for a spouse, a sibling, or a child.

It is important to note that there is no prohibition against mourning other relatives. If a grandchild wants to participate in the *shiva* and recite Kaddish for a grandparent, there is no *halakhic* (legal) reason to deny this. There may be strong taboos rooted in the folk religion against having those whose parents are still alive participate in mourning rituals. But, should a grandchild, a cousin, an aunt or uncle, a niece or nephew, an in-law, a grandparent, or even a very close friend wish to show special respect for the deceased by joining in some of the practices of Jewish bereavement, there is no reason to prevent it.

Making Funeral Arrangements

RICHARD LOPATA: When Laurie died, I called Rabbi Schulweis and set up a meeting. I took a whole bunch of people with me, and it was wonderful. Not only did they give me support, each one of them contributed stories about Laurie. The rabbi got a much better idea of her life than if it had been just me talking about her. As a result, his eulogy for my daughter was overwhelming.

Meet the rabbi

If you belong to a synagogue, one of the first calls to be made following a death is to the rabbi. Contact the synagogue. If the rabbi is away from the office, his or her secretary or the executive director will likely talk with you. The rabbi will want to know when it would be convenient to meet with you, usually at your home, but sometimes at the synagogue. In setting this time with the rabbi, it is advisable that the closest members of the family be available to join the meeting.

When you meet with the rabbi, he or she will, of course, offer condolences to you and the family. The rabbi will probably ask you to tell the story of the death. Your first question is likely to be "What do I do now?" The rabbi will explain the steps in the ritual of Jewish burial and the reasons for them. You will need to discuss which of the rituals you would like done. Then, you will likely talk about the funeral itself and the *shiva* to follow.

Don't be afraid to ask questions about anything. There is no such thing as a "silly" question about Jewish practice. You may have seen things done at other funerals that you don't understand. You may want to have things at the funeral that you aren't sure are okay with the rabbi. Now is the time to make known any special requests in order to save embarrassment or misunderstanding later.

By and large, you will find most rabbis are insistent about some points of Jewish burial practice, while flexible on others. For example, many rabbis will not officiate at a service when the casket is open for viewing, but will not mind if flowers are displayed. Most rabbis will encourage, but not require, lowering the casket and placing dirt in the grave.

The rabbi also will ask you to talk about the deceased in order to prepare the eulogy. You will be asked to give a brief family history and to share anecdotes that illustrate the essence of the loved one. Rabbis take the job of crafting a eulogy very seriously; the information you give at this meeting will be the basis for the talk. This is a very important time of reflection, and it is useful to have the immediate family participate with you. The discussion will help crystallize the memories of the deceased as well as give the rabbi the information needed to prepare a eulogy that will succeed in representing the life of your loved one.

The rabbi will want to know the Hebrew name of the deceased. Let's use the example of a woman named Deborah Schwartz whose parents' names are Abe and Shirley. Hebrew or Jewish names have three parts.

1. The given name of the person. Deborah's Hebrew name is *Devorah;*
2. The Hebrew word for "daughter of" is *bat;* for "son of" *ben;*
3. The Hebrew names of the person's father and mother. *Devorah's* father's Hebrew name is *Avraham,* and her mother's Hebrew name is *Sarah.* The two names of the parents are connected with the Hebrew conjunction *v* or *oo,* which means "and."

Thus, the entire Hebrew name is *"Devorah bat Avraham v'Sarah."*

If you do not know the Hebrew name(s) of the deceased's parents, ask a senior member of the extended family. Sometimes, the deceased was never given a Hebrew name. Ask the rabbi to suggest a name to use. In the past, only the father's name was used as an identifier, but today many include the mother's name as well.

You may also find yourself asking the rabbi "why" questions. "Why did he have to suffer?" "Why me?" "Why did God do this?" The rabbi will offer you answers from Jewish tradition and psychology. He or she may bring along or suggest books that will be helpful such as Rabbi Harold Kushner's *When Bad Things Happen to Good People* or books containing reflections and readings designed to console the mourner.

Don't expect to be easily satisfied with quick answers. You will have an extended period during the mourning process to confront these questions and to seek answers that console you.

Mortuaries and funeral homes

BEN DWOSKIN: In the early days, funeral directors were generally people who lived in the community. As time went on, it became more and more of a business. Of course, as in any profession, there were and are people who will take advantage of a situation. It doesn't take too many of those to besmirch a whole industry.

Then Jessica Mitford's book, *The American Way of Death*, began a wave of consumerism. People began to ask questions, associations developed, standards were established. Most importantly, Mitford recommended that people look into preneed arrangements to avoid being pressured into choices they didn't really want.

In many communities in North America, a Jewish funeral home serves the mortuary needs of the Jewish population. A mortuary provides the services of care for the body upon death until the burial. This may include retrieving the body from the deathbed or hospital; preparing the body for burial; offering a choice of casket; transporting the body, and sometimes the family, to the place of the funeral service; organizing the logistics of the burial; and assisting in the conduct of the funeral itself.

Although most people think of the Jewish funeral home as a "community" institution, many are, in fact, for-profit businesses owned by individuals. As such, they are not accountable to any community organization and have free rein in establishing prices and procedures. Except for the major centers of Jewish population, there is little competition.

In his excellent book, *A Plain Pine Box,* Rabbi Arnold Goodman details the experience of a Conservative congregation, Adath Jeshurun in Minneapolis, in establishing its own memorial society to offer low-cost traditional burial to its membership. The <u>Hevra Kevod ha-Met</u> (Society to Honor the Dead) consists of laypeople from the congregation who themselves take on the tasks normally offered by a mortuary, including conducting *tahara* (preparing the body), acting as *shomrim* (guards), even sewing *takhrikhin* (shrouds) and building caskets. The impact of this effort on the local Jewish funeral home, the congregation, the community, and, most especially, the lives of the members of the <u>Hevra</u> itself has been extraordinary. The Minneapolis experiment is now more than fifteen years old. Other congregations have established bereavement committees to provide some of the services of traditional hevra *kadisha societies,* but usually not to the extent of the Adath Jeshurun model. Rabbi Stuart Kelman of Congregation Netivot Shalom in Berkeley, California, is an important exception.

Contact the funeral home

ARNOLD SALTZMAN: Often, people call us from the hospital or from home and simply ask, "What do I do?" People are so terribly vulnerable at this moment. Our job is to let them know that everything will be taken care of with sensitivity.

BEN DWOSKIN: When the person comes in, we ask them to bring the deceased's Social Security number, any veteran's papers, Hebrew name, and certain vital statistical information such as name and birthplace of parents ...

A funeral arrangement counselor will sit with the family members. The process is explained to them so they are comfortable with what will happen. Certain questions have to be asked to fill out the death certificate, even though the medical portion is completed by the doctor. A burial cannot take place without a proper death certificate accepted by and filed with the health department. After the necessary information is recorded, the arrangements for the funeral itself are made. The first question: Does the deceased have cemetery property? If not, a plot must be chosen and purchased. Then, there is a series of questions: Who is to officiate at the funeral? When would they prefer to have the service? Does the family want *tahara* performed? What about embalming? Will there be flowers or music? Where and when will the *shiva* be held? Who will be the casket-bearers? What is the disposition of jewelry or other personal effects brought with the deceased? Will the family want a limousine? Then, if the family so wishes, an obituary needs to be written and placed in a newspaper of its choice. Of course, a casket has to be chosen. All of this is done at a time of great stress. Yet, there is a very positive aspect about this. The minute they come to the funeral home or mortuary, they become actively involved in doing their grief-work by participating in making the final arrangements for the deceased.

ARNOLD SALTZMAN: So much of the experience of making arrangements depends on the family and its history. One might think on this day of all days, brothers and sisters are going to get along. Well, if they haven't been getting along, this will not solve their problems. In fact, sometimes the battles continue and at a time when emotions are very raw. This is another strong argument for making arrangements in advance.

BEN DWOSKIN: I think it's important that the bereaved not be alone. In most instances, a relative or dear friend can be a major help to them. However, there are some who feel they know the answer to everything and try to take over. They are well meaning, but making decisions for the bereaved may not always be in the best interest of the family.

DAVID TECHNER: I like to give people the "home-court" advantage. I meet the family at home. That's where family members are most comfortable. I also want all the key people in one place. There are too many decisions that need to be made. I guess my practice is somewhat unusual, but by having the initial meeting in the home, the entire family support system is there.

Representatives of the mourning family will need to meet with officials of the funeral home to make arrangements for the funeral. If the meeting is held at the funeral home, choose carefully who should go to this meeting, for during it, you will be making important decisions ranging from choice of plot to the disposition of personal property of the deceased. Funeral counselors report that usually a surviving spouse and one or more children make the arrangements, sometimes accompanied by other relatives or friends.

If the death certificate has not already been filled out at the place of death (hospital, convalescent home), you will need to bring with you vital information about the deceased, including his or her Social Security number, birthplace, date of birth, maiden name of mother, name of father, and names of immediate family. If you plan to request a traditional Jewish burial, bring the deceased's *tallit* (prayer shawl).

The meeting to arrange the funeral can take as long as two hours, especially if cemetery property must be purchased. In communities with standardized traditional procedures, the arrangements can be made fairly quickly. Here are some of the major decisions to be made when making funeral arrangements:

The plot

A Jewish cemetery is considered "hallowed ground." It is called *beit olam*—an eternal home, or *beit ha-ḥayim*—a home for the living, indicating the Jewish view that the soul continues to live on even after the body is gone. It is consecrated in a special service that demarcates the ground as set aside for Jewish burials. The cemetery is to be separated from unconsecrated ground by a wall, fence, or hedge. It should have its own entrances and exits.

In practice, one of the first places most Jewish communities establish is a Jewish cemetery. Often, the cemeteries are owned by a synagogue or by cemetery associations. In some very small Jewish communities, the cemetery is located in a separate section of a larger secular cemetery. For example, in Salt Lake City, Utah, Brigham Young offered a separate section of the large Mormon cemetery to the Jewish community in the late nineteenth century.

In most cases, the Jewish cemetery is owned and operated separately from the Jewish mortuary or funeral home. Thus, in securing funeral arrangements, two separate institutions must be engaged.

Cemetery property is sold by the cemetery association to the consumer just as any other real estate transaction. You take title to the property for the purpose of burial. Cemetery plots are sold from the inventory of available land.

If the deceased had not previously purchased a plot, you will need to buy cemetery property. You will probably want to visit the site to see if you are satisfied with the location and environment surrounding it. Some people want the plot to be near trees, benches, pathways, even driveways for easy access during visits.

Often, family plots are purchased by families who plan to be buried next to each other. The family plot may consist of two side-by-side graves or a number of plots reserved for family members. Sometimes, family plots are purchased, and then, due to the expansion of the family, the graves are not used. An example is my family in Omaha. When my grandmother died, the family purchased a plot containing ten graves, enough for my grandparents and their four daughters and sons-in-law. However, when Uncle Morton died, his children established their own family plot in a different section of the same cemetery so that, when the time comes, they can be buried next to him.

Depending on the tradition of the community or the rules of the cemetery association, there may be a variety of "property" for sale in different locations at different prices, or it may be one that allots you the next plot(s) in line. Cemeteries also vary as to the types of gravestones allowed: Some insist on uniform flat markers while others allow all kinds and sizes of monuments.

The scarcity of space in many Jewish cemeteries is leading to the increasing development of double burials in a single space, one coffin above another. This is known in Jewish tradition and is permitted as long as there is sufficient distance between the caskets.

A significant factor in choosing cemetery property is the location of the cemetery itself. When there is a choice of Jewish cemeteries, people often select one based on its proximity to the family. Several people interviewed for this book said that an earlier generation would choose a cemetery based on whether it was close to a bus stop!

Mausoleums

When I was a teenager, my mother traveled from Omaha to California to attend the funeral of an aunt who had married a top executive of a movie studio in Hollywood. She was shocked when, at the ceremony, the body was interred in an above-ground mausoleum and not in the ground as was customary in Nebraska and in most Jewish communities.

The tradition of burying the dead in the earth is so strong within Judaism that the very idea of storing the body above ground is considered an aberration. As we shall see, even the traditional coffin is designed to decompose in order to hasten the atoning effect of returning to dust. In Israel, a coffin is not used at all; the body is buried in shrouds alone.

Within some traditional communities, the idea of an above-ground interment is so abhorrent that most rabbis would simply ignore the request or refuse to participate in such a ceremony. The Conservative movement's official position is that, although burial in a mausoleum is not against Jewish law, it should be discouraged. Some Conservative rabbis will officiate at an interment in a mausoleum, although they will likely suggest placing some sort of earth in the coffin. The Reform movement allows burial in a mausoleum.

The casket

ARNOLD SALZMAN: I must alert people before I open the door to the casket room. Even then, you can see a look of fear and fright, and they back away.

BEN DWOSKIN: There are any number of attitudes. Some people have gone into the casket display area with a sense of bravado and say: "Well, let's go in and select the furniture." Others will think about what the deceased would have wanted. Those who are familiar with tradi-

79

tional practice will say: "We know that the casket is supposed to be simple so we want the simplest." Interestingly, the simplest is not always the least expensive. We always let the family make this choice in private, without pressure. They are escorted into a room where the caskets are displayed and contain a written description of construction and the price of each casket. The counselor explains the various types of caskets available and then leaves the selection room so that the family may make their decision. When they have decided, they take a small card from a holder on top of the casket that indicates their choice, and they give it to the funeral counselor after they leave the room.

DAVID TECHNER: Some people worry about what happens to the body in the ground. They have all kinds of ideas about it. A few years ago, I was treated for a cancer that is now in remission. Since I was around the hospital, I had a friend arrange a meeting with a professor of anatomy. We met in the cafeteria, and he was clearly not interested in my taking up his time with this question. He said to me, "I understand you want to know what happens to the body in the ground?" I said, "Exactly." He said, "Look, your body consists of two-thirds water and one-third bone. What happens to water when it sits still and has no place to go?" I said, "It evaporates." He said, "What's left?" I said, "Bones." He said: "Can I leave now?" It was the most reasonable and decent answer I've ever heard.

Death is the great equalizer. The rabbis were quite concerned that the rituals and objects of Jewish burial indicate the fact that every human being is created equal and every human being is equal in death. This notion of democracy in death is illustrated best by the following quotation from the Talmud, *Moed Katan* 27 a–b:

Formerly, they used to bring food to the house of mourning: the rich in baskets of gold and silver; the poor in baskets of willow twigs. The poor felt ashamed. Therefore, a law was established that all should use baskets of willow twigs ...

Formerly, they used to bring out the deceased for burial: the rich on a tall state bed, ornamented and covered with rich coverlets; the poor on a plain bier. The poor felt ashamed. Therefore, a law was established that all should be brought out on a plain bier ...

Formerly, the expense of the burial was harder to bear by the family than the death itself, so that sometimes they fled to escape the expense. This was so until Rabban Gamliel insisted that he be buried in a plain linen shroud instead of costly garments. And since then we follow the principle of burial in a simple manner.

Judaism is also concerned that the body return to the earth as soon as possible. "For you are dust, and unto dust you shall return" (Genesis 3:19). This value is reflected in the preference within Jewish law for a simple casket (*aron*) constructed of wood. Wood naturally decomposes while a metal casket would prevent the body from "returning" to the earth. Although metal nails and handles may theoretically be used, traditional caskets use wooden pegs, the interior is unlined, and some have four holes in the bottom that allow the body to come into contact with the earth.

The type of wood used in the casket is not important. In some areas, a "plain pine box" is used; in others, a redwood casket is common. The wood may be polished or natural. Sometimes, a wooden *Magen David* (Star of David) is attached to the top of the coffin.

The choice of coffin is often a task that causes emotional reaction among the bereaved. Most large funeral homes have a "casket room," a display area filled with a variety of available coffins. For many, walking into this room brings the bereaved into stark confrontation with the reality of death facing them. For some, it can be a terribly disconcerting experience. For others, it brings a sense of peace and relief. Whatever the reaction, it is a task that must be done.

Rabbinic authorities recommend the selection of the simplest of caskets, both to reflect the value of democracy in death and to avoid unnecessary expense. The range in cost of caskets is extraordinary—it ranges from several hundred to thousands of dollars. It is preferable to donate monies to *tzedakah* rather than to spend it on lavish caskets.

Traditionally, nothing is buried with the body in the casket except for some earth from Israel, the Holy Land, and the person's *tallit*. However, some families ask to bury small mementos, such as photos or letters, with the deceased.

BEN DWOSKIN: Most people know nothing about the ritual preparation of the body. We ask, "Do you want to have *tahara* performed?" and they say, "What's that?" So, we explain it to them and they may say, "Well, he wasn't that Orthodox," or, "Oh, that's what they did for my grandfather." If they ask, "Is it the appropriate thing to do?," we say "Yes, it is," and many people will choose to have it done.

DAVID TECHNER: When I explain the source of *tahara*, its meaning, and its beauty, most people want it.

Tahara—Preparing the body

The notion of *kevod ha-meit* extends to the actual preparation of the body for burial. This involves a ritual cleansing of the body known as *tahara* (purification), dressing it in the traditional burial shrouds called *takhrikhin*, and placing the body in the casket.

Tahara is a unique *mitzvah* performed by the staff of the Jewish mortuary or by the *hevra kadisha*—literally, the "holy society." The *hevra kadisha* members are Jews who have been specially trained in the ritual of *tahara*. They are unusually dedicated Jews who respond with love and devotion when called upon to do this ultimate *mitzvah*. Detailed procedures are followed with the utmost care and concern. Men attend male deceased and women attend female deceased; modesty is a Jewish value that continues even after death. Psalms and prayers are recited as the body is washed with warm water. The body is handled with such reverence that the face of the deceased is never allowed to face downward. And, at the conclusion of the ritual, the members of the _hevra kadisha_ ask forgiveness from the deceased.

Although many people have never heard of _tahara_, it is considered one of the ultimate kindnesses accorded the dead. In some Jewish communities, _tahara_ is done as a matter of course. In others, particularly the larger cities, you may need to specifically request the performance of _tahara_ when the funeral arrangements are made.

Jacob Neusner offers a moving testimonial to the members of a _hevra kadisha_ who performed _tahara_ for his father, Mordechai, before burial in Jerusalem.

> These men showed me more of what it means to be a Jew, of what Torah stands for, than all the books I ever read. They tended the corpse gently and reverently, yet did not pretend it was other than a corpse. At the end of the process, the head of the _hevra kadisha_ said in a loud voice, that the dead should hear, and the living: "Mordechai ben Menahem, all that we have done is for your honor. And if we have not done our task properly, we beg your forgiveness."
>
> Jacob Neusner, "Death in Jerusalem," in Jack Riemer,
> _Jewish Reflections on Death_

Takhrikhin—Shrouds

Jewish tradition stipulates dressing the deceased in plain linen shrouds for burial. This ancient tradition is yet another way to demonstrate equality in death. The Talmud says this practice was designed to protect the poor from embarrassment since they did not have the fancy clothes of the rich.

The _takhrikhin_ themselves are sewn from white linen cloth by hand and consist of a shirt, pants, a thin overcoat called a _kittel,_ a head covering, a veil (for women), a belt, and a large sheet. Traditionally, a male is also wrapped in his _tallit,_ the four-fringed prayer garment he has worn during life; however, one of the _tzitzit_ (corner fringes) is cut, a sign that the tallit can no longer be used. Women who wear a _tallit_ in life may certainly wear it in death, although, depending on the religious orientation of the _ḥevra kadisha,_ you may have to insist on this.

One of the most striking characteristics of the shrouds is that they have no pockets. No pockets means that, in the end, we are all equal. No matter how much or how little we have acquired, none of us leaves this world with material possessions.

Some families prefer having the body dressed in a suit or dress, although clearly the tradition stipulates the use of the shrouds.

Embalming

Embalming is a surgical procedure that replaces bodily fluids with chemicals in order to "preserve" the body. Unlike the stereotype of ancient Egyptians embalming their dead, this procedure does not prevent the body from decomposing; it only temporarily slows the process and prevents the body from turning black and blue. Embalming is anathema to the Jewish way of burial, which considers the return of the body to the "dust" from which it was fashioned a high priority. Moreover, embalming results in the disposal of blood. In traditional Jewish practice, the entire body, including its fluids, is to be buried. (In fact, if blood should be spilled on the clothes of the deceased, the clothes are to be buried as well.)

Many Jewish funeral homes today offer embalming services even though the tradition frowns on its use. In some states, the law requires the mortuary to inform you of its availability, and you must sign a waiver requesting no embalming to be done.

The _shomer_

BEN DWOSKIN: In many larger funeral homes, there is staff on site twenty-four hours a day, and the body is never left alone. Of course, traditional people will ask for a _shomer_ to say Psalms through the night. We contact the people who will act as a _shomer_ for anyone who requests this service. If the bereaved are comforted knowing that the _shomer_ is there, it is psychologically helpful. Some smaller communities may not have people willing to take on this responsibility. Then, volunteers are essential.

An important part of *kevod ha-meit* is not to leave the body unattended from the moment of death until burial. While originally this custom may have developed for the practical protection of a body or animals, Judaism considered the body the abode of the soul, and thus to be respected and guarded, even after the soul has departed.

The person who guards the body is known as a *shomer* (guard). The *shomer* sits next to the body or in a room nearby from the moment it reaches the mortuary until the funeral (including through Shabbat or holidays), reading from Psalms and studying. More than one person can act as *shomer* during this period.

Who can act as a *shomer?* Anyone who wishes to perform a great *mitzvah,* another act of kindness that can never be repaid by the deceased. Usually the funeral home will contact those who are willing to act as *shomrim.* However, it is perfectly acceptable for a close relative or friend, for example a grandchild, to act as *shomer* for her or his loved one. This can be an act of great comfort to the bereaved, knowing that someone the deceased knew, rather than a stranger, performed this *mitzvah.*

The obituary

According to accounts in the Talmud, in ancient days every funeral was announced to the community by blowing a funerary bugle. When people heard the sound, they knew that their presence at a funeral was required, involving them in the burial and comforting process.

Today, placing an obituary notice in the daily newspaper(s) is probably the best way to inform the community of the funeral arrangements. Your friends and coworkers will want to know about your loss. People feel terrible when they do not find out about a funeral in time to attend. And you will be comforted by the people who come to honor the deceased and console you with their presence.

When making arrangements for the funeral, the funeral director will assist you in writing an obituary for the local papers. There are general formats used in most communities into which you can insert the basic information of the funeral. Usually, obituaries consist of some or all of the following:

- Name of the deceased
- Date of death
- Survivors' names, relationships to deceased, and places of residence
- Place, time, and type of funeral service (chapel or graveside)
- Instructions for those wishing to make a gift, e.g. "in lieu of flowers, friends may contribute to such-and-such charity, address."
- Place and times of shiva visits and/or services
- Name of officiating rabbi and/or cantor
- Name of mortuary

You may want to discuss the contents of the obituary with your family before it is submitted to a paper. Remember, you are likely to be in an anxious state when you do this task, and you certainly don't want to leave out important members of the family in the notice. Have a member of the family help you write this and double check it for accuracy and completeness. You will also want to determine which charities you wish to recommend for contributions in memory of the deceased. The funeral home should be able to submit the obituary notice for you, or you may wish to place it with the paper directly. In either case, there will be a charge for the space, usually determined by the number of lines in the notice. If you run the notice for more than one day, the paper will charge you for each day it appears.

You may also wish to place an obituary notice in your local Jewish press. Since these papers appear weekly, the notice will most likely appear after the funeral has occurred. Nevertheless, friends who are readers in other towns or have been out of the city will appreciate this announcement.

An interesting question has been raised in some communities concerning whether it is proper for a Jew-by-choice to submit an obituary notice for a non-Jewish relative to a Jewish newspaper. Since the Jew-by-choice is fully Jewish, and since he or she is in mourning for one of the seven relatives, he or she has every right to sit *shiva* for the non-Jewish deceased. There would be no reason, therefore, not to alert the community to this death so that the mourner can be comforted with condolence visits.

The death certificate

If the mortuary is acquiring the death certificate, you may be asked how many certified copies you require. You will need a copy for nearly every financial transaction necessary to settle the deceased's business affairs with any of the following: credit card companies, insurance companies, auto leases, banks, pension plans, stocks and bonds, etc. For most of these, however, photocopies usually suffice, so three or four certified copies may well be enough.

The time of the funeral

Judaism places a high value on the speedy burial of the deceased, often within twenty-four hours of death. Rabbis and Jewish mortuaries are geared up to make this happen. However, in setting the time of the funeral, several factors must be considered:

- **Availability of the rabbi and cantor.** Check with them first if you wish to have their participation. Usually they will try to accommodate, but there may be circumstances that will prevent them from being available at specific times.
- **Available times at the funeral home chapel and/or cemetery.** In smaller Jewish communities, it is rare to have more than one funeral a day, except perhaps on Sundays since there is no burial on Shabbat. In larger cities, this can be a problem.
- **How fast the family can gather.** With the increasing mobility of the Jewish community, family members often must travel great

distances to attend a funeral. If the decision is to wait for relatives, this will affect when the funeral can take place.

- **Transfer of the deceased from local authorities.** In some cases of death (homicide, suicide, accidents), an autopsy may be required by the coroner. Depending on how busy the coroner's office is, the body may not be released for some time. Usually, the rabbi and funeral director can explain the importance of an expeditious procedure for religious reasons, and the coroner's office will cooperate, although we know of cases where political pressure had to be brought to bear to get rapid action.

- **Transporting the body to another location.** Sometimes, the death occurs in one city and the burial takes place in another. This transfer will take time and needs to be considered.

- **Personal preference.** Think about the time of day that would be best for the family. Remember that the family will likely return to the *shiva* home for the meal of condolence. If the funeral is on a weekday, friends will be more likely to attend during the lunch hour or in the late afternoon.

Given these considerations, choose one or two options for when you would like the funeral to be and then clear the time with the rabbi and the funeral home. Or consult with the rabbi, who will in turn tell the funeral home. If you don't know a rabbi, let the funeral home make the arrangements and set the time.

The place of the service

Most services are held either in a funeral chapel, in a synagogue, or at graveside. In some places, the synagogue is used only for the funeral of an especially esteemed member of the community. Ideally, even if the service begins at a synagogue or chapel, most of the attendees will accompany the deceased to the graveside. However, in reality, often a significant percentage of attendees will not go to the graveside after a chapel service. Other factors determining the choice of site:

- **Time of year.** Clearly, if the weather could be inclement, a chapel service is a better site at which to begin the funeral.
- **Anticipated number of attendees.** If the funeral is likely to be large, a chapel or synagogue service will usually be more suitable for the participants. Conversely, if you anticipate a small number of people, you may wish to hold the service at graveside.
- **A processional.** If the service is held in a funeral chapel or synagogue that is a distance from the cemetery, a motorcade will be necessary. This adds time to the entire ceremony and, as noted above, some people will not proceed to the graveside. By having a graveside service, this step is eliminated.

Limousine

The funeral home can often arrange to pick up the immediate family at one location by limousine, transport them to the service and the cemetery, and return them to the original location. In areas where parking near a funeral chapel is difficult and there are great distances between the chapel and the cemetery, this service is quite welcome. In other areas, the geographic spread of the community is so huge that it is usually more convenient for the family to come in its own car. You will probably be asked if you would like a limousine to pick you up.

Announcements of the *shiva*

The funeral director will ask you about your plans for *shiva* calls and/or services after the funeral. You should have already discussed with your family where you will be sitting *shiva* and the times you will receive visitors. If you are holding services in the *shiva* home, you should determine what days and times they will be held. This information will be announced by the funeral director at the service.

Pallbearers

The funeral director will want to know the names of those being honored as pallbearers. They will be called forward at some point to accompany or carry the casket to the grave. In the Ashkenazic tradition, sons do not act as pallbearers, but in the Sephardic tradition, they do. The Orthodox will give this honor only to men, but there is no reason why women cannot be pallbearers in non-Orthodox services. Usually, six to eight people are needed to do the actual carrying of the casket, but you can name additional close relatives and friends "honorary pallbearers."

Guest book

One of the most common refrains heard in the limousine on the way to a cemetery is "Look who came! I haven't seen him in twenty years!" You may be astounded at who shows up for a funeral. Depending on the number of people, you are not likely to see everyone who is there. The funeral home may or may not provide you with a means of knowing who attended the funeral. At a chapel service, there is usually a guest book stationed at the front door for attendees to record their names.

Flowers

Jewish tradition frowns on the use of flowers at funerals. A donation to a good cause is preferred. However, in some communities this is a matter of personal choice. Should you wish flowers—anything from a floral display to a single red rose—most funeral homes can arrange for them. Even when you alert the community to the preference for donations, sometimes flowers are sent to a funeral, so you may be asked whether you want them displayed or not.

Music

In traditional Jewish practice, the only music at a funeral is the chanting of the cantor. Yet some funeral homes will ask you if you would like music played as the attendees gather in the chapel for the service. "Funerary" or classical pieces are usually played.

Recording the service

Many families report that having an audiotape recording of the service is a great comfort to them during the mourning period. Particularly helpful is listening to the rabbi's eulogy. However, it is a little awkward to ask the rabbi to record the service. Instead, request that the funeral director arrange for the recording of the service, even if you need to provide the tape recorder.

Once the recording is made, it can be duplicated and shared with relatives and friends who cannot travel to the funeral.

Telephone hook-ups

With widespread mobility dispersing families to many different locations, it becomes difficult for some to travel to attend a funeral. David Techner suggests that with speakerphones, it is now possible to hook up a phone line to the funeral chapel so that anyone in the world can listen to the service as it happens.

Gravestone

At some future time, you will need to compose the inscription for a gravestone. You may be asked about this at the meeting to arrange the funeral.

Costs and contracts

BEN DWOSKIN: People have no idea how much time it takes to arrange and conduct a funeral. And cemetery property is becoming more and more scarce. Selecting cemetery property and making funeral arrangements is a major business transaction, and unfortunately it's done at a time of considerable stress. You sign a contract with all sorts of disclosures and legal conditions. One of the reasons we encourage people to make before-need arrangments is to enable them to make these decisions without the time pressures and emotional stress present at time of need.

The cemetery property and mortuary services do come with a price tag. In fact, an average Jewish funeral in a major city can cost many thousands of dollars. The cost may be less in smaller Jewish communities or in various areas of the continent. But there is no question that these costs will increase in the years ahead.

The funeral industry is regulated by the Federal Trade Commission, which requires mortuaries to detail exact costs for each of their services on a line-item basis. You should be shown a menu of mortuary services and the corresponding cost of each of the items before the funeral is arranged.

When all the arrangements have been completed, the mortuary and/or cemetery association will complete a legal contract that will obligate you to pay for the property and/or services provided. As with most consumer transactions, this contract will stipulate precisely the services and/or document the property purchased and the cost of each. Most mortuaries will expect payment in advance or at the service, although some may offer financing.

Burial in Israel

Occasionally, a person who dies in the diaspora has expressed a desire to be buried in the Land of Israel. Most Jewish funeral homes maintain contacts with Israeli authorities and can arrange for the transportation to Israel for interment.

Helping Grieving Children

RON WOLFSON: Did your grandchild go to the funeral?

ALLEN BROWN: Yes. My daughter Dawn got a book out of the library called *The Badger's Parting Gift* and read it to Sara Beth before the funeral. It's about an old badger who dies. It helped her to understand what was going to happen.

Later, during *shiva,* Sara Beth and I had a talk about the funeral. She said, "Grandpa is like the badger." I said, "Tell me more about it, Sara." So she started telling me about how this badger was getting old, and how it related to Grandpa. Then she said, "Do you think Grandpa is watching us right now?" I said, "I don't know if he's watching us right now, but I know he's with us right now." "What do you mean?" she asked. "Well," I said, "we're thinking about him and we're talking about him and when we remember things about him, he's with us." She understood that. Then she looked up at me and said, "Papa, I'm glad it wasn't you, but I really miss Grandpa."

When Dianne's father had passed away, our daughter Dawn, Sara's mother, was only twelve, and we decided not to take her to the funeral. We always felt it was a mistake not to take her. Dawn, too, always felt left out when we didn't take her to the cemetery. So with Sara, we all felt it was important for her to go as long as she was prepared for what was going to happen. That's why the book was so valuable. She was upset when the coffin was lowered, but overall she held up pretty well. It was the right decision.

RON WOLFSON: When people ask you, "Should I bring a child to the funeral?" what do you say?

HAROLD SCHULWEIS: By all means. The child should not be denied his or her right to mourn. Not taking the child to the funeral may emotionally be interpreted by the child as a form of rejection. This is his or her grandfather, the one who played with him or her and gave him or her gifts. Should grandchildren be exempted from the need to mourn their loss?

DAVID TECHNER: Parents usually start a conversation with me by saying, "My child is very sensitive and he can't possibly understand." I have yet to meet a Jewish parent who didn't think his or her child was sensitive, brilliant, and gifted. My response is always the same, "Tell me. What is it about death and dying that you understand that your kid can't?" That's not to say there aren't things we adults might understand better, but then our job is to help the kids learn. That's why when a child becomes bereaved, I offer to take that child on a tour of the funeral home sometime before the burial. I show them what a shroud is, where the *tahara* is done. I answer all their questions. My goal is to give them an idea of what will happen during the funeral.

CAROL STARIN: When people talk about how to help children deal with death, they often think only of small children. My boys were teenagers when Joel died—fourteen and sixteen. They each reacted within their own personalities.

Joel died at home. When the medics told us there was nothing more they could do, I asked the kids if they wanted to go up and say good-bye. One did and one didn't. One stayed home for the entire *shiva* period; one went back to school after two days—and I let him. Yet, the one who went back to school was sitting with me in my room one night during the *shiva* and in the midst of tears said, "Daddy is never gonna get to see me play varsity basketball."

One of the most challenging tasks confronting mourners and comforters alike is how to explain death to a child. In the midst of one's own grief or in the attempt to comfort another, a child's need to know and understand is often overlooked. Or adults decide that a child simply won't comprehend what is happening. Or the tremendous upheaval in the normal routines of the household throws the child into a kind of chaos of unexpected events and uncertainty about his or her future. Yet psychologists tell us that children today, shaped by the constant barrage of death portrayed on television and in the movies, are far more aware of death and its consequences than many adults realize.

The decision about what to tell children will depend largely on the age of the child, her or his sensitivity to the subject, and the child's relationship to the deceased. As with the "phases" of grief, much of the actual response of a child will depend a great deal on the relationship between the parent and child and how the parent chooses to discuss the death itself.

Children under the age of two will have no concept of death, but will know something is wrong. They will sense the upset in the house, the commotion of the preparations, and the changes in parents. They need attention, love and time. They need holding, touching and reassuring gestures and words.

Three-to-five-year-olds will know that something bad has happened. They may ask about what death means, what makes people die, and where dead people go. Children at this age have difficulty understanding the concept of finality. For them, death is like sleep—they expect the deceased can wake up again. This explains why some children don't understand the sadness around them. "Grandpa will be back. He's just gone for a while." If they have had an experience with the death of a pet, a reference to that time can be helpful, "Remember when the hamster died and we buried it in the backyard? Sometimes even people die." Long explanations that the child will not understand are unnecessary. But a brush-off "you're too young to understand" can add to a child's sense of mistrust about what can happen.

Six-to-eight-year-olds will ask questions, lots of questions. "Can I see Grandma again?" "Will I die too?" Children at this age exhibit some understanding that death is a physical experience, but in their vivid fantasies they think of the dead person transforming into an angel, skeleton, or ghost. Death is accepted, but it only happens to old people.

After age nine or ten, a realistic concept of death based on information gained through personal experience leads the child to the understanding that dead is dead. Death is final and universal. It will happen to everyone, although some teenagers tend to live life as though they could never die.

Rabbi Sam Joseph has worked with thousands of grieving children in his work at the Fernside Center in Cincinnati. Here are his thoughts:

When someone dies, you should inform the child as soon as possible. They should be told clearly, simply, and honestly what caused the death. Never lie to a child; avoid euphemisms. Don't say, "Mommy went to sleep and won't wake up." Use language the child can understand, "She was very, very sick. The doctors couldn't make her any better. Her body stopped working. She couldn't breathe anymore."

One of the things we hear from the kids we deal with is that they felt not included. If the child is old enough to not be disruptive to other mourners, he or she should be included in the funeral. The child should be told what to expect. "There will be lots of people crying. Grandma will be in the casket." Children five and older can be included in the planning; let them write something, draw something, choose a piece of music. Children should be allowed to invite a teacher or a friend to be with them at the funeral. Often, a surviving parent is so taken with his or her own grief that it becomes important to have someone close to the child throughout the entire ceremony to explain, comfort, or even leave early if necessary.

On the other hand, a child should be given the opportunity to opt out. The child can be told, "The funeral for Mom is tomorrow. It's going to be very sad. I'm going to cry, other people are going to cry. The rabbi's going to say some prayers and talk about Mom. If you would like to be there, we would like you to be part of it. But, if you don't want to be there, you can help in other ways. You can be back at the house, you can help open the door, or get people's coats." Give the child a task; don't whisk them away.

Let the child grieve. Don't set time limits for their grief. Well-meaning people who deal with grieving children sometimes say the worst things to them, even teachers and rabbis. The kids in our groups tell us how painful it is to hear a teacher say, "Your brother has been dead for two months already. It's time you forgot about him and stopped wearing his shirt." "I know it's painful that your mother is not here, but you have to stop crying because she's in a better place." "You have to stop misbehaving in Hebrew school. We know your father died, but you can't keep looking for attention from us." The research is clear that every person recovers from grief at his or her own pace, and it often takes a very long time.

A surviving parent needs to spend a lot of time with each child. There should be family conferences each week to check how things are going. Big changes should be put off, like who's going to take over the empty room. If there are temper tantrums, this is normal. Provide a punching pillow or wooden pegs to pound or let the kid scream in a bathroom instead of at the parent.

How do you know what's troubling a kid? You have to listen really carefully. Concerns get overblown in children's minds if they are not addressed. One of the big questions kids have when a parent dies is, "Who's going to take care of me if you die?" They may become very protective of the surviving parent and become scared if they just leave the house for an errand. You have to address the concern and say, "I know you're scared that something might happen to me and then you wonder what would happen to you. Well, I'm going to be extra careful because I love you, and I don't plan on anything happening to me." Or, if someone died in a hospital, they may freak out if they have to go to the hospital to get their tonsils out. "Your brother went into the hospital because he had cancer. But, not everyone who goes to the hospital dies. Most people who go into the hospital come out of the hospital."

The bottom line is that children who lose parents or siblings and parents who lose children are never, ever the same. Never. If our synagogues would only realize that. Every holiday that comes along, they think of that loved one. *Yizkor* may be the only time that the name of that child is said out loud. We counsel families to take out photo albums of the good times at holiday time.

Finally, it is not uncommon for children, and especially teenagers, to retreat inside themselves in the face of the death of a family member. It is frustrating for family and friends who desperately want to help the child bring the grief into the open and deal with it. In the face of such a retreat, the most important message to give to the child is, "We will not give up on you. We love you. We care about you, and we are not going to let you shut us out. No matter how hard you try, you can't do it, because we love you too much. We're always going to be here."

DAVID TECHNER: A child once called me with this question, "How long does it take for my grandfather to turn into a dinosaur?" It turns out that shortly after her grandfather's funeral, her class had visited the University of Michigan's Natural History exhibit on dinosaurs. The guide stopped in front of this huge skeleton of a brontosaurus and said, "This is what happens to people when they die."

The most touching experience I had in talking with a child about death happened on a jumbo jet 35,000 feet in the air. I noticed a little kid looking intently out the window of the emergency exit. He stood there for about a half-hour. I was intrigued and asked him, "Excuse me, what are you looking for?" While still looking out the window, he answered, "I'm looking for my grandpa. My grandpa passed away and my mother told me grandpa is now up above the clouds." I asked, "Have you seen your grandpa?" He said, "Nope." All this time, he never looked at me— just out the window. Finally, I asked, "Have you seen anybody else?" All of the sudden, the kid turned to me, tears welling up in his eyes, and said, "I'm not gonna see my grandpa, am I?" It was a very emotional moment. I said, "That's a very interesting question. Tell you what. I want you to close your eyes and tell me about the best, most favorite story you can re-member about your grandpa." Well, the kid began to tell me that every summer his grandfather would take him to the amusement park and go on the children's roller coaster with him and how much fun they had rid-ing on that roller coaster together. The kid went on and on about his grandfather. When he was done, I said, "Okay. Now, open your eyes. Did you just see your grandpa?" He smiled and said, "Yeah, I did." Then I told him that I had a daughter who died, but she is with me always—in my mind and in my heart, not above the clouds.

These stories all share certain basic characteristics that teach us how adults can talk to children about death:

- **Avoid euphemisms.** Earl Grollman tells the story about a young mother who was extremely careful not to say the word *dead* in explaining to her three-year-old the death of a grandparent. She said, "We lost Grandpa today." The child responded simply, "So let's go find him!" Grollman explains in his excellent book *Talking with Children about Death*:

    > People don't die anymore. They "pass on," "pass away," "perish," "expire," "go away," "are lost," or "depart." Euphemisms get in the way of children's understanding just as they are attempting to distinguish reality from a world of fantasy.

    Actually, the use of these euphemisms is a way adults avoid talking about death. Kids need trust and truth. They get neither when euphemisms for death are used in talking to them, or anyone else for that matter.

- **Death is forever.** So much of the life of children is pretend and make-believe. Every child wants a happy ending. In fairy tales, the prince can kiss the sleeping beauty and she will awake. In real life, no one can kiss Grandma and make her wake up again. "Grandma will never come back." As painful as it sounds, it is true.

- **Death cannot be denied.** "As much as we don't want to believe Grandpa is dead, he is." Denial works as a defense against death for children as well as for adults. This is a natural reaction, and sometimes children will act as if nothing has happened, fully anticipating the time when the deceased will return. When adults are silent and secretive about death, this contributes to denial. It is important to discuss the event, no matter how hard it is to believe it actually happened.

    Another way denial works is to suggest a loved one "went away on a long trip." While this might afford temporary relief and an explanation of an absence, it leads to a misconception that can easily backfire. What does the child learn when Grandpa never returns from the journey? That other living people may not return when they go away either!

How about "Grandpa is sleeping"? The child may never go to sleep again! Many kids have trouble falling to sleep, fearing they will never wake up. Again, these ideas feed into denial. Death is real; separation is painful. Grandpa is not on a journey or asleep. Grandpa is dead.

- **Not all people who are sick die.** Sometimes adults explain to children that "Grandma died because she was sick." Well, that is probably true, but the lesson learned might be that all sick people die. The child becomes terrified of getting sick. The adult must reassure the child that almost everyone who becomes ill gets better, almost everyone who goes to the hospital gets to come home. Make the distinction between very serious illness and common ailments and reassure the child that he or she should live for many, many years.

  After the death of a grandparent, children often wonder if Mommy or Daddy will die too. According to David Techner, one of the greatest things you can do for your child at that point is to schedule a physical examination as soon as possible after the *shiva* and take them with you. When everything checks out fine, your child will know that you will be okay.

  Among children who suffer the loss of a parent, the concern is often about what will happen if the other parent dies. After all, children have seen *Annie;* they know about orphans. Experts suggest that a surviving parent should assure the child that, God forbid, if anything did happen to you, "Aunt Libby and Uncle Danny will take care of you." In other words, children, like most of us, want to be reassured that they won't be left alone.

- **Explain what death really is.** For many children, the best approach is to relate examples of death from their own experience. A pet dies, a flower dies, bugs die. Children grow up with the phenomenon of death all around them. Adults can use these incidents to explain how living things eventually become quite still, no longer breathing or living. Change is part of life. Death is part of life. (See the Bibliography for books about the death of animals and plants that can be read to children.)

- **Let children grieve.** Most children have had the experience of a pet dying. One of the most important preparatory lessons adults can give children about death is to let the child give the pet a funeral. Ritual is as important to children as it is to adults. Usually there will be some expression of grief, particularly if the pet has been especially loved by the child. This, too, is a valuable experience for the child. Validate the sadness that children experience when death occurs. It is important for them to be reassured that the emotions of grief are natural. The child will learn that grief helps to heal the wounds of separation and that, eventually, the pain subsides, although the memory remains. This, in short, is the ultimate lesson of healthy bereavement for all of us.

You may want to include children in the mourning process. They can participate in a number of ways:

- Often a grandchild will want to read a poem or reading at the funeral. Some teenage grandchildren might even want to offer a eulogy. This should be discussed with the officiating rabbi. This can be a very moving part of the service. However, it is likely to be a highly charged moment for the young person, who may have difficulty controlling emotions. Some rabbis have encountered situations when several grandchildren wanted to speak; a good solution is to suggest that these eulogies be given at the *shiva minyan* during the week.
- Children can be allowed to place dirt in the grave, although some may not want to do so. If a child shows any hesitancy at all about participating in any part of the funeral, they absolutely should not be forced to do anything.
- Children can be asked to help in the *shiva* home. No one likes to feel left out. Let them answer the phone, do light chores, etc. They may want to participate in the *shiva minyan*.

Of course, if a child is very apprehensive about attending the funeral, certainly they can be allowed to stay home or go to a friend's house. Don't be surprised if, after a discussion about what will happen at the funeral, a child changes her or his mind several times about attending. If the child does not attend the funeral, do not make the young person feel guilty or shameful about not going. Gently suggest that perhaps you will visit the cemetery together at another time.

David Techner suggests that parents talk with the child's teacher about what can be done when the child returns to school. Often the teacher is also at a loss about how to handle the situation. He recommends that immediately after the opening moments of the school day, the teacher welcome back the child, recognize the loss, and offer a contribution previously collected from the classmates to the charity the family has designated. Books can also be given to the child, the surviving parent, and a sibling as a gesture of comfort. These are signs that the class cares for the child. It breaks the ice so that everyone can talk about and deal with the loss.

Another helpful idea is to encourage the child's friends to make a *shiva* call. Teenage peers can gather on a particular evening to visit their bereaved friend, who needs the support a visit can bring as much as the adults.

Ultimately, exposing children to the reality of death is a very important part of what might be called "death education." Just as parents and family are the first to address sex education, learning about death is an important part of life. Knowing about death is the only true preventive from fearing death. Psychologists overwhelmingly agree, encouraging educators and clergy to teach children about death through experience and study. In the end, our children will acquire their attitudes and knowledge about death from our example. So think carefully about how you will talk to them about the death in your family.

Preparing for Shiva

HAROLD SCHULWEIS: Many people are totally unprepared for the *shiva*. At *shiva,* the home becomes a synagogue. What is to be done? Who is to lead the services? The fear of the unknown may be rationalized: "I'm not that religious." The mourner needs help, friendship from the community, ritual support.

The mourner in his or her grief may say, "I don't want anybody around. I want to be alone." But the tradition will not abandon the mourner, isolate them. At first, the mourners are tentative, but they report after the *shiva* that the *minyan* was a source of comfort and that they never knew how caring the synagogue is.

RON WOLFSON: What do you say when people tell you they only want to sit *shiva* for three days, or one day, or not at all?

HAROLD SCHULWEIS: The mourning period is not the ideal time to talk about Jewish philosophy and theology or ritual behavior. But when I explain that "seven" recalls the number of days in which the world was created and that in death a world was destroyed, they can understand the need for the seven days of *shiva* to recreate the world for themselves.

A significant moment such as death requires time to work out one's grief and one's relationship to family and self. But mourning is more than obeying the law. It is a private matter and I am respectful of the reasons of the heart. They must know the "law" and its rationale, but their mourning cannot be ordered or qualified. I would rather they observe the *shiva* with personal meaning and seriousness than add on another day or two without feeling and with resentment.

Among the families we interviewed, several options seem to emerge as popular adaptations of the *shiva* experience. In some families, the decision to sit *shiva* for seven days is honored; however, the family goes to the synagogue for the morning *minyan,* hosting an evening service in the *shiva* home. There are obvious reasons for this: It is much more difficult for people to come to an early morning *minyan* than to an evening service—people need to get to work, the *minyan* by necessity must be quite early, and, unfortunately, many people simply have lost the art of the morning service and its requirement for *tallit* and *tefillin.* It is also more difficult for the family to get up early in the morning to host a morning *minyan* than to open the house in the evening. The *shiva minyan* in the evening is an easier service to lead and often more familiar to participants.

Some families, particularly those who are less comfortable with the idea of holding religious services in their homes, or are worried that there will not be enough knowledgeable people to lead and participate in these services, decide to hold just one service on the evening of the funeral day, attending *minyanim* throughout the week at the synagogue. This is not a preferable option, particularly because the truncated week does not allow for the all-important grief-work to happen over time. The tradition was quite wise when it understood that it takes a good three days for the mourner's initial numbness to subside. Only then can the work of comforting truly begin. As for the concern that there won't be enough knowledgeable people to lead the *minyan* service, most synagogues have bereavement committees that will help organize such a service. In smaller Jewish communities, when a death occurs, the entire daily *minyan* will often take place in the *shiva* home rather than at the synagogue. Let the rabbi or other synagogue official know you want this help and it is likely to be offered.

One other critical decision should be made at this point. You, the mourner, should not worry about having enough food or supplies for your family and your visitors throughout the *shiva*. However, someone else should. Someone, a family member who is not an "official" mourner or a friend, or several people together, should take it upon themselves to organize everything that needs to be brought to the home during the course of the *shiva*. (A list of these items is included in the section for Comforters.)

FOR COMFORTERS

When a Friend Experiences a Death— The Art of Jewish Comforting

Can I see another's woe

And not be in sorrow too?

Can I see another's grief,

And not seek for kind relief?

—WILLIAM BLAKE

From the instant you hear a friend has died, you want to help, to respond, to make the pain go away. Yet you don't know what to do. Should I go to the house—but what if I'm in the way? I'll send over something—but what do I send? I'll make a *shiva* call—but what do I say? I'll send a card—but what do I write?

Why is it so hard to comfort? What causes the uneasiness, the loss of words, the stumbling, the nervousness? For some, it is the confrontation with one's own mortality. For others, it is the painful reminder of our own losses. For most, it is the uncertainty about what truly comforts—what words, what deeds will ease the way for the mourner?

Yet, when we do offer condolence, it is a great *mitzvah*—not only for the mourners, but for us. Comforting can itself be a transformational experience—we feel good, we feel needed, we feel real when we comfort others.

Moreover, we feel connected to the common bond of humanity. After all, death is the great equalizer, a destiny we all face. The very word *condolence* expresses this value. It comes from the combination of two Latin roots: *cum*, "together" and *dolere*, "to grieve." To grieve together—that is what we do when we offer condolence. Through our empathetic grief, we comfort and console.

What Can You Do?

SARALIE FOOTE: I got a call from a mutual friend who said, "I don't think Allen's father is going to make it through the night." I immediately said, "We ought to do for them," because I knew that even though they have many, many acquaintances, I just grabbed the bull by the horns ...

I had to go to work the next day, so I began to make phone calls. I guess I called about five different gals. Allen's sister-in-law did all the shopping for the meal after the funeral. Others made the standard things—tuna fish, hard-boiled eggs, kugel. Once I knew the meal after the funeral was taken care of, I began to work on the dinners for the week of *shiva*. Everyone I talked to worked during the week, so it became clear that no one could make a dinner to send in. So I called the kosher caterer—because the meals had to be kosher for Allen—I said, "Listen, I want you to prepare cold-cut trays one night, chicken one night," and so on. Even though it was only a twenty-four-hour notice, he was great.

Then I called Dianne and said, "Listen, I just want to let you know that I've got everything under control. Don't even think for a minute what's gonna be done." She was relieved, because you do want to know. Dianne said, "Thank you so much. You know, my sister from Washington wants to do something." So I said, "Just have her call me." She did and she wanted to provide another dinner later in the *shiva*.

When Allen was at the funeral parlor making arrangements, I went over to the house, and we did an inventory of what they needed—coffee pots, paper goods, sheets to cover the mirrors, a water setup when they returned from the cemetery ...

I went to the funeral, but Dianne's sister-in-law stayed back to help set up the meal of consolation. When we got back from the cemetery, a few of us fed the family and cleaned up. The next day, I left work early to pick up the food at the caterer. I called another friend and said "Listen, do you think you could come over and give me a hand?" She did, and the two of us served the family before the *minyan* started. We didn't even hang around for the *minyan* since they were *davening* early. The next night the caterer delivered the meal the sister from Washington ordered, but there was no one to serve it. So I went over to do that, too. Four straight days, you know, tons of food, but everything was organized and cleaned up. But, actually, I really don't feel like I did that much ...

Since bereavement in the Jewish tradition occurs in the context of a caring community, you as a member of that caring community need to act. Your actions will depend in large measure on how close you are to the bereaved. By close, we don't necessarily mean how you are related to the deceased. Usually, family members rally to the side of a relative who is bereaved, but not always. We know of situations in which the comforters who do the most work in preparing a *shiva* are friends of someone whose parent has died who never knew the deceased. Close here means how deeply you feel about your friend and how keenly you feel the obligation to help in his or her hour of need.

For the purposes of our discussion, let us divide comforters, be they relatives or friends, into two categories: close friends and friends. Close friends will most likely take on the major responsibility for organizing the *shiva,* while friends will engage in the normal actions comforters do to show their support for the bereaved. Clearly, there will be overlap between the two; this distinction only helps clarify the various roles to be played.

Close Friends

SARALIE FOOTE: Normally, you hear someone passes, the first thing you do is run to the store and you make tuna and eggs and all that. I figure, how am I gonna do that with work, so that's when I called the caterer. If the caterer was not available, I would have gone to Plan B: made out a grocery list, assigned dishes to people, tried to coordinate it all. With everyone working, it was just easier to have everyone contribute $40 or $50 and have the caterer do it. I guess the women of the nineties are so busy with the rest of their lives; you know, we're typical yuppies, "Just order it." I mean, we got the meal after the funeral together ourselves. But, truthfully, with work and our own families to worry about, I don't think I could have cooked a whole meal for eighteen people and sent it over myself.

When close friends learn that a friend has sustained the death of a family member, the first reaction is to be there. If the deceased is a member of the extended family or a very close friend, the first instinct is to drop everything and go to those who are in mourning. In most cases, this means to the home designated as the center of the funeral preparations. Some will call first for permission to come over. But if you feel close enough not to call, you should probably go.

If you do call first, it is likely that someone other than the bereaved will answer the phone. Identify yourself clearly, explain that you have heard the news, and briefly express your sympathy and your wish to come over or to help in some way. If the answer is not to come over, you will probably get some sort of assignment related to the *shiva*. As much as you want to speak to the bereaved directly, in most cases, it is probably not a good idea to ask them to come to the phone. It adds pressure to an already difficult burden for them and, remember, it is not yet time to "comfort." If you must, suggest to the person answering the phone to ask the bereaved if they wish to come to the phone. Be prepared to be told no. Yours is probably just one of many calls, and as we suggest to the mourners, it is best for them to take only calls that are essential.

Of course, if you are a close friend or relative living in another city, by all means call as soon as you hear the news. You will want to let the bereaved know if you can attend the funeral or *shiva;* in some cases, the funeral may be arranged to allow your presence.

If you find yourself wanting to travel to a funeral on a moment's notice, you will discover that airlines have specific policies on waiving advance purchase requirements that enable you to travel on the least-expensive fare. Each airline differs slightly in these requirements, but most include the following:

- Only immediate family members are eligible for special fares in case of death. Amazingly, this is usually defined as Jewish law defines mourners: spouse, parent, child, or sibling. Aunts, uncles, cousins, and even grandparents are not normally included.
- You will have to give the airlines proof of death and proof of your relationship to the deceased. This can be done by providing a copy of a death certificate, an obituary notice, or by having the airline call the funeral home to verify the information.
- You may not know when you will return. Ask the airline to allow for an "open return" to give you maximum flexibility.

Speaking of out-of-towners, it would be good for a close relative or friend of the bereaved to take on the job of coordinating travel arrangements for those coming to town for the funeral. Often, this requires making hotel reservations and trips to the airport.

Sometimes, the opposite happens. Your friend has lost a relative who lives in another town and must travel to the funeral. You can offer to help make travel arrangements, pack, drive to the airport, watch the house, feed the pets, cancel the paper, change appointments, collect the mail, and so on, while they are away.

In the house of an *onen*, there are many decisions to be reached and much preparation to be organized for the funeral and the *shiva* following. In many cases, this involves making phone calls for the bereaved. Get a pad of paper to put next to the phone to record what calls were made and who is doing which task. Since there might be several people involved in this work, it will help to keep a record of the arrangements. Here are just a few possible ways you can offer to be helpful:

- Contact the rabbi or another synagogue official.
- Contact the mortuary or funeral home to make arrangements.
- Accompany the bereaved to the funeral home to complete arrangements for the plot, the casket, and so on.
- Organize the *se'udat ha-havra'ah*—the meal of condolence served the mourners immediately upon returning to the home after the funeral. The traditional menu for this meal includes: hard-boiled eggs, bread, dishes such as gefilte fish, tuna fish and herring, fresh fruit, and coffee or other beverages. This meal is supposed to be served to the mourners and their closest family and friends *only*, not to dozens or even hundreds of friends after the funeral. However, in some communities, the custom is to invite those who wish to come to the mourners' home immediately. If that is the case, quantities will be quite different than if just serving the immediate family.

   In some congregations, the Sisterhood or a bereavement committee can provide the meal of condolence, and sometimes additional meals as well. In some cases, you can organize a menu and ask friends to provide specific dishes. Or you may need to put the meal(s) together yourself.

   A word about caterers. Many caterers offer "*shiva* trays," "*shiva* baskets," or complete meals. Certainly, when many face frenetic and busy lives, finding the time to prepare dinners or shop for food may be difficult. With no time to bake, we buy cakes at the bakery. With no time to cook, we call the caterer. The caterers themselves know that this market exists; we counted ten ads for "*shiva* trays and baskets" in a recent edition of the *Detroit Jewish News*. However, we caution against turning the *shiva* into a nonstop party with food for all. The obligation here is to feed the mourners, not the visitors. On the other hand, some will feel the obligation to offer a light breakfast to those coming to participate in a morning *shiva minyan,* and certainly, offering cake and coffee during an evening *shiva* session is also appropriate. The families we spoke to overwhelmingly felt the most moved when friends took the time to personalize this *mitzvah* rather than rely on a caterer.

- Offer to do a light shopping for immediate needs: juice, milk, bread, coffee.
- Shop for quantities of paper goods (plates, cups, napkins), tablecloths, garbage bags, paper towels, cutlery, coffee, sodas, and even toilet paper needed during the *shiva*. Don't worry about the bakery—many people will bring cakes and cookies. Large urn coffee pots, folding chairs, and a coat rack and hangers can be brought over.
- Prayer books and *kippot* (head coverings) are usually provided by the Jewish mortuary or the synagogue; the kit they provide (usually in a large briefcase) will often have a set of twenty books. The mortuary or synagogue will need to be contacted if more are needed. The kit also will include a seven-day memorial candle to be lit upon returning from the funeral.
- Ask if you can help with important routines, particularly those involving children. One of the most wonderful ways to comfort a mourner is to relieve concerns about car pools, appointments, school assignments, afterschool activities, and so on. After a few days of the *shiva,* you might also offer to take a child to the park, for a walk, to a movie, or for a sleepover.
- Make phone calls to family and friends. These calls will have two purposes: to let people know the details of the funeral and

shiva and to give people an opportunity to offer to do something. If they do offer, keep a list of names and phone numbers of the volunteers and the days they are responsible for helping out. You might also check the bereaved's calendar for the week ahead and make calls to cancel appointments.

- Answer the phone. The telephone rings constantly in a *shiva* home, and it is very helpful to have someone screen the calls to the mourners. Ask the mourners if there is anyone in particular they are waiting to hear from. You can also avert the embarrassment of someone who has not heard about the death calling to talk to the deceased. Keep a list of all those who called and their messages—word for word.

- Organize evening meals for the days of *shiva* and the *Shabbatot* following. Ask friends to take responsibility for preparing or providing a complete dinner for the family on one of the nights of *shiva*. Have the provider deliver the meal at an agreed-upon time. If you are providing the meal, just drop it off—don't stay and eat with the family. This is not the time for the mourners to entertain you. Keep a list of those providing meals to give to the mourners after the *shiva* so they can send thank-you notes.

Friends

ALLEN BROWN: One of the most comforting things for me during the *shiva* was reading Elie Wiesel's book *The Forgotten*. Rabbi Charles Simon told me about it. The book is about a father and son. I cried through it. I laughed through it. It brought me very close to my father. In fact, one evening between *Minḥa* and *Maariv,* I read a particular section to everyone at the *minyan*. It was so comforting to read it.

Normally, friends will not come to the house upon learning of the death. But you can still be extraordinarily helpful to the bereaved without their even knowing it. Here are some things you can do:

- Call a mutual friend. If you know a close friend or relative of the bereaved, you can call them to get information about what you can do.
- Once you make contact with those arranging the *shiva,* you may be asked to pick something up, bring food, supplies, or chairs and tables, or do other errands. Choose something that you definitely can do—people are depending on you.
- If you are bringing something to the home for *shiva,* ask when you can bring it. Someone will be in the home to accept food and other items the evening before and the morning of the funeral.

Depending on the item, you may be able to bring it with you after the funeral.

Baked goods, especially coffee cakes, are always needed during *shiva*. Fresh fruit is always welcome. Generally, liquor, wine, and candy are considered more festive gifts and are rarely served in a *shiva* home. You may want to make a casserole, a kugel, or a quiche. However, you should always be aware of issues concerning *kashrut*, the Jewish laws of legally permitted foods.

A complete description of *kashrut* is beyond the scope of this text, but what you need to find out is whether the home in which the *shiva* is being held has a kosher kitchen. If the family does "keep kosher" and you do not, you will most likely be advised to limit the food you bring to baked goods from a kosher bakery. Since you may not know how stringently the family follows the laws of *kashrut*, it is best to stick with certified kosher products. If you know the home is strictly kosher, find out which bakeries would be acceptable to the family or bring something other than food, or food that is unprocessed, perhaps a fruit basket. If the family is less stringent, you would be well advised to bake or prepare food that is dairy or pareve. If you do bring homemade food to a *shiva* home, be sure to label the dish with your name so the bereaved will know who sent it.

- Flowers are not usually sent to a Jewish funeral or brought to a house of mourning.
- A very appropriate gift is a charitable contribution in memory of the deceased, either to a cause specified by the bereaved family in the obituary notice or to one of your favorite charities. Have the charity send an acknowledgment card to the bereaved so they know of your thoughtfulness.
- Some people like to bring a book to the bereaved. There are "books of comfort" that contain sensitive readings and poems for mourners. Alan Kay's *A Jewish Book of Comfort for Mourners* is a personal story and an anthology of readings. A book on coping with grief might be appropriate for some. Dennis Gura read *What Helped Me When a Loved One Died* by Earl Grollman every night of *shiva*. Many people find comfort in Harold Kushner's acclaimed book *When Bad Things Happen to Good People*.

Often, the mourner's interest in Jewish topics is heightened during *shiva*. Two well-known volumes on Jewish bereavement are Jack Riemer's *Jewish Reflections on Death and Dying* and Maurice Lamm's *The Jewish Way in Death and Mourning*. Several children's books are very helpful in explaining death to young people. A bibliography can be found in the back of this book.

- Another idea is to bring a blank journal or book in which the bereaved and visitors can record memories about the deceased. We found a book published in Germany in 1915 entitled *A Mourner's Album* that was designed for a mourner to record vital details about the death, dates for subsequent *yahrtzeit* observances, a family tree—it even has a page for a photograph of the deceased. Since one of the most important objectives of *shiva* is to crystallize memories of the deceased, this is a very creative idea that should be encouraged.

- Other creative ideas for remembering the deceased include donating a book to a library, planting a tree in Israel, placing a memorial notice in a newspaper or bulletin, creating or donating to a scholarship fund, acquiring ritual objects for a synagogue (contact them about current needs), and donating items to a school.

PART 5

The Funeral

FOR MOURNERS

It is the morning of the funeral. You have slept restlessly, if at all. You awake feeling numb. You question whether you are just in the midst of a bad dream, not a terrible reality. You look to the other side of the bed, and your beloved is not there. Suddenly, waves of sorrow overcome you. Yet you must get control of yourself and prepare for the ceremony.

You pick at your food, unable to eat. You get out your dark suit or dress, the somber black reflecting your mood. Your closest family comes to the house to be with you, to accompany you to the synagogue, the funeral home, or the cemetery. You pass the time fitfully, waiting for the limousine to arrive. It comes, and you begin the awful ride to the funeral. No one speaks; it's a time for silent reflection, punctuated with the soft sobbing of the mourners.

As the limousine pulls into the cemetery, a wave of emotion overcomes you. You've been here before for other funerals, but this time, it is for your beloved. You know it, but you don't want to believe it.

The limousine stops at the side entrance of the chapel where the ceremony will be held. Just as you've regained control of yourself, you see the hearse and begin sobbing again. Your family escorts you into the waiting room of the chapel where the rabbi, cantor, and officials of the funeral home await you. The rabbi tells you the order of the service and what to expect. The funeral attendants explain their procedures. You wait as the crowd begins to gather.

Then, suddenly, it is time. You are taken into the chapel—to the front row, to a side area. It matters little, for in front of you is the casket, and another wave of intense grief overcomes you. You cry and reach out to those around you for support. You sit down, face to face with the reality that in the coffin lies your loved one.

The service begins. The cantor chants Psalm 15 in a plaintive voice. The rabbi recites verses from the ancient tradition, and then asks the congregation to join in reading "Yea, though I walk through the shadow of the valley of death, I fear no harm for You are with me ..." The rabbi begins to talk about your loved one, where she came from, the kind of person she was, the accomplishments, the dreams, the joys, the hopes. Names are recalled, your name, the members of the immediate family who have sustained this loss. As the rabbi speaks, memories begin to flood your mind; a lifetime of memories races before you. A family member rises to offer a personal eulogy, a reflection of love. You are moved beyond tears, exhausted from the waves of grief. The cantor sings *Eil Malei Rahamim* ... in a voice that reminds you of *Kol Nidre* in its sorrow. The Hebrew name of your loved one is chanted in the prayer, asking God to grant perfect peace to the soul on her way to the eternal home. The funeral attendant announces the place and times of the *shiva* to follow and invites the pallbearers to come to the casket. The first part of the service is over; it is time to take the beloved to the final resting place.

As you walk behind the casket to the gravesite, you begin to see your family and friends who have come to be with you in this time of sorrow. You are comforted knowing that you are not alone; rather, the community has come to be with you, to surround you with love. You reach a row of chairs set up in front of the grave, and you must sit down, for you have seen the empty hole with its pile of dirt to the side, awkwardly covered with a green carpet, unable to conceal its contents. The coffin is placed on the steel contraption used to lower it into the grave, which the funeral attendants do as the rabbi and cantor recite verses of Psalms.

The crowd gathers behind and around you as the graveside service begins. The rabbi explains the *k'riah,* the rending of garments, and attaches a black ribbon to your clothing. With a tiny scissors, the rabbi cuts the cloth, while reciting the words "Praised are You, *Adonai* our God, Ruler of the Universe, the Judge of Truth ... *Adonai* has given, *Adonai* has taken away, praised be the name of *Adonai.*" The cantor sings once more, and then it is time to recite the Mourner's Kaddish. You rise in your place, steadied by the loved ones around you, and say the ancient words, *"Yitgadal, v'y-itkadash, shmei rabbah ..."* The comforting word *Amen* drifts from the crowd as you follow the rabbi in the rest of the prayer.

Now, the final act of love, the ultimate gesture of *kevod ha-meit,* honoring the dead. The rabbi explains that it is not up to strangers to bury the dead, but up to each and every one of us to provide the blanket of earth for the final slumber. You are taken to the grave itself and handed a shovel. As difficult as it is, you fill it with earth and empty it into the grave. The dirt hits the top of the coffin with a thud that shudders through your entire body. You stand aside as your family and friends each take turns fulfilling this ultimate *mitzvah,* this *mitzvah* for which there will be no repayment, no reward, except the knowledge that you have brought the deceased to a final resting place. Friends approach you with hugs and words of condolence. As you leave the cemetery, the community forms two rows in the crowd, forming an aisle for your departure. They offer you the ancient words of hope and consolation, "May God comfort you among the other mourners of Zion and Jerusalem." You reach the limousine and collapse in tears into the back seat, numbed and humbled. As you leave the cemetery, you take one look back at the gravesite, knowing that with this ending comes a beginning. The funeral is over, but the mourning has just begun.

The Service

ALLEN BROWN: The funeral was very simple. Just before it began, Rabbi Skopitz cut the ribbons. Then, they lowered the casket. That's when my granddaughter started to cry, and of course, everyone else began to cry, too. The rabbi said the prayers and then gave the eulogy. My son Marc had written a poem that the rabbi asked him to read, but Marc told him he'd never get through it. So the rabbi read it, and even he broke up. Everyone broke up.

We said the Kaddish. That was a tough one. Then the rabbi took three scoops of dirt and threw it into the grave. I was next and grabbed three handfuls of dirt and threw it onto the coffin. My body shook each time I did it. I waited until the dirt hit the coffin with that noise, that thud.

TAMARA GREENEBAUM: It was a gorgeous day. The cemetery is located on a bluff overlooking the ocean. The funeral was really very simple. The rabbi and Gary co-officiated, which meant that they each said a prayer. Then, the custom in this town is that when someone dies, anyone who wants to says something about the deceased. At least half the Jews in town were at the funeral, and they just went around, and people talked about my mother.

We said the Kaddish. I had explained to the mortician that we wanted to lower the casket and cover the grave with earth. So, it was very simple, very graphic, very moving, and very satisfying. My father and sister and I took shovels of dirt and placed it in the grave, and then, three-quarters of the people shoveled dirt, or threw flowers or pine branches, or whatever sixties California thing into my mother's grave. Then, two men decided they wanted to finish filling the grave themselves. When they were just about done, we finally left. I loved the gesture that the whole community buried my mother. I really did.

I was really very satisfied by the whole experience. Even my father felt gratified at the participation of the community. It turned out to be not so burdensome for him to handle the little ritual that there was.

But the best thing for me was to get to hear people talk about my mother. I don't live there. It was nice to see that other people saw her as I did. It was so comforting to hear other people say that they loved her and that they missed her.

SANDY GOODGLICK: My mother wanted a private funeral and we agreed. It was an error—for us. She thought she was sparing us, but in fact, to grieve alone is probably the most difficult way to grieve.

The Hebrew word for funeral is *levayah*—"accompanying." Jewish tradition places a great value on the interactive nature of burying the dead. The rabbi doesn't bury the dead. Neither does the cemetery worker. Rather, the bereaved family, assisted by the community, is responsible for this most important *mitzvah* of bringing the dead to the final resting place.

When is the funeral held?

The burial should take place as soon as possible. The biblical injunction is to bury on the same day as the death. The rabbis of the Talmud considered a speedy burial to be among the most important ways to honor the deceased. They believed that final atonement depended in part on the body returning to the dust of the earth and did not want the process delayed. By the time of the Middle Ages, since embalming was forbidden, it became a matter of hygiene and public safety that the body be buried expeditiously.

Yet, today it is difficult to hold a funeral on the day of the death itself. Proper preparation for burial and the need to notify the community require the funeral be held the day after death at the earliest. In addition, further delays are allowed in the following special cases:

- When close relatives must travel long distances to attend the funeral. As the Jewish community has become more and more mobile, families have scattered all over the continent, indeed the globe. Even though airplanes can bring together families in a matter of hours, the funeral may have to be delayed a day or two to allow for such travel.
- When Shabbat, the High Holy Days of Rosh Hashanah and Yom Kippur, and the *Yom Tov* days of the pilgrimage festivals of Sukkot, Passover, and Shavuot occur.
- When a suitable casket or shrouds are not available.
- When civil authorities require unavoidable postmortems, documentation, etc.

Funerals are almost always held in daylight hours (although in Jerusalem, burials do take place at night). Times are chosen that are convenient for the family and for a maximum number of friends to attend. Preferred times seem to be near the lunch hour and late afternoon.

Where is the funeral held?

The place of the funeral varies according to the custom of the local community. Here are the options:

- **The home.** It is possible to have the service in a home, but very few people do this today.
- **A funeral home.** Many communities have a Jewish funeral home that houses the mortuary and a chapel for services.
- **A synagogue.** In some communities, the service begins in the synagogue sanctuary or chapel, and then proceeds to the cemetery. However, some congregations do not allow these services in the sanctuary, unless the deceased is an outstanding member of the community.

- **The cemetery.** In the larger Jewish communities, the cemetery will usually have a chapel for services on site.
- **At graveside.** In some ways the simplest of alternatives, it is absolutely appropriate to conduct the entire service at graveside. Of course, season and likely weather should be taken into consideration when choosing this option. Often, the cemetery will have some tenting for the immediate family, but usually not enough for the entire funeral party.

Is there a standard funeral?

Surprisingly, the answer is no. There is not a single standard for the service, although there are the following basic components:

- **Readings.** Generally, a funeral begins with several readings about death from Jewish sources. Psalm 23 with its famous verses, "*Adonai* is my Shepherd, I shall not want. God has me lie down in green pastures ... God revives my soul for the sake of God's glory ... Though I walk in the valley of the shadow of death, I fear no harm, for You are with me ..."

  Psalms 15, 24, 90, and 103 are also often recited. At the funeral of a woman, the *Eishet Hayil* (Proverbs 31) is sometimes included. These readings offer comfort and reflection about the deceased and the survivors.
- **The eulogy.** The eulogy (*hesped*) is designed to recall the life, characteristics, and accomplishments of the deceased. Most often, it is offered by a rabbi who has been furnished information about the deceased in an earlier meeting with the bereaved. This is seen as a sign of respect and an honor to the deceased and the family.

  Yet, increasingly, members of the family request the opportunity to speak about the life of the departed. These personal eulogies are often delivered with great emotion and with a degree of insight that is difficult for a third party to achieve. In every case we know of, a eulogy offered by an adult child for a parent, or a brother for a sister, or even a grandchild for a grandparent has been a source of great comfort and honor for the mourners and a tremendously moving experience for the listeners. Some rabbis will welcome this contribution to the funeral (as long as not too many people want to speak), while others would prefer that personal eulogies be given at a *shiva minyan*. Tips on how to write and deliver a eulogy can be found below.

- **The memorial prayer—***Eil Malei Rahamim.* Among the most well-known prayers in Jewish liturgy, the *Eil Malei* asks God to grant perfect peace to the departed and to remember the many righteous deeds he or she performed. "May this soul be bound up in the bond of life (*b'tzror hahayim*) and may he or she rest in peace." The cantor normally chants this memorial prayer in a plaintive, mournful voice.

Generally, this concludes the formal service held in a synagogue or chapel, and the funeral party moves to the gravesite.

It is a great honor to be named a pallbearer. Generally, the honor is offered to close relatives and friends. The coffin is actually carried by hand or guided on a special gurney to the gravesite by the pallbearers who, traditionally, pause several (usually three or seven) times before reaching the grave. This indicates our unwillingness to finally take leave of the loved one. The rabbi or cantor recite verses from Psalm 91 expressing confidence that God watches over us at each of these stops. It is considered an important responsibility of the community to follow the casket for at least a few steps on the way to the grave.

At the gravesite, the final steps of the funeral ritual are performed. The mourners take their places by sitting in a row of chairs placed before the grave. If *k'riah*, the rending of garments, has not taken place before the earlier service, the mourners stand and it is now done by the rabbi. The cantor may chant another Psalm, and the rabbi often offers another reading from Psalm 91. Then, in traditional burial, the casket is lowered by hand or mechanical device and the rabbi says in Hebrew, "May she [he] go to her [his] resting place in peace." Some rabbis will also say the traditional prayer *Tzidduk ha-Din,* justification of the divine decree, which acknowledges acceptance of the inevitability of death.

The climax of the service is when the mourners are asked to rise and recite the Mourner's Kaddish (sometimes a version called the Burial Kaddish is said), the ancient prayer that reaffirms our belief in the greatness of God. Then, mourners and those in attendance are invited to fill the grave with earth. Since this practice is not universally observed, the rabbi usually explains what is about to happen and the reasons why the community fulfills this ultimate *mitzvah* of burying the dead. When the mourners are ready to leave the cemetery, two parallel rows are formed by the participants, creating an aisle for the bereaved to pass through on their way from the gravesite. As the mourners walk through this corridor of consolation, the community offers the traditional prayer of condolence, *"Ha-Makom y'na-hem etkhem b'tokh sh'ar aveilei Tzion v'Y'rushalayim"*—"May God comfort you among all the mourners of Zion and Jerusalem." It is customary to wash the hands upon leaving the cemetery.

Two customs associated with filling the grave are (1) to use the convex side of the shovel and (2) not to pass the shovel from hand to hand, but to replace it in the earth for the next participant, "lest death be contagious."

Another interesting custom is to ask the deceased for forgiveness for any hurt one might have caused her or him. Some also pluck grass from the ground, which they throw behind them as a sign of their renewed awareness of human mortality.

How to Write and Deliver a Eulogy

One of the most wonderful ways to honor a departed friend or family member, and one of the greatest gifts you can give to a bereaved relative, is to write and offer a personal eulogy at the funeral or at a *shiva minyan*. Here are a few tips on how to do it:

1. First, discuss your desire to offer a eulogy at the funeral with family memebers. In most cases, they will be touched and thrilled that you want to do so. However, you should have the unanimous agreement of all members of the immediate family to avoid any unpleasant feelings of competition.
2. Write down your thoughts, memories, and stories about the deceased. Let the words flow onto a page. You can edit and organize the talk later.
3. Seek the advice of the rabbi. He or she is a professional at this and can be of enormous help. Most rabbis will be more than willing to assist you.
4. Great eulogies have the following elements:
   * What happened to the deceased.
   * A brief history of the life—where was the deceased born, where did he or she grow up, marry, settle down, what business or profession did he or she work in, what major accomplishments was he or she the most proud of?
   * Stories that illuminate the characteristics of the person—don't be afraid to tell humorous incidents that reveal the humanity

of the person. The knowing laughter will release some of the tension of the moment.

- Stories that tell of the relationship the deceased had with you and other members of the family.
- Personalize your feelings at the loss of the deceased. The audience will identify closely with your emotions.
- Ultimately, ask yourself if the listeners will better understand the personhood of the deceased at the end of the eulogy.

5. Decide whether or not you can deliver the eulogy. The emotions generated at a funeral are often overwhelming. As confident as you might be that you can "get through" the speech, you may be overcome with emotion as you speak and literally be unable to continue. As moving as that may seem, it is ultimately not helpful to the bereaved or the listeners. In fact, such a scene can become embarrassing and uneasy for all concerned. This is not to say that expression of emotion during the speech is avoidable or even undesirable; rather, it is to warn against a situation of total breakdown. If you do offer the eulogy, and find yourself cracking under the emotional strain, pause to collect yourself before continuing.

If you are quite sure that you cannot deliver the eulogy without breaking down, you can still write it and have it spoken in your name by someone else. Often, the rabbi or another family member can read the words for you. In this way, your important and meaningful words are heard by everyone, even though you are not speaking.

The Kaddish

One of the most famous prayers in all of Jewish liturgy, the Kaddish is a magnificent statement of faith in God. Even if the words are not understood, nearly every Jew knows its rhythms and responses.

Originally, the Kaddish had nothing to do with mourners. Its five different variations are used to divide major sections of prayers and to conclude the services. It is not even written in Hebrew. Except for the last line, the prayer is written in Aramaic, the vernacular language spoken by Jews from the time of Ezra in the fifth century B.C.E. through the time of the Rabbis of the Talmud.

Kaddish literally means "sanctified." It is related to the Hebrew term *kadosh,* meaning "holy" or "special." There is no mention of death in the prayer. Rather, it praises God. At the moment of the supreme test of our beliefs, the tradition asks us to stand and proclaim our faith in God and our hope for *shlaimoot*—"completion"—in a world that now feels terribly unwhole.

The Kaddish is said in the context of community. Traditionally, a *minyan* (quorum) of ten is required to recite Kaddish. In Orthodox and most Conservative synagogues, only the mourners stand during Kaddish. This identifies their special status within the community. In most Reform, Reconstructionist, and some Conservative synagogues, the entire congregation rises to recite Kaddish to show support for the mourners, to remember friends and relatives who have died, and to recall the memory of those victims of the Holocaust who left no one behind to say Kaddish.

The Mourner's Kaddish

Magnified and sanctified is the great name of God throughout the world which was created according to Divine will.

May the rule of peace be established speedily in our time, unto us and unto the entire household of Israel and let us say: Amen.

May God's great name be praised throughout all eternity.

Glorified and celebrated, lauded and praised, acclaimed and honored, extolled and exalted ever be the name of the Holy One, far beyond all song and psalm, beyond all hymns of glory which mortals can offer. And let us say: Amen.

May there be abundant peace from heaven, with life's goodness for us and for all the people Israel. And let us say: Amen.

May the One who brings peace to the universe bring peace to us and to all the people Israel. And let us say: Amen.

Mourners say:

Yitgadal v'yitkadash sh'mei raba   יִתְגַּדַּל וְיִתְקַדַּשׁ שְׁמֵהּ רַבָּא,

Congregation responds:

Amen.   אָמֵן.

Mourners continue:

B'alma di v'ra khir'utei,   בְּעָלְמָא דִּי בְרָא כִרְעוּתֵהּ,
V'yamlikh malkhutei   וְיַמְלִיךְ מַלְכוּתֵהּ,

B'<u>h</u>ayeikhon u-v'yomeikhon

בְּחַיֵּיכוֹן וּבְיוֹמֵיכוֹן,

U-v'hayei d'khol beit Yisrael

וּבְחַיֵּי דְכָל בֵּית יִשְׂרָאֵל,

Ba-agala u-vi-z'man kariv

בַּעֲגָלָא וּבִזְמַן קָרִיב,

V'imru:

וְאִמְרוּ:

Mourner and congregation say:

Amen.

אָמֵן.

Y'hei sh'mei raba m'varakh

יְהֵא שְׁמֵהּ רַבָּא מְבָרַךְ

L'alam u-l'almei almaya.

לְעָלַם וּלְעָלְמֵי עָלְמַיָּא.

Mourners continue:

Yitbarakh v'yishtaba<u>h</u>,

יִתְבָּרַךְ וְיִשְׁתַּבַּח

V'yitpa'ar v'yitromam

וְיִתְפָּאַר וְיִתְרוֹמַם

V'yitnasei v'yit-hadar,

וְיִתְנַשֵּׂא וְיִתְהַדָּר,

V'yit'aleh v'yithalal

וְיִתְעַלֶּה וְיִתְהַלַּל

sh'mei d'kudsha

שְׁמֵהּ דְּקֻדְשָׁא

Congregation and mourners say:

B'rikh hu.

בְּרִיךְ הוּא,

Mourners continue:

L'eila (On High Holy Days add: l'eila mi-kol)

לְעֵלָּא (לְעֵלָּא מִכָּל)

Min kol birkhata v'shirata

מִן כָּל בִּרְכָתָא וְשִׁירָתָא,

Tushb'<u>h</u>ata v'ne<u>h</u>emata

תֻּשְׁבְּחָתָא וְנֶחֱמָתָא

da-amiran b'alma

דַּאֲמִירָן בְּעָלְמָא,

V'imru:

וְאִמְרוּ:

Congregation and mourners say:

Amen.

אָמֵן.

132

Mourners continue:

> Y'hei sh'lama raba min sh'maya
>
> V'ḥayim aleinu v'al kol Yisrael,
>
> V'imru:

יְהֵא שְׁלָמָא רַבָּא מִן שְׁמַיָּא
וְחַיִּים עָלֵינוּ וְעַל כָּל יִשְׂרָאֵל,
וְאִמְרוּ:

Congregation and mourners say:

> Amen.

אָמֵן.

Mourners continue:

> Oseh shalom bi-m'romav
>
> Hu ya'aseh shalom aleinu
>
> V'al kol Yisrael,
>
> V'imru:

עוֹשֶׂה שָׁלוֹם בִּמְרוֹמָיו,
הוּא יַעֲשֶׂה שָׁלוֹם עָלֵינוּ
וְעַל כָּל יִשְׂרָאֵל,
וְאִמְרוּ:

Congregation and mourners say:

> Amen.

אָמֵן.

When saying the last line of the Kaddish, mourners take three steps back, bow left, right, and forward, as if leaving the presence of God the Sovereign, then three steps forward to their original position.

A Commentary on the Kaddish

My friend, mentor, and rabbi, Bernard Lipnick, rabbi emeritus of Congregation B'nai Amoona in St. Louis, offers this perceptive interpretation of the Kaddish:

Why is it that the mourner recites the Kaddish at the end of the service? After all, there isn't a word about death in the prayer. It is a kind of benediction, a last "good word" before ending the service so people will go home feeling uplifted. The words remind us of what we came together to do, namely praise God, and they encourage us to look forward to the establishment of God's kingdom, when there will be completion, peace. But, why should the mourner be given this honor?

My theory is that there are three problems that mourners face that the Kaddish speaks to in a most direct manner. The first problem is loss of faith. If there is a God in this world, how could my loved one die? Maybe there is no God in this world; maybe the world is rudderless. The blow to faith is never more pronounced than it is at the moment when you bury a loved one. Yet, here comes the Kaddish and proclaims faith in God. It isn't that the mourner is talked back into faith by reciting the Kaddish. But the fact that a mourner says the Kaddish in a *minyan* of Jews three times a day for a period of eleven months keeps the mourner in the community of faith. By standing up and proclaiming publicly, *"Yitgadal v'yitkadash sh'mei rabbah"*—"Magnified and sanctified is the great name of God"—the body and soul of the mourner have a chance to recuperate, to go through a healing process. The perspective changes from that first day, that first week, that first month. The mourner begins to see that there are magnificent mountains and blue skies and gorgeous flowers and lovely birds. You don't know that the day you bury your mother. But a month later you do; two months later, you certainly do. The denial of the existence of God which wallops the mourner like a sledgehammer during that first week is blunted some by the recitation of the Kaddish, as the mourner gradually regains perspective.

Okay, so you say there's a God in the world? But, what kind of God can it be? A good God would not have taken my child. A congregant called me last night to tell me that his nineteen-month-old grandson has a tumor on his brain the size of a baseball. It's malignant. The chances of a nineteen-month-old baby surviving this are very, very slim. Maybe one in five. This same man's wife died two years ago at the age of fifty-six. He says to me, "Eleanor, I can understand. Fifty-six years old, with children and grandchildren. But, a nineteen-month-old baby? Come on, what kind of God are we dealing with?"

The Kaddish speaks to this problem, too. It says, *"B'almah divrah khi'rutei"*—"Throughout the world which He created according to His will." There is a certain pattern to life and death in this world which seems to be inherent in creation. If God is the author of creation, then God created it as a place where people live and then die. I once talked to a doctor and asked him about the mortality rate. He said, "It's still 100 percent!" The point is that the world was created according to God's will. Now, if you had created it according to your will, people, especially babies, wouldn't die. But, you didn't create the world. God did. It's not that God is a bad God. Death happens when microbes get the better of us, or when accidents happen, when immune systems aren't what they ought to be. In this world which operates according to the rules of physics and motion, which seem to have inherent time clocks, people die. God didn't choose that your father should die rather than somebody else; "somebody else" will die too. Your father died because his liver stopped working, or because he had bacteria that infected it—not because of a bad God. God really had nothing to do with it. God created the world which operates according to certain rules. People, even nineteen-month-old babies, die because they get sick, because the cells go haywire. Now that it's happened, what we have to do is find a way to cure it. Let's call upon the divine powers within us and the universe to help us find a solution. The Kaddish says first that there is a God in the world, and second that God created a world according to Divine will, in which death is the inevitable conclusion of life.

The third problem is: What's it all for? If this is the way it all ends, why beat your head against a wall? Whether it's eighty-nine years, or fifty-six years, or nineteen months, it's all over too rapidly. Now, people have different reactions to this awareness. Some say, "Eat, drink, and be merry, for tomorrow we die." Others say, "Withdraw from life. It will all be over soon anyway." The issue is: If it's all over so soon, why break our necks?

The Kaddish speaks to this. *"V'yamlikh malkhutei b'hayeikhon u-v'yomeikhon u-vhayei d'khol beit Yisrael"*—"May God establish His kingdom during our lifetime and during the lifetime of the house of Israel." When the prayer says "establish His kingdom," this is theological language for a perfect world, the Messianic era. God's rule is to be perfect and complete. So, the mourner at this moment when he or she is most sensitive to the issues of life and death and to his or her own in-evitable demise, stands up and says, "There is a God who declares that it is our obligation as Jews to establish God's rule on this earth in our lifetime."

Jews are very sensitive to words. Words are very precious in Jewish tradition. This is saying that we undertake to solve all the problems in the world in our lifetime. Now, I'm sixty-six years old. If I live a normal life span, I've got another eleven years or so, maybe twelve. But, I've had a heart bypass, so who knows? Even if I make it to one hundred and twenty, is it realistic to expect that all the social problems of the world, all the political problems of the world, all the medical problems of the world, all the psychological problems of the world will be solved—all in the next twenty to thirty years!? It would take that long just to list the problems! Yet, the tradition asks the mourner to stand up and make the statement, "I'm expected to work toward the establishment of God's complete and perfect world in my lifetime." What does that say? It says, "Mourner, you have never been in a better position to appreciate the brevity of life, and the fact that you have a mission in this life—to estab-lish God's kingdom—and you don't have very long to do it! You must therefore redouble your efforts to bring God's kingdom into existence."

Who is more in touch with the realities of the human condition than the mourner? That's why Judaism decided that it should be the mourner who proclaims in the benediction to the service the ultimate meaning of human existence.

Questions about the Funeral

RON WOLFSON: My father is a guy from Brooklyn. His father was a pious Jew, but my dad wasn't into Jewish things. When his father died, my dad tells a story about his burial that sends shivers down my spine. The funeral was the standard sort of thing, and then they get to the grave. My dad is a young man. He doesn't know what's going to happen. He's an emotional person; he's staring at his father's grave trying to cope with his grief. Suddenly, a rabbi with a beard turns to my dad, hands him a shovel, and says, "Here, dig." It broke him up completely. It was a complete trauma; he had no warning. He did shovel dirt into the grave. He talks about the terrible thud of the dirt on the coffin, that it reverberated through his whole body. To this day, he has trouble approaching a grave; he even shakes when he talks about it.

HERMAN FEIFEL: Your dad was not truly emotionally mobilized for the death of his father. All of a sudden, he was given a shovel, and it was like he was transferred to an express train when he was traveling on a local. His denial of what had truly occurred was just ripped away. There was no warm-up nor emotional preparation for him, and his coping capabilities were overwhelmed. This is a case where the wisdom of the tradition in underscoring the reality of death by the shoveling of dirt on the coffin didn't work for your dad, perhaps because of his personal situation and emotional needs.

BEN ZION BERGMAN: Placing dirt in the grave, literally participating in the burial itself, is a *mitzvah* called ḥesed shel emet—an act of true loving-kindness—because there is no reciprocal favor from the deceased.

MOSHE ROTHBLUM: I find placing the casket in the grave and putting earth on the coffin very comforting. It's like a blanket, not leaving the casket uncovered. I know some people find it barbaric and I really have to work hard at understanding why they feel that way. I don't insist on it at all, but I would say more than 95 percent want the casket lowered, and a great majority now put earth in the grave. For me, having strangers fill in the grave is barbaric.

HAROLD SCHULWEIS: I recall a man who didn't want to shovel dirt upon his mother's casket. He felt it was callous. I explained to him that the ritual was a form of closure and a mark of respect. He abhorred the sound of the dirt and gravel. I took the shovel and threw the earth on the casket. After he saw me, he came forth, knelt to take a scoop of earth into his hands, and dropped it gently into the grave. He explained that he felt his gesture was less mechanical, less utilitarian. I leave that gesture as an option for those who feel as he did.

TAMARA GREENEBAUM: You know, when we got to the gravesite, there was this mound of dirt with a shovel sticking out of it. No Astro-turf covering it up; just a mound of dirt. And the sound of the dirt hitting the top of the coffin is the most horrible sound in the world, but without it, it doesn't seem real.

HAROLD SCHULWEIS: When I was a young man in the rabbinate, I wanted to be as compassionate as possible. I would say to the family at the end of the service, "I'll remain here and you go to the car." As they walked to the car, they looked back almost longingly. I could see that there was no closure for them—in the very literal sense of closure. Some people have ambivalence about nature. So I try to explain before the funeral that the earth is not our enemy, that nature is not alien to us. This is the soil of creation. We attach ourselves to creation, and the deceased is part of the cycle of creation. In the end, as difficult as it is for some, the actual process of burial is one of the most comforting things we can do. We are drawn from the earth and return to it and to the ground of our birth.

BEN ZION BERGMAN: I've had people who didn't stay for the burial say to me later, "You know, Rabbi, I feel like I abandoned them."

Where do the mourners sit during the service?

In some funeral chapels, a small room just to the side of the *bimah* (pulpit) is available for the family to sit in during the service. Usually, a thin curtain is drawn to conceal the family from the view of the others attending the ceremony. The idea of the room is to allow the mourners some privacy as they grieve during the service. Some rabbis advise family members to sit in the front pews of the chapel surrounded by their community, rather than be isolated in a separate room. The tradition encourages the public expression of grief; the emotions of the moment are not likely to be hidden in any case. But, if the option exists, it will be left to the mourners to decide where they want to sit.

Must I shovel dirt into the grave?

For most people who have received a proper explanation of this practice, shoveling dirt into the grave brings a closure to the funeral that is literally rooted in the reality of the moment. However, others feel the custom is potentially psychologically troublesome. The placing of earth on the casket or in the grave is a matter of personal choice.

Where is the torn garment worn?

Traditionally, the *k'riah* is made on the left side of the garment for parents (over the heart) and on the right side for other relatives. You may choose to have a tie, blouse or shirt, or suit lapel torn, or a black ribbon worn on a garment.

How long do I wear the *k'riah* garment?

The tradition calls for the mourner to wear a torn garment during the *shiva*. On Shabbat, Holy Days, and festivals, no public signs of mourning are worn.

What about flowers at a funeral?

Although descriptions of flowers at funerals are found in the Talmud, most rabbis discourage the use of floral decorations at the funeral or on the casket on the grounds that the money spent on such displays is wasted. Instead, sympathizers are encouraged to send donations to favorite charities or to a charity specified by the bereaved family in the obituary notice. These charities will let the mourners know of your donation to the living, a more appropriate way to express your solidarity with the family. If flowers are sent, you might suggest to the funeral director that they be donated to a hospital or nursing home after the service. In another reflection of differing burial customs, flowers are common at funerals in Israel.

I've seen the coffin covered with a cloth during the service. What's that?

At some funerals, a large cloth, similar to the kind of cloth used to cover the lectern on a synagogue pulpit, is placed over the coffin. At Valley Beth Shalom, this cloth, called a *miktze,* is used at funerals of members. It is embroidered with the Hebrew words *Tzedakah tatzeel mimavet,* "charity redeems from death." The cloth remains on the coffin from the beginning of the service until it is lowered into the grave.

HAROLD SCHULWEIS: One of the most commonly asked questions is about the permissibility of a public viewing of the deceased. They claim to have seen it even at Jewish funerals. I explain that the Jewish tradition is sensitive to the status of the deceased. The deceased is a *mirch v'ayns roch,* someone who is seen but who cannot see. To open the casket and allow people to look at the deceased is to turn the comforters into spectators and the deceased into an "it." We remember those we loved when they were free and active human beings, not as objects to be observed. Rarely, after the explanation of the ritual tradition, have the mourners objected to the practice.

Why is the coffin not opened for viewing at Jewish funerals?

One of the major goals of the funeral and mourning rituals is to solidify memories of the dead in the minds and hearts of the living. We hope to re-member them as they were in the fullness of their lives—vigorous, hearty, beautiful—not as they often are at the end of their lives—weak, frail, help-less. Traditional Judaism argues against embalming or cosmetic surgery to the body. The deceased is not dressed in the finest of clothes. No, the Jew-ish way is to let the photographic image of the best of times be forever bla-zoned in the memory.

Isn't it true that sometimes mourners are asked to identify the body in the casket before burial?

Yes, especially if the body had not been positively identified before prepa-ration for burial. In the past, most people died at home, surrounded by loved ones. Today, most people die in hospital rooms with family members scattered in many different places. Thus, in some communities, the request to view the deceased has become more common. This viewing of the de-ceased is strictly reserved for the immediate mourners, not the assembled friends and family. For some, this encounter is a comforting final goodbye and a chance to see the beloved at peace. For others, the idea of looking into a coffin is not comforting at all.

Is it possible to bury personal items with the body?

According to Jewish law, each person receives equal burial and there is no need for physical items to be buried with the deceased. Some people request that a small memento be placed in the casket.

What about earth from the Holy Land of Israel?

An age-old wish among Jews in the Diaspora during the past two thousand years of dispersion was to be buried in the hallowed ground of Eretz Yisrael. For those not able to be buried there, a bit of earth from the land of Israel can be placed in the coffin. Some families actually gather a sackfull of earth from Israel especially for this purpose. One of the most moving experiences I have had on my many trips to Israel was the time Susie and I collected such a sack of dirt at the same time we planted trees. We brought some of it to Omaha to place on the grave of Susie's mother, who had died the year before. You might also ask the funeral director if some dirt from the Holy Land is available.

I see people walking on graves to get to graveside services. Is that proper?

People should not step on graves as a matter of respect. In some cemeteries, walkways are provided for visitors to avoid inadvertently stepping on a grave. However, the need for maximum use of space in some cemeteries creates a situation when walking on a grave is unavoidable. Jewish law was sensitive to this and allows stepping on a grave if there is no other way to reach another gravesite.

Why can't a *kohen* attend a funeral?

Those Jews who trace their ancestry back to Aaron, the first Jewish priest (*kohen*), brother of Moses, traditionally did not come into contact with any dead body. In the Israelite religion, such contact rendered the priests "impure" and disqualified them from their priestly duties. To this day in traditional practice, *kohanim* do not enter a funeral home or a cemetery in order to avoid being in proximity to the dead. Of course, exceptions are made when the *kohen* must bury one of the seven immediate relatives. Many Jews who are *kohanim* will attend a funeral; others will enter a cemetery but will not come close to the grave. In any of these cases, you may attend a funeral where some Jews stand just outside the chapel. They are most likely *kohanim*.

How do I let my friends know that donations to a favorite charity in memory of the deceased would be appreciated?

There are three ways to get this information to the community: a line in the obituary, an announcement during the funeral service, or a card containing this request given to attendees at the funeral.

Sephardic Burial Customs

The Jews known as the Sephardim, descended from the Jewish communities of Spain, Morocco, Syria, and Iran, follow most of the traditional burial and mourning practices set forth in Jewish law. Among the Syrian Jews, surviving children ask forgiveness from the deceased parent. A *shofar* (ram's horn) is sounded at the funeral of a man with children before the recitation of the Kaddish. Traditionally, women weep and wail openly at the news of a death, although, as the community becomes Americanized, the pronounced wailing has diminished. In some Syrian communities, men and women are buried in separate sections of the cemetery and are placed in the next available grave without regard to position or wealth. *K'riah* is performed when the mourners return home, not at the cemetery.

In some Moroccan Jewish communities, an interesting custom involved preparing the body for burial. Four coins were thrown in different directions of the room or were placed on the coffin while a verse from Genesis 25:6, "And to the children of Abraham's concubines he gave gifts," was recited seven times. This was believed to ward off any potential evil spirits. In Morocco, coffins were not used to bury the dead, similar to current practice in Israel. The tradition of not handing a shovel from one person to another when filling the grave with earth probably originated with the Sephardim.

Among Spanish Jews, an unusually moving custom after the death of a parent is the gathering of the surviving children in the presence of the rabbi for a final blessing. The rabbi asks the children to ask for *meḥilah* (forgiveness) from their parent, and they then kiss the hand of their father or mother for the last time. The rabbi then lifts the hand of the deceased, places it upon the head of the child, and recites the Priestly Benediction and offers other words designed to strengthen the bereaved. This symbolically marks the final blessing children receive from their parents.

Instead of flowers, Iranian Jews sprinkle rosewater on the grave. Intense wailing is characteristic of Iranian funerals. If *k'riah* has not been performed immediately upon the news of a death, the mourners tear a shirt at the grave. Fifty years ago, the Iranians would also drink *arak*—a strong liquor—at the gravesite to help blunt the agony of grieving.

In the Spanish Portuguese community, traditional customs are followed, and *k'riah* is performed at the cemetery. As with other Sephardim, there is a strong preference for the tearing to be done on an actual article of clothing, not on a black ribbon. Until recently, it was unusual for women to accompany the deceased to the grave. In some communities, it was the practice immediately after the Kaddish for the rabbi to say *"Tzedakah tatzil mi-mavet"*—"Charity saves from death"—and to put some coins in a *tzedakah* box, the congregation doing likewise as people left the chapel.

Special Cases

Suicide

BEN ZION BERGMAN: It's true that suicides used to be buried outside the cemetery, and there were even questions about a eulogy and *shiva*. The Rambam (Maimonides) says no *shiva*, the Ramban says no eulogy, but *shiva* is okay if the family wants it. Among later commentators, the <u>Hatam</u> Sofer says you can assume that anyone who commits suicide must not be in his or her right mind at that moment, and therefore all mourning rituals are observed. All mourning rites and standard funeral rituals are observed when a person commits suicide. Modern mental health experts consider the conditions leading to taking one's own life symptomatic of serious psychological conflicts. Moreover, the rabbis were always aware that the mourning process is designed as much for the living as for the dead. Thus, it would be counterproductive to deny survivors the right to bury their dead.

In an earlier time, those who committed suicide were denied the usual respect for the dead reflected in Jewish burial rites because they were seen as literally destroying God's creation. Only God can give life or take it. Suicide was considered such a moral wrong that the body was buried in a separate section of the cemetery. Even so, the rabbis were aware that the suicide's loved ones should not be shamed, embarrassed, or hurt by denying them the honor of public mourning.

Thus, with an enlightened understanding of the causes of suicide and a compassionate view of the needs of survivors, a person who commits suicide is accorded the full honor of Jewish burial practices, and the family participates in all aspects of Jewish bereavement.

Divorce and remarriage

RON WOLFSON: What happens if there's a remarriage? Who are you buried next to?

BEN ZION BERGMAN: The basic *halakhah* is that even if it is a widow who gets remarried, she's buried with her second husband. Now, this is most often observed in the breach because the children want their father and mother together. In a divorce, the problem generally doesn't arise because they usually want to be buried with the second spouse. Listen, if they didn't get along when they were alive ...

With the widespread phenomenon of divorce and remarriage in the Jewish community, interesting complications sometimes arise when a spouse dies. If the couple has purchased a family plot before the divorce, decisions need to be made about the disposition of this property. In some cases, the couple will sell both plots or one person will take possession of the plots. In any case, it is advisable to resolve this issue at the time of the divorce.

What happens if a spouse dies and the surviving spouse remarries? Where shall the surviving spouse be buried—near the first spouse or the second?

If at all possible, the surviving spouse who remarries should indicate a preference for where he or she wishes to be buried. This may avoid unpleasant arguments between children of the first and second marriages or between the second spouse and the children of the first marriage. By respecting the wishes of the deceased, these arguments may be avoided.

Non-Jewish family members

According to Jewish law, a person not of the Jewish faith may not be buried in the consecrated ground of a Jewish cemetery. Of course, those non-Jews who convert to Judaism are fully Jewish and are accorded full Jewish burial rites.

The problem arises in the case of a mixed marriage where the non-Jewish spouse has not converted. Even if the couple is raising the children to be Jewish, the non-Jewish partner may not be buried in most Jewish cemeteries. What if it is known that a Jewish community cemetery allows burials by Reform rabbis of non-Jewish spouses of their members? In a recent responsum accepted by the Committee on Jewish Law and Standards of the Rabbinical Assembly, Rabbi Ben Zion Bergman concludes that the interment of non-Jewish spouses and children does not vitiate the Jewish character of the cemetery or its sanctity. While a Conservative rabbi may not officiate at the burial of the non-Jewish spouse, nor should the burial be allowed in the section owned by the congregation, the rabbi may officiate at the burial of Jews in that cemetery.

In the case of a Jew-by-choice suffering the death of a non-Jewish relative, it is appropriate for the convert to Judaism to engage in the observance of *shiva* following the burial of the deceased. After all, he or she is fully Jewish and has sustained the loss of one of the seven relatives for which *shiva* is mandated, even though the relative was not Jewish.

FOR COMFORTERS

You heard the news in a phone call from a friend the day before. This morning, you open the paper immediately to the obituary page and read the notice. You dress in somber colors, something appropriate for a synagogue service. You've changed appointments to clear your calendar. The funeral is at 11:00 a.m.

You arrive at the cemetery gate at 10:45. A funeral attendant is there to direct you to the chapel. You park your car in a line that will later become the processional to the gravesite. You enter the chapel, and an attendant offers you a card on which to record your name and a message to the bereaved. You see friends to sit with and share whatever news you have of how the deceased died, how the family is doing, and the normal small talk while waiting for the service to begin. The various conversations create a low, but audible, crowd noise.

A curtain opens, you see the casket, the bereaved take their seats, and the chapel becomes immediately silent. The rabbi asks the congregation to take the prayer booklet, and the service begins. You participate in the responsive reading and answer "Amen" to the chants of the cantor. The rabbi's eulogy recalls warm and wonderful memories of the deceased, and you begin to sob. As at weddings, you always cry at funerals, so you've come prepared and reach into a pocket for a tissue. You rise for the *Eil Maleh Raḥamim,* and when the departed's name is recited in Hebrew, your mind is filled with memories the name evokes.

The service concluded; the funeral attendant announces when and where the *shiva* is to be held. You make a mental note of the times, thinking ahead to when you can make a *shiva* call. The pallbearers bring the casket through the chapel; the mourners follow behind. You are moved to tears again, this time by the site of your bereaved friends. You exit the chapel, handing the attendance card to an usher, feeling good that the family will know that you were there.

As the casket is put into the hearse, you greet friends by the lineup of cars awaiting the processional to the gravesite. Once there, you stand around the bereaved family as the rabbi and cantor conduct the remainder of the service. When invited to participate in the actual burial, you line up for your turn to shovel some earth into the grave. Finally, you and your friends, representatives of the broader community, form an aisle through the crowd for the mourners' departure from the grave. As they pass, you offer the traditional words of condolence, "May God comfort you among the other mourners of Zion and Jerusalem."

How to Attend a Funeral

BERNARD LIPNICK: It is very important to attend a funeral. A person shouldn't die alone and shouldn't be buried alone. The community envelops the individual Jew into its warm embrace from birth to burial. To be at the funeral is also a tremendous comfort to the mourners. I have sat with the family in a limousine with tinted windows—you can see out, but the people can't see in. The main topic of conversation at that point is: "Look who came!" "I haven't seen her in twenty years!" "How did he get here all the way from New York?" Being there is the most important act of consolation. Beyond that, at most funerals, you are offered the opportunity to perform one of the really great *mitzvot*— physically burying the dead by actually shoveling earth into the grave— which is the highest form of *kevod ha-meit*—honoring the deceased.

SANDY GOODGLICK: Even though you may not know the deceased, you still have an obligation to be with the bereaved. You may be inclined to say, "I didn't even know this person's father. I don't think I'll go to the funeral." But, of course, we all know you go for the people who are left behind. Whenever there's a death, there's pain. And if you care about the person in pain, you've got to be there one way or another.

You will hear about a funeral. Bad news travels fast. And the news of a funeral travels at the speed of light. You will likely get a phone call from someone. Or in a true sign of advancing age, you may have reached that time in your life when you regularly read the obituary column in the newspaper.

Once you hear the news, here are the steps to follow in attending a funeral:

1. **Decide whether you're going.** Since there is often such short notice of a funeral, you may very well need to clear your calendar or make the necessary arrangements to attend the service. Most employers are understanding and will allow you time off to attend a funeral. If you have young children, you may need to arrange child-care. If you don't drive, you may need to ask someone for transportation to the funeral.

2. **Dress appropriately.** Proper attire for a funeral is a dress for women and a coat and tie for men.

3. **Arrive early.** Funerals almost always start exactly on time. Try to arrive at the site sometime between a half-hour to a few minutes before the announced time.

4. **Follow directions.** A funeral director will tell you where to sit or stand for the service. He or she may give you an attendance card to fill out or ask you to sign a guest book when you enter the chapel. Write your name and, if you wish, a brief message of condolence.

5. **Do not greet the mourners.** With few exceptions, now is not the time to approach the mourners. They will either be in a "waiting room," seated in the front pews, or exiting from a car at graveside when the service is about to begin. As much as you want to reach out to comfort them, this is not the time. You may want them to know you are there—that's what the guest book is for— or let them know how you reacted to the eulogy when you see them during a *shiva* call.

   If you are very, very close family or friends, it may be appropriate to see the mourners before the service begins or approach them after the graveside service.

6. **Talk softly.** In the minutes before the service, as people come in and see friends and relatives, a low rumble of conversation develops. Often, the coffin is already in the room. Try to talk softly

and appropriately. This is definitely not a time for swapping jokes or boisterous talk.

7. **Participate in the service.** The rabbi and/or cantor will lead the congregation in prayer during the service. Reply with "Amen" at the appropriate places. Participate in any responsive readings. React as you may to the eulogy—it is designed to touch you emotionally. Bring a handkerchief or tissues—like weddings, it's not unusual to cry at a funeral, even if the deceased was not well known to you.

8. **Note the times and place of the *shiva* and preferred charities.** The funeral director will announce the times and the address of the home where the family will receive visitors. Preferred charities for donations in memory of the deceased will also likely be announced. It's a good idea to bring a pen and a piece of paper on which to note this information.

9. **Decide to go to the graveside.** If the service has been held in a synagogue, a funeral home, or chapel on the grounds of the cemetery, there will be a processional to the gravesite. If at all possible, go. It is a great comfort to the mourners to accompany them to the grave.

10. **Follow directions to the cemetery.** In situations when a processional is formed to go from the place of the service to the cemetery, you will be directed to join the line of cars following the hearse and the family. A sticker identifying your car as part of the funeral may be placed on the windshield, and you will probably be asked to turn on your headlights. A police officer may escort the procession for traffic control; follow any directions he or she may give you.

11. **Surround the family at graveside.** When you reach the cemetery, you will be directed to the graveside. There you will find a row of chairs for the mourners. Stand behind and around the graveside. When the family arrives, do not greet them. Often, this is the most difficult part of the entire experience. Let them take their places for the graveside service.

12. **Participate in the ritual at graveside.** Those officiating at graveside will say several prayers; respond in the appropriate places. At the end of the service, the casket may be lowered and friends

invited to place dirt into the grave. Normally, the officiants begin this ritual, followed by the mourners and their family members. Then, you can take a place in line to do this most meaningful and important *mitzvah*. When your turn arrives, pick up a handful of dirt with your hands or with a shovel and place it into the grave. Some do this three times. Place the shovel back into the pile of dirt; do not hand it to the next person.

13. **Offer your condolences.** As the mourners leave the gravesite, form two rows in the crowd creating a path for their exit. As they pass, say the ancient words of consolation:

הַמָּקוֹם יְנַחֵם אֶתְכֶם בְּתוֹךְ שְׁאָר אֲבֵלֵי צִיוֹן וִירוּשָׁלָיִם

Ha-Makom yenahem etkhem b'tokh sha'ar aveilei
Tzion v'Yerushalayim

May the Omnipresent comfort you among all the mourners of
Zion and Jerusalem

Generally, you do not approach the mourners at this time. If you do, they must acknowledge your presence rather than cope with their own grief. Of course, if the mourner reaches out to you, respond with a hug and an additional word of condolence.

14. **Visit the graves of family and friends.** Since you are already at the cemetery, take the opportunity to visit the graves of family members and friends. Besides being a wonderful *mitzvah,* this will give the mourners time to return to the *shiva* home before visitors arrive. It should be noted, however, that in some communities it is emphatically not the custom to visit the graves of others when attending a funeral.

15. **Wash your hands.** It is customary to wash hands when leaving a cemetery. You may do this as you leave or before you enter the *shiva* home, or in your own home if you are not going directly from the funeral to the *shiva* home.

PART 6

Shiva

For Mourners

ALLEN BROWN: When we returned from the funeral, the limo dropped us off at the bottom of the driveway, and we walked up to our house. When I saw the water and the towel at the front door, I broke up again. Another reality hit me.

When I got into the house, all the little small chairs were there. And the mirrors were covered, even the TV, so we couldn't see our reflections. I went to light the *shiva* candle. They had given me the choice of electric or wax; I chose the wax because of tradition.

Then, the rabbi said we had to eat. None of us wanted to eat, but we had to do it. He insisted we eat hard-boiled eggs. First the immediate family ate, then everyone who wanted ate.

RICHARD LOPATA: There must have been two hundred people at the house after the funeral. It was unbelievable. I can't begin to tell you how comforting it was for me to have all those people here. Call it a wake or whatever; it was just such a relief, such a tremendous help to get over that day.

The ride home from a funeral is interminable. You are feeling numb, exhausted from the nearly constant emotions generated by the funeral experience. When you reach the house, you find a table set with a pitcher of water and a basin next to the front door. You wash your hands and enter the home where you will be "sitting *shiva*" for the next week.

By the amount of activity going on in the home, you would think someone was about to have a large open house. Friends are in the kitchen, busily preparing food. A table has been set for a meal. Extra chairs have been brought into the living room. The limousine driver, an employee of the funeral home, has brought in a large case filled with the prayer books necessary for the services to be held during the *shiva*. A large urn of coffee is brewing.

People begin to arrive, entering the home through the unlocked front door. They come to you immediately, offering a hug, a kiss, a pat on the back. Their look is one of sympathy and empathy. Some say, "I'm sorry." Others say a few words about the goodness of the deceased. Some say nothing at all.

The trickle of people becomes a torrent, and suddenly, the house is filled with people, each one trying to reach you to offer gestures of condolence. In a curious way, the quality of your response to each person varies markedly depending on a number of factors: your relationship to the person, the relationship between the comforter and the deceased, how tired you are. When some people approach you, the memories of these relationships leads to an overwhelming emotional response, "Oh, Bruce, how Morton loved you!"

Someone leads you to the dining table where a simple meal of hard-boiled eggs, fish, and bread has been set out for the mourners. This is the "meal of condolence." You're not hungry at all, and you don't feel like eating; yet, the tradition insists you take this step of slowly returning to the business of living.

By the time you return to the living room, the visitors have turned to the usual small talk of conversation. But, you are not in the mood to talk about the weather or the Dodgers or the latest movie. You want to talk about your dearly departed. You begin to tell stories. Others join in with their memories. The words wash over you like a blanket of comfort. Occasionally, emotional waves lead you into the quiet sobbing that has been with you since the early morning. Your friends and family understand and reach for you with reassuring hugs and hands.

By late afternoon, you are truly exhausted. Most of the visitors have left. You try to take a nap, but falling asleep is difficult. A friend has brought over dinner, but you can barely eat. A half-hour before the appointed hour for the evening service, visitors begin to return. They ask, "How are you doing?" What can you say? The rabbi arrives to lead the service. He or she explains the evening prayers and asks the group to participate in an English reading. The climax of the service is the Mourner's Kaddish, which you and the other mourners recite together, following the rabbi's lead. The visitors help themselves to the coffee and cake offered to them, standing around and schmoozing. Your closest friends and family come to you, hold your hand, offer words of comfort, ask if they can do anything for you. You feel overwhelmed by the love and support in the house.

Finally, the last guests have left. You are drained, numb. Someone has offered to stay with you through the evening. You climb into bed and drift off into a nervous, fitful night, hoping that the coming week will see the gradual diminution of the intense grief of the first day.

Shiva

The Bible records several instances of the seven-day mourning ritual. In Genesis 50:10, we learn that when Jacob died, his son Joseph "wailed with a very great and sore wailing, and he made a mourning for his father seven days."

The real work of mourning and comforting comes together during the *shiva*, the seven-day period of prayer, reflection, and memory. The bereaved now leaves the state of *aninut* and enters the stage of *aveilut* (mourning). If the tradition regarded the *onen/onennet* as incapable of personal "grief-work" because of the total focus on the need to honor the deceased, it considers the *shiva* as the beginning of intense mourning that centers on the bereaved. The bridge between the stages of *aninut* and *aveilut* is the gauntlet of comfort created for the mourners as they leave the gravesite.

How Long Is Shiva?

ALLEN BROWN: I wanted to sit *shiva* for the full week. My sisters who don't live in Rochester had different ideas. One sister lives in Arizona and has young children, so she only wanted to sit for three days before she returned there. My sister in Baltimore said, "Mom doesn't want to sit for seven days; she only wants to sit for three days." I said, "If Mom wants to sit for three days, she can sit for three days. She's got to come here for dinner anyway. What's the difference?" A lot of people are only sitting for three days, or even just one day. But there were four *shiva* houses going in the neighborhood when we sat, and all four sat for seven days.

HERMAN FEIFEL: With an elongated dying process these days, the need for the whole *shiva* may be somewhat mitigated. On the other hand, psychologically I think the Jewish tradition is mostly on the beam. Even if anticipatory grief has occurred to some degree, there still is a difference between anticipating and the actual reality of death. To short-circuit the *shiva* is by and large not good or fully therapeutic. Funeral and ritual are important because they accentuate the reality of death, bring the support and warmth of fellow human beings when needed, and provide a transitional bridge to the new circumstances facing the mourners. We are learning that if we do not lament close upon the death of a loved one, we shall do so later on—only more inappropriately.

JACK RIEMER: *Shiva* means "three" if you don't know Hebrew! But now it means "one." Many people have one *shiva minyan* at home the night of the funeral, and then they come to the synagogue, if at all. Of course, I know a lot of people who don't have time to sit a week who end up spending many times that much time sitting on a couch working out what they didn't have time to work out then—years later, years later.

Shiva—literally, "seven"—refers to the seven-day period of mourning that begins immediately after the funeral. Since according to Jewish law a fraction of a day can be counted as a full day, both the day of the funeral and the morning of the seventh day are counted as full days. Thus, one normally "sits *shiva*" from the moment one returns home from the funeral until after the morning service six days later. On the intervening Shabbat, the rules of *shiva* are suspended, and the mourners are encouraged to join the community in the synagogue, returning to the *shiva* after *Havdalah,* the concluding service of Shabbat.

However, there are several factors that can reduce the days of *shiva*. If the major holidays of Rosh Hashanah, Yom Kippur, Passover, Shavuot, and Sukkot come during the seven days, the *shiva* is cancelled. For example, if *shiva* has begun on a Sunday and the festival begins on the subsequent Wednesday night, the remainder of the *shiva* is nullified. In fact, if the *shiva* began on Wednesday morning and the holiday begins that evening, the few hours in the day are considered equivalent to the entire seven days of a "normal" *shiva*. While this might seem counter to the purpose of the seven-day grief cycle, the holidays and Shabbat were deemed so important for communal solidarity that their observance superseded the requirements of *shiva*. If someone dies on the first day of a major festival, the funeral takes place on the morning after the *yom tov* is over (i.e., during ḥol ha-moed), but the *shiva* does not begin until after the entire festival is over. When holidays fall during the *shiva* period, it is best to consult your rabbi to determine what you should do.

Traditionally, the *shiva* was divided into three time periods: the first day (the day of the funeral), the first three days of intense mourning, and the rest of the week. Again, the tremendous psychological insight of the rabbis is revealed; they knew that the grief-work of the first three days (really the day of the funeral and two additional days) would be intense, with a corresponding diminution of the intensity of grief during the remaining days.

The psychological wisdom of seven days of intense grief has been recognized by virtually every bereavement expert. Vast experience with mourners validates the notion that the first days of grieving often find the bereaved exhibiting shock and numbness. It is only after a few days that the mourner can begin to truly accept the consoling actions and words of those seeking to comfort.

Although festivals cancel official mourning, the obligation to extend comfort to the mourner is still in effect. Certainly, it is permissible to visit with the mourner or see to it that the mourner has appropriate festival meals (see *Shulḥan Arukh Yoreh De'ah* 399:1).

This phased pattern of grief over the week is one of the things lost when mourners truncate the *shiva* period to fewer than seven days. It is an undeniable fact of modern Jewish observance in the non-Orthodox movements that the observance of *shiva* is often reduced to three days, one day, or, in some cases, eliminated completely. There are many reasons for this: the "trouble" of opening the home to visitors, the difficulty of getting a *minyan,* the desire to go back to work and normal living as soon as possible, the need of out-of-towners to return home. These are reasons of inconvenience. However, there are two more serious problems threatening the traditional observance of *shiva.*

One theory that may explain the desire to shorten *shiva* in some families can be traced to a phenomenon known as "anticipatory bereavement." The enormous success of medical technology now keeps people alive for months and years longer than they would have survived a generation ago. Many families must cope with the slow death of loved ones. During this painful process, it is not uncommon for those attending the terminally ill to begin mourning for the loved one well before the actual death.

There are, of course, serious pitfalls when anticipatory bereavement begins to happen. Most problematic is the tendency of some to "abandon" the terminally ill patient, at least mentally if not physically. Then there is the long vigil at the bedside, often with the patient in a coma or uncommunicative, sometimes for months.

In some of these cases, when the death finally occurs, there is the inevitable confrontation with the reality that the loved one is really gone. The process of grief begins, and the *shiva* proceeds in much the same way it would in the case of sudden death. But, in other cases, much of the grief-work has already been done. The need for seven days of *shiva* may not be as acute. The family is just plain exhausted and cannot face the idea of sitting for seven days. The decision may be to sit for less time.

The second serious problem threatening the traditional observance of *shiva* is a widespread lack of knowledge about its practices and meanings. A new generation of Jews simply does not know much about *shiva* and its value, both religious and psychological. Many Jews choose to observe a full *shiva,* complete with daily *minyanim,* when the ritual is properly explained. Our hope is that the information that follows will help you make an informed decision about observing shiva in a way that will assist the healing process for you and your family.

The Observance of Shiva

The *shiva* period is usually observed in the home of the closest relative to the deceased. For example, if an elderly parent dies, the *shiva* is held in the home of the surviving spouse. By staying in familiar surroundings, the mourning spouse is saved the discomfort of moving in or traveling to another home. However, sometimes it is more suitable to hold the *shiva* at the home of an adult child. If there is only one person sitting *shiva* at a residence, the family and community can organize a rotation of people to stay with the mourner throughout the majority of the day, if not overnight.

Over the centuries, a number of observances and customs developed to enable the mourners to do their grief-work. Many of these customs also have their roots in the folk superstitions commonly found during the time between the redaction of the *Mishnah* (200 C.E.) and the Middle Ages (1500 C.E.) when most of these practices were codified in the *Shulḥan Arukh,* the Code of Jewish Law. Of course, modern commentators have attempted to reinterpret the traditional customs in order to make them useful and meaningful for today's mourner.

- **Washing hands.** Jewish law stipulates the washing of hands before entering a *shiva* house upon returning from the funeral. The reason dates to a time when contact with the dead was deemed to make a person ritually "impure." The issue of spiritual "purity" was of great importance to the ancient rabbis.

    The folk superstition held that spirits were afraid of water, and this washing would remove any lingering spirits picked up at the cemetery. The *Shulḥan Arukh* reveals this theme when it stipulates the recitation of this prayer while washing the hands:

"Our hands have not shed this blood, neither have our eyes seen it ... Forgive, *Adonai,* Your people Israel ... so shall you put away the innocent blood from Your midst."

Today, the washing of hands is an act of spiritual cleansing. Unlike the washing of hands before a meal *(netilat yadayim),* there is no *b'rakhah* (blessing) recited, nor is there a particular procedure for washing the hands. There is simply a pitcher of water and a basin set out on a table in front of the house for those who wish to wash hands before entering the home.

- **The *shiva* candle is lit.** A special candle is lit immediately upon returning to the *shiva* house from the cemetery. It is designed to burn for seven days, the entire length of the *shiva* period. Candlelight is universally recognized as an antidote to spiritual darkness. The folk religion taught that light prevented the spirits from doing their work since they are unable to operate in the light. Some modern commentators have pointed to the analogy of the wick and flame to the body and soul. The *shiva* candle is also a foreshadowing of the *yahrtzeit* candle, the memorial flame that will be lit on the anniversary of the death and on major festivals.

  Most Jewish funeral homes will provide this large *shiva* candle to the family as part of their services. Some will offer an electric light as an alternative, but most people prefer the authenticity of a real candle. Again, there is no *b'rakhah* to be recited when lighting the candle, but it should be placed in a prominent place within the *shiva* home.

- **Grooming of the body is prohibited.** Jewish tradition offers guidelines on personal grooming during the *shiva* that restricts haircuts, shaving, showering, and the use of cosmetics. Why? Because the rabbis wanted to remove from the mourner any concern for appearance as the grieving process took its course. By prohibiting the ornamentation of the body, the mourner symbolically withdraws from society, in a way, simulating death itself.

  Thus, among the most traditional of Jews, a "luxurious bath" in hot water "for pleasure" is not allowed, but washing separate parts of the body in cool water is. Shaving is not permitted, nor is the trimming of nails, nor is the use of perfumes. Yet there has always been a tension between pleasure and basic hygiene. A shower is certainly different than a luxurious bath. Clearly, the idea here is for the mourner to be in a state of social withdrawal. It is up to the individual to determine how to express this value.

- **Mirrors are covered.** This ancient practice requires that all mirrors and shiny surfaces that reflect a person's image are to be covered. The most common reason cited is that the mourner should not be concerned with issues of vanity. Without a mirror to look into, the concern with one's appearance is moot. Other commentators point out that the image of God within the human being has been diminished by this death, and it would be inappropriate to view a human/divine reflection in a mirror at this time.

  The popular practice of covering mirrors reveals a primitive understanding of both the soul and ghosts. One theory is postulated by James Frazer in his definitive study of folk beliefs about the subject, *The Belief in Immortality and the Worship of the Dead* (pp. 455–456). He states: "The soul, projected out of the person in the shape of his reflection in the mirror, may be carried off by the ghost of the departed, which is commonly supposed to linger about the house till burial."

- **Mourners stay home.** The predominant reason for the extraordinary effort on the part of comforters to provide for all the mourners' needs during the week of *shiva* is to enable the bereaved to focus exclusively on the grief-work that must be done in order to return to living. Traditionally, then, the mourners had no reason to leave the *shiva* home during the week. They generally did not work (unless dire economic consequences would result); all food and provisions were provided by the community, and a *minyan* of Jews would come to the home morning and evening to conduct prayer services in which the mourners could recite Kaddish.

  Observant Jews maintain this practice today. However, many people report the most difficult challenge to be confronted during the *shiva* is to recruit a *minyan* of at least ten adult Jews in the morning. (Tips on how to get a *minyan* follow below.) The tradition does allow for this problem and permits mourners to go to the synagogue for services and to return to the *shiva* home immediately. Of course, on Shabbat and festivals, *shiva* is suspended and mourners go to the synagogue for services.

- **Pleasurable activities are limited.** Of course, when one is in mourning, the idea of attending a party, watching a movie, or even listening to favorite music is often the last thing one wishes to do. Therefore, the tradition limits a number of obvious—and not so obvious—"pleasures":
  - Attendance at weddings, bat and bar mitzvahs, circumcision ceremonies of relatives (except one's own son), and any other "party" is curtailed;
  - Wearing shoes, specifically leather shoes, is not allowed. Leather is considered a luxury and comfort, and as on Yom Kippur when we approximate the feeling of death by not eating or wearing leather, the idea here is to identify symbolically with one's own personal mortality. Cloth shoes or slippers, however, are permitted.
  - Studying Torah is not allowed since it is assumed to be a source of great enjoyment. Nevertheless, it is deemed appropriate to read from the books of Job, Lamentations, and Jeremiah, laws pertaining to mourning, and other appropriate readings of comfort.
  - Wearing new clothes and laundering soiled clothes is to be avoided. Surely, the mourner is allowed to wear clean clothes, but not brand-new or even especially laundered garments. Again, the point is that the mourner should not be concerned with appearance during the *shiva* period.
  - Watching television, playing games, and listening to music are considered inappropriate since they are pleasurable activities.
  - Sexual intercourse is considered inappropriate during *shiva*. This does not mean expressions of intimacy and affection are forbidden, just the physical act itself.
  - Sitting on a regular chair is curtailed. In fact, the very term "sitting *shiva*" probably refers to the practice of mourners sitting on low stools or benches during the week, an ancient sign of grief that emphasizes the bereaved's lowly state. Sephardic Jews traditionally sit shiva on the floor, emulating the original custom of sitting on the ground. This practice is

derived from the description of the three friends who comforted Job, "for seven days and seven nights they sat beside him on the ground" (Job 2:13). "*Shiva* chairs" or "*shiva* stools" are often available from a Jewish funeral home. Old-timers might remember mourners sitting *shiva* on wooden orange crates. As with other *shiva* traditions, today some mourners forgo sitting on low chairs.

It is important to emphasize that the term "sitting *shiva*" does not mean that mourners must sit all the time during the *shiva* period. It is perfectly permissible to stand, walk, and even sit in a chair at a regular table to eat a meal. However, the mourner is not obligated to rise from her or his chair to greet any visiting comforter. This is perhaps the clearest indication to all that the normal roles of host/hostess and guest are inverted during *shiva*.

- **Shabbat.** Shabbat, Friday sundown to Saturday sundown, is counted as a full day of *shiva*, but a number of the restrictions of the mourning period are lifted.

ALLEN BROWN: Going to *shul* on *Shabbes* was really tough. First of all, everyone knew my dad, and everyone wanted to come up and say something. I remember on Shabbat morning, right after the preliminary prayers, the mourners were supposed to say the *Kaddish d'Rabanan*. I had never said that before. All the men came up to show me the pages; they had even marked up a book where the Kaddish is found. When the Rabbi announced the *yahrtzeits* and the recent passings, it was very difficult when Dad's name was mentioned. At the end of the service, even though there was a big bar mitzvah, we just snuck out the back door.

RICHARD LOPATA: You know what really hurt? All these people who came to my house for the *shiva*—not one of them came to the synagogue to be with me on Friday night. Here they're gonna mention my daughter from the *bimah* and no one was there. If my two brothers and their wives had not come, my son, Cynthia, and I would've sat there all by ourselves.

Shabbat has such an important status in Jewish religious and communal life that mourners are encouraged to participate in the celebration of the holiday even during the midst of *shiva.* Thus, mourners are permitted to leave home to attend services in the synagogue on Shabbat.

Since the celebration of Shabbat is joyous, mourners remove any public signs of mourning, such as the *k'riah* garment or ribbon. Normal clothes and regular shoes are worn. Mourners can sit on regular chairs during Shabbat. However, sexual intercourse is not permitted, and men do not shave.

At the *Kabbalat Shabbat* (receiving the Sabbath) service in the synagogue on Friday night, mourners are greeted by the community at the conclusion of the *L'kha Dodi* hymn. The rabbi announces the death by saying something like, "This week, our community sustained the loss of _____," and then gives the names of the survivors and their relationships to the deceased. Then the congregation expresses its condolences to the mourners by reciting the formula for comfort:

הַמָּקוֹם יְנַחֵם אֶתְכֶם בְּתוֹךְ שְׁאָר אֲבֵלֵי צִיּוֹן וִירוּשָׁלַיִם

Ha-Makom y'nahem etkhem b'tokh sh'ar aveilei Tzion v'Y'rushalayim

May God comfort you among all the mourners of Zion and Jerusalem.

Mourners participate in the service and recite the Kaddish. However, they generally do not accept an *aliyah* to the Torah. Of course, mourners will be approached by members of the congregation who will offer personal condolences. Some mourners report that going to synagogue on Shabbat fills them with comfort, while others feel uncomfortable, finding it difficult to confront the many sympathizers. After all, the mourner may have just spent the better part of a week isolated from the community. This first tentative step back into the community can be fraught with very mixed emotions.

Mourners attend services Friday night, Saturday morning, and Saturday afternoon/evening, resuming *shiva* on Saturday night after the *Havdalah* service concluding Shabbat.

MOSHE ROTHBLUM: A lot of the customs of *shiva* are very positive but some of them just aren't very meaningful to me. Not shaving was very meaningful to me. I hate not shaving. This was clearly for me a statement of mourning. I really didn't care how I looked. You're not supposed to take a shower because it's a "pleasurable experience," although the *halakhah* says you can if not doing so makes you "sick." I guess one could say even psychologically or emotionally upset ... then you should take a cold or lukewarm shower. Well, I took a hot shower, but I was in and out very quickly. I couldn't have stood not taking a shower.

Covering the mirrors is another one. The real origin of the custom was a superstitious belief that the angel of death was lurking there. I understand the rabbinic interpretation of covering the mirrors to avoid the concern with vanity, but I didn't feel that was important for me, so we didn't do that. The stools too, I don't know ... I didn't have a strong feeling about that either. On the other hand, I didn't wear leather; I wore slippers and a cloth belt. I guess I did pick and choose from these customs ...

The Open House
—or—
Who's the Host? Who's the Guest?

BERNARD LIPNICK: Contrary to what many people think, the entire
tone of the *shiva* is set by the mourner. The mourner should think of
him- or herself as a guest in his or her own home, not as a host. Those
who come to visit should act as hosts, not the other way around. A case
in point is food and drink. If mourners think of people coming to their
home as guests, they think that it is their place to offer them food and
drink. Once that happens, the tone is set, "I am your host, you are my
guests." The drinks flow, the food is eaten, there is boisterous conversation (what do you talk about with a drink in your hand?), the evening
passes, and the guests leave. And the mourner feels as though he or
she's been clobbered, run over by a Mack truck. Why? Because all the
emotions he or she has had and wants to give vent to and wants to sort
out have been denied. He or she's been the host when he or she should
have been the guest.

In the traditional *shiva* house, you, the mourners, are to be served,
waited on hand and foot, so that you can deal with your grief. All your
physical needs are to be taken care of by family and friends.

That's why I always recommend that absolutely no food be offered
to visitors in a *shiva* home. Not even a cold drink. Not even coffee.
Nothing. Zero. When it comes to meal time, a friend can say, "Excuse
us, the mourners have to eat their dinner." And the mourners can get

up and go to the kitchen or dining room to eat the meal. Most consolers will get the message and say, "Excuse me, I didn't realize it was dinner time" and leave. The consolers will always follow the lead of the mourner.

LOIS ROTHBLUM: Maybe it's because Moshe is a rabbi, but people wanted to come over all hours of the day. The *shiva* itself is so exhausting that we felt we had to try to put some limit on people's visits. So we typed up a note that said, "Dear Friends, We will be receiving visitors beginning at 7:00 p.m., one hour before the *minyan* at 8:00 p.m. Thank you for understanding. Moshe and Lois." We put the note on the front door in the afternoon so Moshe could take an undisturbed nap from three to five.

We also didn't want hordes of people over after the funeral so we announced at the service that we would be receiving visitors beginning at 8:00 p.m. that evening. We said, "Please limit your visits to the *minyan* times of eight in the morning and eight in the evening." People were very respectful of that for the most part.

Seudat Ha-havra'ah—
The Meal of Condolence

JACK RIEMER: It's not a party. It doesn't have to be a catered affair. Serving the food to mourners enables them to withdraw, to be taken care of, just for this week. There's a great, great story in the Bible about this tradition. King David's child is very ill. For weeks he's fasted and wailed and sat on the ground. The child dies and the people are afraid to tell him. He guesses what's going on and he asks, "Is the child dead?" They say, "Yes." So David gets up, changes clothes, goes to worship, comes back, and asks for food. The people say, "We don't understand. When the child was ill, you wept and fasted and mourned. Now the child is dead, and you eat?" David tells them, "As long as the child was alive, there was hope. I thought if I cry hard enough and pray hard enough, maybe the child will be saved. Now that he's gone, I must go on living. Someday I will go to him; he will not come back to me." It's called *seudat ha'havra'ah*—the meal of recuperation. And the law is that friends serve it to you. Why? Because left to yourself, you wouldn't do it. You don't want to go on living. But you must. So your friends reach out to you and say "we care about you" and provide you with food.

LOIS ROTHBLUM: The Adat Ari El Sisterhood provided the *seudat ha-havra'ah,* which was wonderful. Our friends were marvelous; they arranged meals for us for every single night. People contributed to a central fund and ordered dinners from kosher restaurants. They'd bring over the food at 5:00 p.m., and they'd just drop off the meal, tell me how to prepare it, and then leave. It was wonderful.

TAMARA GREENEBAUM: We had one *shiva minyan* with the community at the synagogue behind Mendoza's Market on the night of the funeral and everyone who came brought some dish for a California-style potluck *shiva* dinner that everyone shared in. It was very comforting to be surrounded by the community that night.

RICHARD LOPATA: I felt and understand that a significant number of people came to my home for the *shiva* because they too lost somebody that day. It wasn't just me. They were mourners, too. For me to sit in the kitchen and eat a sandwich and have them have to go down to the corner and get something to eat is wrong.

JACK RIEMER: That's okay. That makes great good sense. Sure, it's a shared meal. It's literally a communion. That's okay. What I am concerned with is when these trays get so lavish, and when everyone is so preoccupied with the food that the mourning and the mourners get overlooked. They're sitting in the corner while everybody is eating—at that point it's pointless.

The last thing you will want to do when you return home from the funeral is to eat. But, eat you must, says the wise tradition. You have spent the last twenty-four to forty-eight hours in an intense state of shock and numbness, totally focused on the funeral, on affording your beloved deceased a proper burial. Now, as you return home from the gravesite, the attention shifts to you and the other bereaved members of the family. You have begun the long road back to the living, the long road back to a feeling of normalcy. It is a road that may take months, even years.

It begins, though, with a simple meal.

The *seudat ha-havra'ah*, meal of condolence, usually consists of very basic foods, often foods that are round, representing *galgal ha-hozer ba-olam*—the wheel of fortune that characterizes all human beings, the wheel of fate that brings everyone to the same end. A hard-boiled egg, an ancient sign of mourning, symbolizes fertility, the circularity of life, and hope. Round lentils and chickpeas (garbanzo beans) were traditionally served in some areas of Eastern Europe. Bread is served, the staff of life. Certainly bagels fit the theme of the meal. Other dairy and pareve foods—gefilte fish, herring, noodle kugel—can be offered. And there will inevitably be a wide selection of baked goods brought to the *shiva* home.

This meal can be eaten at a regular dining table and should be served to the mourners by family and friends. The meal of condolence is not the Jewish version of a wake. Unfortunately, in many communities, the meal after the funeral has become exactly that—a large gathering of friends and family, characterized by platters of food—often supplied by caterers—that inevitably turns into a "party" atmosphere. The tradition did not intend this at all. There is no obligation to feed visitors to the *shiva* home. In fact, comforters are to serve mourners, not the other way around.

Yet, conditioned as we are by social mores, it doesn't feel right if we don't serve something to those who have been kind enough to make a condolence call. Moreover, some families are so large that it is easy to end up with dozens of people in the house even without opening the home to visitors. So, here are some options for serving food after the funeral:

- Offer a simple meal. Bagels, cream cheese, baked goods, and coffee are enough for anyone. If friends send fancy platters, save them for the family meals during the week.
- Offer only coffee and cake.
- Offer nothing at all. Bernard Lipnick taught his congregation in St. Louis that they should not expect food to be served at a *shiva* home.
- If you don't want people to come to the house after the funeral, make it clear at the funeral that visitors will be welcome at the first *shiva minyan*. If you want close friends to be with you at the meal of condolence, they can be invited privately.

On the other hand, a number of people we interviewed felt strongly that to have extended family and friends with them immediately after the funeral to share in the meal of condolence was of tremendous comfort. It is not unusual to find a *shiva* home filled with dozens of people who return to the house after the funeral to sit with the mourners and partake of the meal. In some cases, the mourners are taken into the kitchen to sit at a table for the meal, while guests help themselves to a buffet set out for them. Or the mourners may feel more comfortable sitting with the gathered guests in a living room.

Even when large numbers of people are in the *shiva* home following the funeral, the tone of the meal is set by the mourners. If they fall into the usual social role of host, greeting the guests, making sure they're eating, the message to those assembled is to "party on," to feel free to eat and drink. If, however, the mourners let the comforters serve them the meal of condolence, sit and accept the sympathies of the guests, a quieter atmosphere prevails. It is up to the mourners to set this tone.

Sometimes the type of death dictates the social climate of the *shiva*. It is undeniably true that when an elderly person dies, an event that people expect as a natural part of life, the tendency to treat the *shiva* as a kind of celebration of the life of the deceased is not unusual. However, when a sudden death, the death of a child or a young parent occurs, there is often much less frivolity associated with *shiva* visits.

Food during *shiva*

Knowing that mourners stay home during the week of *shiva,* the most common gift brought to the home by visitors is food. Two categories of food are needed in the *shiva* home: meals for the bereaved and refreshments for visitors.

The mourners who sit *shiva* all week in the traditional style do not leave the house for meals. Thus, someone needs to be sure that food for these meals is available. Many times, those organizing the *shiva* will ask friends to be responsible for bringing or sending a specific meal to the *shiva* home, usually a dinner. Most people report being able to eat breakfast and lunch from the food brought in by visitors. Again, these meals are for the mourners and the immediate family, not for visitors.

Although the meal of condolence after the funeral is reserved for the mourners, there will be occasions throughout the week of *shiva* when food is appropriately served to visitors:

- **At the morning prayer service.** When people arrange their schedules in order to participate in a morning *shiva minyan,* it is generally expected that a light breakfast will be served after the services. The menu can be as simple as coffee, juice, and baked goods or as substantial as bagels, cream cheese, fish, and eggs. This is generally not a sit-down breakfast; rather, people tend to help themselves at a buffet table and stand together in small groups. Since most need to get to work, this is a rather grab-a-quick-bite sort of thing.
- **At the evening prayer service.** As we shall discuss below, the evening service is often scheduled after the dinner hour. It is common practice to have coffee and sweets for visitors after the service.

Prayer Services during Shiva

RICHARD LOPATA: Cantor Fox did the *shiva* service, and he was just amazing. He told everybody what was going on and why we were doing it. He included everybody. He stood in the middle of the group rather than up front. And he had just the right touch—serious, but not so heavy-handed.

    The first night there was this horde of people. The next night it was down by 50 percent. The third night it was down a little bit more. On Shabbat, we went to *shul*. On Saturday night, it was like I had the plague.

MOSHE ROTHBLUM: One of the most comforting experiences I had throughout the *shiva* was the morning *minyan*. It was wonderful.

HAROLD SCHULWEIS: Having a *minyan* in the house is like bringing the synagogue into the home. It is opening oneself up to the healing powers of the community. We were a community of pain. It was comforting to know we were not alone in our pain. All these other people were there, too.

It is traditional practice to hold prayer services in the *shiva* home throughout the week, except on Shabbat. The daily schedule of prayer in traditional Jewish observance includes three services: *Shaḥarit*—the morning service, *Minḥa*—the afternoon service, and *Ma'ariv*—the evening service. The *Minḥa* and *Ma'ariv* services are often held together, with the two services separated by a brief break. (Depending on the time of year, the break may need to be longer to await the fall of darkness when the evening service is offered.) Obviously, the *Shaḥarit* service is held in the morning.

A *minyan* (quorum) of ten adults (a Jewish adult is a girl at least twelve years old and a boy at least thirteen years old—the legal ages of bat mitzvah and bar mitzvah) is required for certain prayers, including the Mourner's Kaddish, to be recited aloud. Many Conservative and all Reform congregations count women equally in convening and *davening* (praying) in a *minyan*. Herein lies one of the significant challenges to those organizing a *shiva*: how to get a *minyan*.

The problem of getting ten people to participate in the service is particularly acute in the morning. Except for the regular *daveners* in a traditional synagogue and for those who attend services to say Kaddish for their deceased or for a *yahrtzeit* (yearly memorial for the dead), most modern Jews rarely attend daily services. The morning service presents three other significant problems: (1) the skill level required to lead the morning service is greater than that of the afternoon and evening services, (2) men (and some women) wear *tefillin* (phylacteries) at the morning service, and (3) although not required at a *shiva minyan*, on Monday and Thursday mornings, a small section of the weekly Torah portion can be read and someone must be found who can prepare the reading.

There are the other problems of getting participants to a morning service. Most people need to be at work by 9:00 a.m. or earlier, so the *minyan* must begin at a very early hour, usually between 7:00 and 8:00 a.m. Even though the service itself lasts approximately thirty minutes, participants must plan their morning to allow for this time.

For these reasons, many of the rabbis and families we interviewed report that some mourners choose to go to the synagogue for the daily *minyan* there. Some *shiva* homes will have a morning *minyan* on Sunday when the time of the service can be later. Some try to hold a morning *minyan* in the home on Tuesday, Wednesday, and Friday, but go to the synagogue on Monday and Thursday mornings when the Torah is read.

While the *halakhah* allows mourners to leave the shiva home for this purpose (*Kol Bo Aveilut*, pp. 286 ff.), it is not the ideal. How, then, can the community help to ensure a *minyan* in the *shiva* home?

Someone—a friend or relative or a layperson at the synagogue—must take responsibility for getting people to the *shiva* home. In some synagogues, the bereavement committee handles this task. In others, the *shammes* (ritual director) who runs the daily *minyan* in the synagogue can help by sending regular *daveners* to the *shiva* home. Or an individual close to the family must get a list of people together who can be called to do this *mitzvah*. Then, as many who have had this task report, at least twenty people should be called to get the ten you need! Of course, don't forget to count the mourners and other family members of age who are likely to be at the service anyway.

Afternoon/evening or just evening services are usually, but not always, easier to organize. People are home from work and are generally more available to make a *shiva* call in the evening. Although mourners often find many people coming to the home in the early part of the week, attendance tapers off toward the end. Thus, whoever has taken the responsibility for organizing the services should be sensitive to this likelihood and be prepared to make calls during the last days of the *shiva*.

Assuming you gather the requisite number of people, what constitutes the prayer service? It is beyond the scope of this book to outline the structure and content of the daily services. Suffice it to say that most Jewish funeral homes will provide a number of prayer books in the *shiva* kit that contain the traditional prayers in Hebrew and English. Do check this out, however. Because so many people do not hold services in the morning, one Jewish funeral home we know sends prayer books that contain only the afternoon and evening services!

It is particularly important to try to have enough prayer books for the anticipated number of participants, or perhaps one for every two people. There is nothing more frustrating than to try to participate in a prayer service without a text. Ask the funeral home or the synagogue to lend you extra books, if available. Or, if you expect a very large crowd, you may want to photocopy a responsive reading to share with the group.

This suggests the first of several creative ideas for enhancing the basic prayer service in a *shiva* home. For many, the memories of *shiva davening* are of old men, racing through the prayers in Hebrew until the Mourner's Kaddish is said at the climax of the service. More often than not, women would be excluded from the *davening,* even the women who were in mourning! Think about organizing a service that not only provides the means for the mourners to say Kaddish, but for them and your visitors to reflect on the meaning of the moment. An appropriate responsive reading in English that everyone can share in, or a reading of comfort from one of the collections of such material, can enhance the experience for all concerned.

Another suggestion is to use the time between the *Minḥah* and *Ma'ariv* services for study and reflection. Sharing readings found in the prayer books, studying a selection from one of the traditional sources dealing with death and mourning in our tradition such as Job, Lamentations, or selections of the *Mishnah* (a lovely custom is to study sections that spell out the name of the deceased or the word *neshamah* [soul]—a play on the word *mishnah*). Bringing poems and other readings that have personal meaning to the bereaved can provide the opportunity for those at the *minyan* to think about the meaning of the experience. You might ask the rabbi or knowledgeable friends of the family or even family members to prepare a brief *d'rash,* a commentary either on an appropriate topic or something in memory of the deceased. During the *shiva* for Jerry Weber, we asked a number of his friends, both rabbinic and lay, to prepare such remarks for each of the prayer services held. These were not eulogies for Jerry; rather, they were brief learning sessions, no more than fifteen minutes each, dedicated to Jerry's memory.

One of the most wonderful ideas at any *shiva minyan* is to take the time to share memories and stories about the deceased. This can be done during or immediately after the prayer service. Generally, all it takes is for someone to ask if anyone wishes to share such a memory and the floodgates open. If you don't think this would work without some advance planning, ask a few friends before the service to be prepared to share a story or anecdote. Often, these stories are quite funny and revealing about the deceased. Inevitably, the memories provide great comfort to the mourners and empower the visitors with the feeling that they have accomplished part of their goal as comforters.

HAROLD SCHULWEIS: I encourage at the *shiva minyan* the reading of poetry that expresses the feelings of the mourners. I encourage the mourners to choose the poetry that consoles, and I have added my own to theirs.

It Is Never Too Late

The last word has not been spoken
the last sentence has not been writ
the final verdict is not in
    It's never too late
    to change my mind
    my direction
    to say "no" to the past
    and "yes" to the future
    to offer remorse
    to ask and give forgiveness

It is never too late
to start all over again
to feel again
to love again
to hope again
It is never too late
to overcome despair
to turn sorrow into resolve
and pain into purpose
It is never too late to alter my world
not by magic incantations
or manipulations of the cards
or deciphering the stars

But by opening myself

to curative forces buried within

to hidden energies

the powers in my interior self.

In sickness and in dying, it is never too late

Living, I teach

Dying, I teach

how to face pain and fear

Others observe me, children, adults

students of life and death

Learn from my bearing, my posture,

my philosophy.

It is never too late—

Some word of mine,

some touch, some caress may be remembered

Some gesture may play a role beyond the last

movement of my head and hand.

Write it on my epitaph

that my loved ones be consoled

It is never too late.

—HAROLD M. SCHULWEIS

Questions about Shiva *Services*

Who leads the services?

The tradition suggests that the mourners themselves should honor the memory of the deceased by leading the *davening*. After all, the visitors are coming to the *shiva* home to enable the mourners to say Kaddish. Thus, if one of the mourners has the skills involved in leading the service, she or he should be encouraged to do so. In many traditional homes, the mourner leads every service.

If not, the friend organizing the services should determine that at least one of the *daveners* is capable of leading the prayers. Often the rabbi or cantor will attend the first *minyan* service and can be asked to lead the *davening*. He or she will usually agree. It is especially moving and meaningful if a grandchild or other relative can lead the service. This is a powerful testimony to the continuity of Jewish tradition and offers great comfort to the mourners and the rest of the family.

Do you need to read Torah at these *minyanim?*

If you decide to hold *minyan* services on Monday and Thursday morning, you will need to decide whether you will have a Torah reading. It is not required, but should you wish to have a reading, contact the synagogue about lending you a Torah scroll. You will also need to ask someone capable of preparing the reading to do so. Be sure you have prayer books with the morning service. If the prayer book does not have the Torah reading in it, you might want to have someone prepare photocopies of the portion to be read. You will need to choose people to have the honors of *aliyot* ("going up" to recite the blessings for a Torah reading), lifting and dressing the Torah. The mourner, however, does not accept an *aliyah* to the Torah during the *shiva* period.

There are other nuances in the content of the *shiva* services. Consult your rabbi or Klein (pp. 287–288,) for details.

Sephardic Customs during Shiva

Among most Sephardic communities, *k'riah* is performed as soon as the mourners return home from the cemetery. The traditional meal of condolence is prepared by the burial society or family and friends. Mourners sit on the floor or on pillows, not on low stools. Daily services are held in the home and the *Zohar* is studied throughout the week.

In the Syrian community, offering Turkish coffee and food to visitors is not uncommon, even though it is not the custom for visitors to bring food or gifts to the mourners. In addition, a unique tradition is followed that stipulates a visitor make either one or three condolence call(s) during *shiva*. A second visit symbolizes the possibility that death could return again to the family. A third visit would indicate that the second visit was only to further offer support to the family.

In the Moroccan community, visitors leaving the house of mourning say, *"Min ha-shamayim tenuhamu"*—"May you be comforted from Heaven." At the end of *shiva*, a special meal and study session, called a *mishmara,* is held, and the deceased is again eulogized and mourners are encouraged to repent. Many mourners immediately begin a year of strict religious observance. Another *mishmara,* complete with food, is held at the cemetery itself on the thirtieth day following the burial.

An interesting Iranian custom is to hold a study session known as *"Tar-ihim"* (derived from the Hebrew *rahamim,* mercy) in the synagogue during the week of *shiva*. The mourners are allowed to come to the synagogue and are often joined by hundreds of friends and relatives. The rabbi will offer words of Torah, and a short eulogy about the deceased will be given.

Children during Shiva

RON WOLFSON: What about the kids?

LOIS ROTHBLUM: We told them that it would mean a lot to Moshe if they were at the *minyan*, not all the time, but perhaps on three mornings. It gave them some choice in a week that was totally out of their control. I let each of them sleep over at a friend's house one night. At one point, the pressure really got to Daniel, and he needed his privacy, which was fine. There were so many people in the house, particularly in the evenings. He felt it to be a real intrusion. I encouraged them to keep up with their activities. After all, they were not in mourning.

Imagine the disruption of a child's life during *shiva*. The house is full of people day and night, your parent(s) and other relatives are struggling with their own grief, and there is disruption of the normal routine of living.

For a child of bar/bat mitzvah age or older who is one of the official mourners, the laws of mourning apply. For younger children, parents or guardians will need to make decisions about how much of the *shiva* will be observed.

If the child is not an official mourner but is living in the house where the *shiva* is taking place, it is advisable to pay close attention to the impact of the mourning on the child. Decisions will need to be made about how involved you want the child to be in the observances. Choices about attending school and participating in the regular routine of activities will be required. If the child needs a break, friends and family can help by taking the children out of the house or having them stay overnight. Clearly, an important change in the family system has happened that must be dealt with, but life must go on.

Dealing with the Aftermath

Most mourners begin to deal with the social and financial aftermath of a death even while the *shiva* is in progress. Sometimes the fact that family members have gathered from disparate places influences the need to have these discussions sooner rather than later. Sometimes it is just too early to talk about what will happen next.

Somehow, mourners know when the timing is right. There are many issues to be resolved when someone dies. Where will Mom live? What shall we do with the business? When will we read the will? How will we divide up the personal effects? Most experts on grief suggest that major decisions not be made during the days immediately following a death. It is a time when emotions are raw and on edge. It is a time of confusion. Thus, if it is possible to delay some of the decisions until nerves calm down and rational discourse can be held, it is probably a wise thing to do.

Nevertheless, as the days of *shiva* grow longer and the week progresses, it may be possible to reach some decisions about matters that must be dealt with immediately, particularly choices about who will care for the survivors.

"Getting Up" from Shiva

RON WOLFSON: Today is the last day of the *shiva* for your mother. How are you feeling right now?

MOSHE ROTHBLUM: I feel really exhausted, very drained. I'm glad that it's almost over. Here I am a rabbi, but really a very private person, so it was difficult to have this week of people coming in all the time. It was also hard to repeat the story over and over again. And I must say I feel somewhat imprisoned by staying home all week. If it had been left to me, I probably would have gotten out of the house. But my commitment to the tradition really made sure I didn't, although I certainly understand people who don't want to stay home the whole time.

But all of the negative feelings are overwhelmed by the sense of comfort I received from the many visitors, the kindnesses, the *davening*, the memories of my mother and her achievements. Now that it's over, I must say I think *shiva* is a really good thing.

JACK RIEMER: You're allowed to be taken care of for a limited time. Then, the law is: *Shiva* has to end. You're not allowed to sit more than seven days. Two thousand years before Freud, the rabbis knew you had to go to the next stage. "Whoever wants to sit more than seven days must be mourning for something else." It's hard, but you've got to get up and go on, ready or not.

Shiva ends on the morning of the seventh day, just after the *Shaḥarit* service. It is traditional for mourners to take a short walk together and/or with friends. This walk symbolizes the beginning of the return to normal everyday life. Then, those who observed the various traditions of the *shiva* begin to restore the house. Mirrors are uncovered, and the *shiva* "kit" is packed up and returned to the funeral home. Mourners may return to work that day, and life begins anew.

This is a time of conflicting emotions for many mourners. On the one hand, sitting in the house all week has been claustrophobic and exhausting. A sense of relief comes with the knowledge that the experience is over. On the other hand, veteran mourners know that the intense attention from family, friends, and community that has characterized the past week is also over. Now, the mourner must face the difficult task of returning to normalcy—a task done without the tremendous support of the community that was evident during the *shiva*. It is a time of transition, a time to beware the inevitable swings of mood and emotion that will characterize the next phase of the bereavement process.

"Sitting Shiva*" out of Town*

SANDY GOODGLICK: We didn't sit *shiva* when my mother died. I stayed with my dad in Seattle for a couple of weeks, but when I returned to Los Angeles, there was virtually no support system. When a a parent dies out of town, I find people feel, "Well, she went to Seattle, she lost her mother, she did her *shiva,* and that's now behind her." There were only a couple of people who really showed up to be of any consolation to me. That was really difficult.

With the tremendous mobility of the Jewish community, many people will be "sitting *shiva*" with family "back home" in a city of origin instead of the current place of residence. Going home for a funeral of a parent or other relative can present a number of problems.

Where do you stay? If you are a mourner visiting from out of town, do you stay with a surviving parent, another family member, or in a hotel? How long do you stay? Ideally, one would stay for the entire *shiva.* Yet, work and school often create powerful tugs to return home as soon as possible. How do you leave? It is often quite painful to leave a surviving parent and return home. Feelings of guilt and abandonment may develop that add to your own grief-work.

Moreover, when you sit *shiva* out of town, your closest friends are not usually around for support. Although family members may gather, you leave your local community behind when going long distances to mourn.

Not only do you miss them, but they miss the opportunity to be there to express their condolences.

In an effort to enable friends to share in the bereavement process, some mourners actually host a "memorial" event back home once the out-of-town *shiva* is over. Our friend and colleague Dr. David Gordis hosted such a gathering in Los Angeles several weeks after sitting *shiva* for his father, Rabbi Robert Gordis, in New York. David invited friends to visit with him during a Sunday afternoon at which time he and others reminisced about his father's remarkable life and career. The experience offered comfort to David while giving those close to him the opportunity to make a condolence call.

FOR COMFORTERS

Shiva calls are never easy for you. What do you say? The words always seem so empty. How can you relieve the pain? It's so hard to watch a friend, a loved one, emotionally hurt. Yet, just being there is more important than anything, so you make plans to go.

You don't want to make the visit empty-handed, so the night before, you bake a cake. Sure, it would be easier to pick something up at the bakery, but you feel the personal effort will be much appreciated.

You approach the door of the house and remember the embarrassment of the first *shiva* call you made. No one had told you that you shouldn't ring the doorbell in a *shiva* home and you did. You felt like such a fool. Now you know that the door of a *shiva* home is never locked when guests are expected.

So, you walk in and immediately take the cake into the kitchen. You've put your name on a piece of masking tape attached to the plate, both so the mourners will know of your gesture and to get the plate back. The *shiva* helpers in the kitchen thank you and stack it with the rest of the baked goods. You notice that the pantry, the breakfast table, and the kitchen counters are loaded with food, paper goods, and beverages, so much so that it gives the impression of a large party under way.

You move into the living room and find your bereaved friend. Here is the moment of truth. What shall you say? You say nothing. Rather, you offer a hug, a squeeze of the hand, and a look that says, "I care for you. I know the pain you must be feeling." The bereaved initiates the conversation, "Thank you for coming. Morton loved you so." You pick up the theme: "Oh, I loved him too. He was a wonderful man. We enjoyed so many wonderful times together. I've been thinking of all the memories we share of him." You notice that the bereaved friend wants to talk about these memories and you continue, "Remember the trip we took to the Grand Canyon with the kids? He had his new camera and *potchkied* with it the whole time." Your friend laughs at the memory. She adds, "Yes, we got home and not one of those pictures turned out!" The ice broken, you engage in a five-minute conversation centered on memories of the deceased. At the end, you kiss and hug your bereaved friend and say, "His memory will be a blessing for you and for all of us." Your friend smiles a knowing smile, a smile of comfort.

How to Make a Shiva Call

DAVID TECHNER: People should know that when they go on a *shiva* call, you need to have a business plan. "Why am I going?" People often show up at a house of mourning, and they haven't the slightest idea why they came except out of a sense of obligation. We need to ask ourselves, "What am I trying to do?" Think about what you want to do and then do it. When people say things like "Well, at least he's not suffering," who are they trying to make feel comfortable? Certainly not the mourner. People say things like that so they won't have to deal with your grief. The comment is for them, not the mourner.

DENNIS GURA: When Rebecca died, the people from the synagogue took care of us for a week. We were in such shock. They literally got us up and put us to bed. They fed us. They brought a *minyan* to the house morning and evening. Without them, I don't know how we would have made it.

    Friends of ours had their second child just a few hours before Rebecca died. So, one day, our *shiva minyan* was much smaller as most went to Shmuel Menaḥem's *brit milah*. He was named Menahem for us. And he has been a comfort, not just because he is a sweet child, but also because we see that a life continues even in the midst of our grief.

SARALIE FOOTE: I think people stay too long. They come, they run into people they know, so they sit. They come and it's an evening.

    As a comforter, making a *shiva* call is one of the most important acts of condolence. Often, those visiting in a mourner's home are not sure what to say, how to act, whether to eat, and how long to stay. Here, step-by-step, is a brief guide to making a *shiva* call:

1. **Decide when to visit.** Listen for an announcement at the funeral for the times that the mourners will be receiving guests. Usually, the options are (a) immediately after the funeral, (b) around the *minyan* prayer services in the evening or morning, or (c) during the day. You need not call ahead to visit at announced times, but should you wish to visit during one of the days of *shiva*, you may want to call ahead. Some experienced *shiva* visitors actually choose to make a call toward the end of the *shiva* week when it is usually more difficult to gather a *minyan*.

2. **Dress appropriately.** Most people will "get dressed" to make a *shiva* call, usually as if attending a synagogue service. Depending on local customs, more informal dress might be appropriate.

3. **Bring a gift.** Food—a cake, cookies, a fruit basket—is the most appropriate gift. Liquor, candy, and flowers are not usually brought to a *shiva* home. An alternative and much-appreciated gift is to make a donation in memory of the deceased to a charity designated by the mourners.

4. **Wash your hands.** If you are visiting immediately after the funeral, you will likely see a pitcher of water, a basin, and towels near the front door. It is traditional to wash your hands upon returning from the cemetery. There is no blessing to say for this act.

5. **Don't ring the doorbell.** The front door of most *shiva* homes will be left open or unlocked. This is a sign that all are invited in to comfort the mourners. It also eliminates the need for the mourners to come to the door to greet you. On a practical level, it avoids the constant ringing of the doorbell, which can be terribly disruptive.

6. **Take the food to the kitchen.** There will usually be someone there to receive your gift of food. Be sure to put your name on a card or on the container so the mourners will know that you made the gift. It also helps to have marked any pots, pans, or platters with your name if you want to retrieve them later in the week.

7. **Find the mourners.** Although there will likely be people you know at the home, go to the mourners as soon as possible to ex-

press your condolences. Spend anywhere from a few moments to ten minutes or so with them. See the chapter on "What Do I Say?" for tips on how to talk with them. Try not to "hog" the mourners; there will be others who want to speak with them. You can always circulate in the crowd and come back to them. If you are the only visitors in the home, then of course spend as much time as you wish.

8. **Participate in the service.** If a prayer service is conducted during the *shiva* call, participate to the extent you can. If you do not know the prayers, sit or stand respectfully while the service is in progress.

9. **If invited to, eat.** Take your cue from the mourners. In some homes, no food will be offered, nor should you expect to eat anything. In others, especially after the funeral, food may be offered. Be sure that the mourners have already eaten the meal of condolence before you approach the food. When attending a morning *minyan,* you will likely be invited to partake of a small breakfast. After evening *minyan* services, coffee and cake may be served. In any case, should you be invited to eat, be moderate in your consumption. Normally, guests are not expected to eat meals with the family during the *shiva.*

10. **Talk to your friends.** Inevitably, you will encounter other friends at a house of mourning. Your natural instinct will be to ask about them—their health, their families, their business—to share the latest jokes, to schmooze about the weather, sports, politics, the *shul,* the neighborhood. If food is served, you may be standing with a plate of food and a drink. If you didn't know better, it would feel just like a party. But, you know better. You know that the purpose of the *shiva* is to comfort the mourners, not to share in the latest gossip. You know that the reason you are in the home is to be a member of the communal *minyan,* to participate in the prayer services. You know that the appropriate topic of conversation in a *shiva* home is the deceased. Reminisce with your friends about the deceased and her or his relationship to the mourners and to you. Of course, human nature being what it is, we tend to fall into our normal modes of social communication. This is not necessarily bad; however, you should be careful to

avoid raucous humor, tasteless jokes, loud talk, and gossip—especially in the presence of the mourners.

11. **Don't stay too long.** A *shiva* visit should be no more than an hour. If a prayer service is held, come a few minutes before and stay for a number of minutes after. Remember, other friends will be right behind you who will want to share their condolences. Mourners uniformly report how exhausted they are by the *shiva* experience; don't overstay your welcome.

12. **Say goodbye.** When you are ready to leave the *shiva* home, you may want to wish the bereaved good health and strength, long life, and other blessings. The formal farewell to a mourner is the same Hebrew phase offered at the gravesite and in synagogue on Friday night:

הַמָּקוֹם יְנַחֵם אֶתְכֶם בְּתוֹךְ שְׁאָר אֲבֵלֵי צִיּוֹן וִירוּשָׁלָיִם

Ha-Makom y'nahem etkhem b'tokh
sh'ar aveilei Tzion v'Y'rushalayim.

"What Do I Say?"

HAROLD SCHULWEIS: Jewish tradition offers great guidance. You don't say *"Shalom,"* for when you're mourning; you are not "whole," and not at peace. It is tempting to circumscribe mourning, to convert the tragedy into something less serious. We want to cheer up people, make them less sad, tell them it's going to be okay. But premature consolation backfires.

I remember visiting a woman whose husband had died about a year after their son's bar mitzvah. She was surrounded by her family and friends, all of whom were desperately trying to make her feel better. I took her into the kitchen and said, "This must a terrible thing for you." She cried with great relief and said, "These people who are my friends and family are telling me 'It could have been worse ... at least he saw the bar mitzvah ...' Each time they try to comfort me like that, it's like salt in an open wound. At least you are allowing me to grieve." She wanted confirmation of her tragedy, the right to cry.

ALLEN BROWN: There was not much to say. People came up to me and hugged me. They started crying and holding me tight. It was difficult for me. Everyone wanted to know how he died, what happened. It was like reliving the whole thing over again.

SARALIE FOOTE: It's a terrible thing to say, but you know, you sit around in a *shiva* home and most of the conversation becomes pleasant chitchat. "Have you seen this one? Have you seen that one?" I've never considered it a morbid experience. I guess the tradition wants you to pay your condolences and have your tush hurt, but I don't look at it that way.

TAMARA GREENEBAUM: People's conversations would begin, "I was really sorry to hear about your mother." My brother-in-law said to me over the phone, "I really liked your mom." I couldn't call one of my childhood friends for days afterwards I was so upset at the thought of telling her. I finally got up the guts to call her; she was very close to my mother. I said, "Sue, it's Tammy. I have some bad news." She said, "When's the funeral?" I said, "It already took place." She said, "Oh God, I loved your mother!" It made me feel terrible and it made me feel great.

RICHARD LOPATA: I can remember how awkward it was for me when I made a *shiva* call in a traditional home. The mourners were kind of isolated, sitting on a couch over in a corner, surrounded by two or three relatives. They were unapproachable. I went over to talk to them, tripping over someone else's legs, bending over. You can't hug them, you can't talk, you can't communicate. All you can do is say, "I'm sorry," and then get out of there because you're standing on someone's toes! I felt foolish and I felt badly because I'm sure I never got to convey my feelings to the mourners.

So when my wife died, I stood near the door, and even though I'm terrible with names, I had 100 percent recall of each person as they came in to greet me. I wanted to be accessible to them, to allow them to offer their condolences.

Perhaps the single most difficult challenge in comforting a mourner is in the initial moment of greeting: What do I say? What can you say that will offer the bereaved some consolation, some measure of comfort? In a way, it is a definition of chutzpah to think that anything anyone can say or do will comfort someone in the throes of grief. You are filled with sincere feelings, but the words seem so inadequate, even petty. So, often, you say nothing.

Ironically, silence is the most powerful language of all. It is perhaps the very best place to begin a conversation with a mourner. A warm embrace, a kiss, an arm around the shoulder, an empathetic look, the sharing of tears together—these are the nonverbal messages to the bereaved that often say more than a thousand words. And, the underlying message sent by these gestures—undoubtedly the single most important act of comforting—is the wordless proclamation, "I am here for you." As God tells Ezekiel (24:17) about mourning, "Sigh in silence."

Being there. Being present. Listening—not speaking. Accepting—not rationalizing. Allowing the mourner to do the important grief-work—not repressing emotions. When asked to name the most helpful thing comforters can do during bereavement, "just being there" is the number one answer reported by mourners.

"Being there" means many things. It certainly means being physically present. It also means being available and accessible. And it definitely means being there not just during the initial aftermath of the loss, but for weeks and months thereafter.

Judaism understands the importance of "being there" for the mourner. We are to accompany the bereaved to the cemetery and physically assist them with the burial—in silence. Not one word of comfort is offered until the bereaved leave the gravesite. We are to be with the mourners throughout the *shiva* period. We are to welcome them to the community when they make the first tentative steps back to normalcy by coming to the synagogue on Shabbat during *shiva*. We are to be by their side at a *shloshim* service thirty days after the burial. We join them to unveil a gravestone. And we gather with them and "all the mourners of Zion and Jerusalem" four times a year at the *Yizkor* memorial service.

Yet, it would be fair to say that even with this cycle of attending to the needs of the bereaved, it is often true that we become "condolence dropouts" once the *shiva* is over. There is so much commotion and activity in the week after the funeral. Dozens of people paying *shiva* calls, coming to the house to be with the bereaved. Then, suddenly, the house is empty, the phone stops ringing, the letters stop coming. One mourner put it this way:

I had returned to work ... I was busy during the days ... but at night and weekends, I was so lonely. I guess my friends didn't realize how

203

much I needed them to be available, how much I needed to hear from them once in a while ...

Of course, the simple answer for those of us who seek to comfort is to call periodically, send a note, visit, invite over, take out, or otherwise connect with those friends who are bereaved. The end of *shiva* is not the end of mourning. It should not be the end of our comforting activity either.

As Rabbi Pesach Krauss and Morrie Goldfischer put it in their book, *Why Me?* (p. 133):

> A mourner feels his greatest despair after sympathetic visitors disperse. His house is empty and his evenings frequently dreary and unbearable. That's when the steadfast friend who is there for the long haul fulfills the greatest need. His contribution goes far beyond his presence, important as it is. By being there, he encourages his friend to express his anger, guilt and depression, and to openly shed his tears.

We emphasize the need to remain available to the bereaved long after the *shiva* at the beginning of our discussion of comforting because it is so often overlooked and so critically important for the mourner's eventual return to normalcy.

"Don't Take My Grief Away"

JACK RIEMER: We don't know what to say. Many a time I've stood outside the door gathering my courage before I go in. Now *shiva* has degenerated into some kind of a party. I remember two teenagers whose father had died suddenly said to me at the end of the week, "Are you not supposed to talk to the mourners?" because everybody talked to everybody else and ignored them.

If the mourner wants to talk, you listen. If the mourner wants to listen, you talk. I remember when Wolfe Kelman, *zikhrono livrakhah,* lost his sister, Dr. [Abraham Joshua] Heschel, *zikhrono livrakhah,* said, "We have to go." We went to the airport, we flew to Boston, got into a cab, and went to the house. Heschel walked in, he hugged them, he sat silently for an hour. He didn't mumble a single cliché, "How old was she?" What difference does it make? "Time will heal." Time won't heal. "I know how you feel." You don't know how I feel. None of the clichés. He just sat there in silence for an hour. And then he got up, hugged them, and we left. I learned that you don't have to be glib. You just have to care.

Grief is often a competitive sport. We hear someone's story and immediately try to top it. My grief is worse than your grief. But, there's a big difference between comparing your grief to another's and identifying with someone else's experience. If someone says to you, "My father died of cancer, too. I'm still dealing with it. It's hard," that's a bond. That's not saying, "I know exactly how you feel."

In a powerful book for mourners entitled *Don't Take My Grief Away from Me,* Doug Manning, an authority on bereavement, recalls the story of a young woman overcome by intense grief, crying uncontrollably in complete despair after the death of her child. Her friends and family, growing more and more uncomfortable with the sight, tried to calm her down:

> "There, there now—get ahold of yourself."
>
> "You can't carry on like this."
>
> "Come on now—stop crying."

Suddenly this brave young mother looked them all in the eye. With fire in her voice she said:

> "Don't take my grief from me. I deserve it. I am going to have it."

Manning concludes:

> Her words have ... done more to change my concept of grief and recovery than any words I have ever heard. I wondered how many times I had tried to take grief away from folks. How many times I had denied them the right to grieve in my presence because I made it quite clear I would not accept such activity (p. 62).

Here are some common well-meaning statements that comforters make that might very well elicit a negative reaction from mourners:

> "You have to get on with your life."
>
> "I know exactly what you're going through."
>
> "It's really a blessing; you must be relieved."
>
> "She lived a long life."
>
> "You're lucky you had her for so long."
>
> "Be thankful you have another child."

"You're young; there's plenty of time to have another child."

"It's just as well you never got to know the baby."

"Don't cry."

"Don't worry."

"It's probably for the best."

"It's a blessing in disguise."

"Don't take it so hard."

"It was God's will."

"I know how you feel."

"Pretty tough. Hey, but how 'bout them Mets?!"

"Why didn't you call me?"

"Get a grip on yourself."

"Calm down."

"Don't fall apart."

"Be strong for the children."

"It'll be all right."

Well, for most bereaved, it is definitely not "all right." A loved one has died, and the grief-work must proceed for the person to be psychologically healed. That is why total acceptance is so important: It allows the bereaved to express the experience of grief, and it validates the naturalness of the response.

These statements can be daggers into the hearts of the bereaved, yet they may sound very familiar. All of them send a message of judgment, advice, and denial—all things mourners do not need to hear. Some of them may be true—perhaps the mourner is relieved that the loved one is no longer suffering. Let the mourner say it, not you. Remember, your best chance at comforting will be to let the bereaved take the lead in sharing feelings and information.

Thus, if you are greeting a mourner for the first time and he or she collapses into your arms sobbing, the first words you say can reflect this acceptance:

"It's okay to cry."

"You must be hurting so much."

Or, say nothing at all. Offer a hug, a hand, a touch that says, "I understand. I accept your feelings and the way you are expressing them. Go ahead. I'll be here for you."

There are different kinds of "being there." Experts on condolence agree that one of the most important gifts you can give to someone in grief is the full, complete, and nonjudgmental acceptance of the person's feelings, thoughts, attitudes, and behaviors, no matter how explosive, no matter how "embarrassing," no matter how much you want desperately to calm the person down, to reassure that things will be better, to take away the grief.

Hearing with a Heart

JACK RIEMER: You don't have to fill the place with noise. We are afraid of silence. I get into the car, I turn on my radio. I get into the elevator, they play music for me. Why? Because we're afraid to be alone for two seconds with ourselves. It's okay to be quiet. It's okay to just sit and listen. It's okay to not fill the air with small talk and cheap talk and sports talk. Just leave enough silence in which something can be felt.

SAM JOSEPH: The single most important thing to remember when around anyone who is grieving is this: Be a listener, not an identifier. The rabbis ask: Why do we eat an egg at the meal of condolence? Because an egg has no mouth. Unlike an apple or an orange or a pear, an egg has no stem, no opening, no *peh*. This is to teach us that there really is nothing to say to the mourner. Just be there.

Jewish tradition offers a specific instruction for initiating conversation with mourners: Don't. The *Shulḥan Arukh* (Chapter 207) says:

> "Comforters are not permitted to say anything until the mourner has first commenced to speak."

This is derived from the example of the three friends of Job who came to comfort him after his ten children were killed:

"And they lifted up their eyes afar off, and [Job was so distraught] they knew him not, so they lifted up their voice and wept; and each one rent his mantle and threw dust upon their heads toward heaven. So they sat down with him upon the ground seven days and seven nights, and none spoke a word unto him; for they saw that his grief was very great. After this, Job opened his mouth ..."

Job 2:12–13, 3:1

Actually, the tradition goes further in detailing the correct approach to the mourner. "During the first three days of mourning, [the mourner] should neither greet anyone [with the word *Shalom*] nor respond to another's greeting, but should inform them that he is a mourner; after three days, he should not offer a greeting, but can respond to another" (*Shulḥan Arukh* 210:6).

The great wisdom in this insight lies in allowing the mourner to focus on her or his grief, not on the social niceties of formal greetings. In the *shiva* home, the normal rules of social etiquette are stood on their heads.

There is a great power in presenting yourself to the mourner as an empathetic listener. It establishes that you are there, ready to hear the story, the feelings, the concerns. Real listening is silent—no interruptions, no judgments, no denials, no problem solving—just hearing with the heart.

This is not easy to do. We all want to fix things, make them better. You see a close family member or friend in intense pain, and you desperately want to make it better with words. But, it is the mourner who must do the grief-work, not you. It is the mourner who must come up with answers, not you. It is the mourner who must speak, not you.

Often comforters report that mourners want to talk about what has happened and what is happening to them. They tell the story of how the loved one died over and over again. They express their feelings of losing control with the hope that a sympathetic listener will reassure them that the response is normal. The need to talk helps the bereaved confront the reality of the loss while at the same time continuing to "hold on" to their loved one during this early stage of grief.

Some visitors to a *shiva* home find it difficult to listen to the mourner. After all, an encounter with a bereaved person may put you in touch with your own unresolved feelings of grief. Or you may feel inadequate to the task of listening or responding to intimate sharing from the mourner, so the best course is avoidance. If you feel this way, you may find yourself engaging in small talk, saying things that you know sound inappropriate, or encourage the mourner to stop grief responses. Of course, the ultimate avoidance is not to be there. There are some people who just cannot make a *shiva* call. Perhaps a condolence card is a safer way for these people to let the mourner know they care.

What You Can Say

SANDY GOODGLICK: When I come into a *shiva* home, I hug the mourner and say, "I'm sorry." I try to get people to reminisce about the person they've lost. There are some people who don't want you to penetrate—they try to put up a good front. We've learned in those instances to back off. Once you begin asking about the deceased, people almost lead you. You can see the weight lift. They may cry, but that's therapeutic. It lets me know they're comfortable with me, and they're comfortable talking.

When you're mourning, there is a canister of tears. When you've emptied the canister, that's pretty much it. No one knows how big the canister is, but it can help to lower the tear level.

SAM JOSEPH: When I'm at a loss for words, I say, "You know, I feel like a child who wishes he had a magic wand, and I could wave it, and it would all be different and better again." Ninety-nine percent of the time the mourner will say, "That's exactly how I feel." Or I'll say, "I just want you to know I'm thinking of you. I feel powerless. I wish I could do more." They hear that and know, "At least he's thinking of me."

GAIL DORPH: I was once asked to be part of a *shiva minyan,* and I went, even though I didn't know the mourners, because they needed a *minyan.* I ended up sitting next to the husband of the woman who died, and we started to talk. His wife had died of cancer—my mother had died of cancer. I said how difficult it is to watch someone die of cancer. So he started talking, giving me the whole saga. Then his daughter came over and I said, "I'm really so sorry to hear that your mom had to go through such suffering." Now, maybe "cancer" was the connection, but the daughter started to talk to me—to me, a perfect stranger. At the end of the conversation, she said, "Will you come back again?" I couldn't believe it ...

You have come to the *shiva* home. You have offered your nonverbal greeting. Now comes the awkward moment when you have to open your mouth and say something. You only hope it is not the wrong thing.

Here are a few suggestions for opening conversation with a mourner:

"I'm so sorry."

"I was so sorry to hear about your loss" (or "your dad," or "David")

"What happened? Was your _____ (mother, brother, or name the deceased) ill for a long time?"

"I don't know what to say. This must be really tough for you."

"Is there anything I can get for you?"

"Do the children need to be taken anywhere?"

"Do you feel like talking?"

If the answer to the last question is no, suggest perhaps another time. Sometimes the bereaved is just too exhausted to talk. Or they may be tired of telling the same story over and over again. Don't feel bad if they put you off. Give them a hug and let them know you're there for them when they are ready.

Sam Joseph gathered statements from children about things teachers and others said to them that were helpful:

"I can't know how you feel, but I want to help you in any way I can."

"I'm ready to listen when you're ready to talk."

"Let's talk about what might make you more comfortable in class."

"I know that you're sad."

"It's okay to cry."

"I can't know how you feel, but I had a death in my family."

"If you feel like sharing any of your writing with me, I'd like to see it."

"I care about you."

If mourners do want to talk, here are some suggestions for helpful conversations:

- **Listen nonjudgmentally.** Mourners don't want to be told that their feelings are wrong. "I didn't tell him enough how much I loved him." You may think that is untrue, but don't say it. Whether it's true or false is immaterial; it's the mourner's feeling and your job is to respect it.
- **Pay attention.** Good listeners give the speaker undivided attention. Establish good eye contact, lean forward, hold hands, nod your head, and use facial expressions to encourage the mourner to continue the conversation.
- **Don't interrupt.** Give the bereaved all the time they need to speak without jumping in to finish a thought or hurry the person along. Also, allow the mourner to be silent if a thought comes to mind.
- **Don't give rational answers.** The death of a loved one cannot be explained away with logic.
- **Don't compare experiences.** The last thing a mourner wants to hear is about your loss, especially in the early stages of grief. Any suggestion that your experience with mourning has been more intense is one-upmanship that will put off and shut up the mourner. Some mourners do feel a connection with someone whose loved one went through a similar illness and death, but it's important to qualify the comparison with the statement, "I can't know how you feel, but when my ..."
- **Ask questions about the deceased.** This helps to assure mourners that you really want to hear about the person; they often assume just the opposite. For example, "When did you meet your husband?" "What's your favorite memory of him?" "Did he ever make you laugh?"

- **Offer suggestions, not advice.** Certainly, you have learned lessons about coping with grief, but it is difficult to tell a mourner how to mourn. You can help the bereaved become more aware of the choices to be made. You can even offer suggestions about where to get information about grief-work or Jewish approaches to mourning. This will help the bereaved find her or his own way.
- **Gently prod the conversation.** As in any good social interaction, the listener can move a conversation forward with soft affirming sounds ("Uh-huh, hmmmm") and by asking for clarification or more information ("Tell me more").

Crisis debriefing

Another approach to conversing with the bereaved can be found in the recent literature on critical incident stress debriefing. Psychologists Leonard Zunin and Hillary Stanton Zunin in their superb book *The Art of Condolence* report on their experience treating survivors of major traumas and events such as accidents, earthquakes, and other natural disasters. They have developed a method of active listening that has proven helpful. This simple technique can be used in fashioning a conversation with a mourner:

- **Ask for the facts, not feelings.** In the first hours and days after a loss, the bereaved may be in such a state of shock that the feelings of grief are more difficult to express than simply stating what happened. Ask the mourner to give you the who, what, when, why, and where of the death. "Tell me what happened." "Where were you when you heard?" "How did you find out?" These questions of fact are usually less threatening and require less trust than a deeper conversation about feelings.
- **Validate feelings.** Once you've covered the facts, the bereaved might offer a comment about how they felt when the death occurred, at the funeral, or during the first hours or days of *shiva*. Then, you might move to current feelings, "How do you feel now?" During the first days of *shiva*, you are likely to hear expressions of hurt, loneliness, fear, anger and frustration. Only

later will the more pleasant feelings of love, tenderness, appreciation, and nostalgia be acknowledged.

- **Reassure and support.** Let the mourner know that the feelings expressed are perfectly normal. This will validate the mourner's experience and reassure him or her that he or she is not "crazy" or
"losing it." Depending on your own comfort in sharing the information about grief-work, you might even begin to discuss the
general psychological stages of mourning and how the Jewish tradition wisely structures the bereavement experience to allow for
the healthy expression of grief. Remind the mourner that you will
"be there" whenever he or she wishes to talk.

A remarkable source in classical Jewish texts illustrates the difficulty of
comforting the bereaved with words. It is a story found in *The Fathers
According to Rabbi Nathan:*

When Rabbi Yoḥanan ben Zakkai's son died, his disciples came in to
comfort him. Rabbi Eliezer entered, sat down before him, and said to
him, "Master, with your permission, may I say something to you?"

"Speak," he replied.

Rabbi Eliezer said, "Adam had a son who died, yet he allowed himself to be comforted. How do we know? For it is said: *And Adam knew
his wife again* (Genesis 4:25). You, too, will be comforted."

Rabbi Yoḥanan said to him, "Is it not enough that I grieve over my
own loss and you remind me of the grief of Adam?"

Rabbi Joshua entered and said to Rabbi Yoḥanan, "May I say something to you?"

"Speak," he replied.

Rabbi Joshua said, "Job had sons and daughters, all of whom died
in one day, but he allowed himself to be comforted. You, too, will be
comforted. How do we know that Job was comforted? For it is said:
Adonai gave, and Adonai has taken away, blessed is the name of Adonai
(Job 1:21)."

"Is it not enough that I grieve over my own son," Rabbi Yoḥanan
said to Rabbi Joshua, "and you remind me of the grief of Job?"

Rabbi Yosi entered and sat down before Rabbi Yoḥanan. He asked, "Master, with your permission, may I say something to you?"

"Speak," Rabbi Yoḥanan replied.

"Aaron had two grown sons," Rabbi Yosi began, "both of whom died in one day. Yet he allowed himself to be comforted, as it is said: *And Aaron said nothing* (Leviticus 10:3). Is not silence consolation? Therefore, you, too, will be comforted."

Rabbi Yoḥanan said, "Is it not enough that I grieve over my own; now you remind me of the grief of Aaron?"

Rabbi Simeon entered and said to him, "Master, may I say something to you?"

"Speak," Rabbi Yoḥanan replied.

"King David had a son who died, yet he allowed himself to be comforted. How do we know? For it is said: *And David comforted Batsheva, his wife, and bore with her a son, and called his name Solomon* (II Samuel 12:24). You, too, will be comforted."

Rabbi Yoḥanan said, "Is it not enough that I grieve over my own son and now you remind me of the grief of King David?"

Finally, Rabbi Eleazar ben Arak entered ... and sat down before Rabbi Yoḥanan and said, "I want to tell you a parable. You are like the man who was given a very precious jewel by a ruler. Every single day, the man would cry out with worry: 'Woe unto me! The ruler has implored me to care for the jewel with a trust unimpaired, but when shall the ruler want the jewel returned?' You, master, had a son. He studied the Torah, the Prophets, the Holy Writings. He studied *Mishnah, Halakhah, Agadah*. And he departed the world without sin. You should be comforted knowing that you returned him with a trust unimpaired."

Rabbi Yoḥanan said, "Rabbi Eleazar, my son, you have comforted me the way comfort should be given!"

—*AVOT D'RABI NATAN*, CHAPTER 14

Sharing Memories

RON WOLFSON: Was there any discussion about your dad's life during *shiva?*

ALLEN BROWN: That was the subject of many, many conversations. People would talk about his accomplishments, things that he shared with them. On Shabbat, we brought out the pictures. We just took out a box of photos from a closet. There were tears and laughter. People started to tell stories about the pictures. There was even a picture of my dad at sixteen that my mother had never seen. Lots of people said my son Marc looked like Dad when he was twenty-one. On Sunday, my aunts brought over albums. We shared an awful lot of stories, stories I had never heard before. It was very comforting. By the end of the week, the really tough first days of *shiva* were over, and I was beginning to feel like myself.

RON WOLFSON: Moshe, tell me why the photos of your mother are on the piano?

MOSHE ROTHBLUM: Oh, the way she was in the last few years is not the way I want to remember her. These pictures are of her in the prime of her dancing career.

Jewish tradition understood that the seven-day *shiva* period would allow for much sharing of the emotions of grief, but it hoped for more than that.

The rabbis knew there would be talk of death, but they wanted talk of life. Rather than small talk about news, sports, and weather, better than petty conversations and gossip, the major topic of conversation in a *shiva* home most appropriately centers on the stories that illuminate the life of the deceased.

At first glance to the comforter, asking questions and telling stories about the deceased may feel awkward. During the first hours or days of the *shiva,* the bereaved may not be ready to hear such stories. Yet, the eulogy at the funeral is designed precisely to stimulate a life review and to conjure up memories of the loved one. Thus, it is entirely appropriate that the comforter come to the *shiva* home prepared to share personal reminiscences with the mourners.

This sharing can be done on several levels and in a variety of ways:

- **Personal sharing with the bereaved.** For example, you approach your bereaved friend and say, "I was thinking back to the time you and Dan and Steve and I went to the Catskills. Do you remember when Dan rented that speedboat and we ..." You will know almost immediately whether your friend will want to hear the story. Assuming she does, continue and help her remember other details, other stories.

  Or, recall a favorite characteristic of the deceased. "I'll never forget what a generous man your father was ..." When the time is right, you might share a funny incident you remember. The laughter you can engender will be quite therapeutic for the mourner.

- **Group sharing.** Many of our interviewees report being at *shiva* homes where small groups of people began to recall stories about the deceased. As each person shares a memory, the words stimulate others to recall additional incidents. These conversations can be held informally at any time during the long *shiva* days. Often, the best time to have such a sharing is when a group gathers for a prayer service—either immediately before, immediately after, or even between an afternoon and evening service. Sometimes, a rabbi will lead such a sharing session as a more formal part of the *shiva minyan* experience.

This sharing of personal stories by comforters is likely to lead the bereaved into sharing their own memories with individuals or groups. Sometimes all that needs to happen is for someone to ask, "Tell us how Grandpa got to America ..." and the mourner is off and running with story after story.

Sometimes, a photo album will spark memories and storytelling, although many mourners report that it is too painful to look at such pictures until later in the *shiva*. Moshe Rothblum's willingness to display photos of his mother, Ruth Zahava, in a prominent place in the *shiva* home was a clear invitation to those who visited to ask questions about her and her life's work. Other such items that might invite conversation and memories include scrapbooks, awards the deceased won, personal documents, and other mementos from a lifetime of work and achievement.

However you do it, enabling the bereaved to share these stories helps them crystallize and record fond memories of the deceased in the heart and mind. As a comforter, you will do the same, often learning a lot of new information about the person. If you didn't know the deceased personally, you are giving the bereaved a wonderful gift in allowing them to share the life of the person with you. Most mourners we spoke to say that this process of memory sharing is one of the most comforting things one can do during *shiva*.

ADDITIONAL REFLECTIONS FOR MOURNERS

ARNOLD SALTZMAN: I remember so vividly the moment I heard Jerry Weber had been shot. I was in a Jewish Family Service meeting, and Sandy Weiner came in and could barely get the words out of his mouth. Everyone sat stunned; no one could believe it. I said, "I'm going to call Sally [his wife]." As I took each step to the phone, I kept thinking, "Could it be true? How do I ask her? If she says it is true, what should I do?" I punched the numbers and said, "Hello, Sally?" The instant she answered I knew it was true. And then she said something that really helped me. She said, "Can you come out to the house?" I said, "Will that be helpful?" And she said, "Yes." It was such a wonderful feeling. I ran into the meeting and said, "I'm going to help Sally." It felt wonderful.

How to Talk to Comforters

Perhaps the single greatest comfort to you as a mourner will be the condolence visits from family and friends during the *shiva* period. It is so important at a time of loss to feel surrounded by those who love you and care for you. These visits are also the most effective means your family and friends have for sharing their support with you.

If it is difficult to know what to say to the bereaved, you, the mourner, will also find it difficult to respond. There will be so many friends and family who will want to offer their words of condolence that, at times, you may feel overwhelmed. Do you remember what a receiving line feels like? Or how everyone comes up to you at the end of a bar or bat mitzvah celebration to thank you for the beautiful party? Everyone wants to express themselves and hear how you are feeling.

The problem with a funeral and *shiva* is that it is *not* a party. You are not feeling happy, elated, successful, proud. You are feeling sadness, anxiety, frustration, and exhaustion. Yet you feel you must talk with visitors, at least most of the time.

What do you say?

We have just reviewed a whole series of strategies for comforters on how to talk to you, the mourner. It may be helpful for you to read these recommendations for it will give you an idea of what people may say to you during a *shiva* call. But how are you to respond?

Jewish tradition clearly puts the focus of conversation on you, the mourner. You are to initiate conversations; the comforter is not to impose her or his need to talk on you. Here are some ideas of what to say. They are not in any particular order; what you say will depend on your relationship to the visitor, the visitor's relationship to the deceased, and how you are feeling at the moment.

- **Go with the flow.** Let your emotions dictate your words. One of the most important objectives in grief-work is to express your feelings, whatever they may be.
- **Tell the story.** Visitors will ask you to tell what happened. You'll be telling the story day after day to visitor after visitor. You may even get through half the story, only to have a new visitor arrive who wants to hear it from the beginning. For some mourners, this is very therapeutic and much easier to do than sharing feelings. For others, by the hundredth time you've told the story, you are pretty much talked out.
- **Thank the visitor for being there.** Acknowledge their friendship and their support.
- **Acknowledge the visitor's relationship to the deceased.**
- **Say nothing.** Sometimes, a hug, an embrace, a kiss is enough said.
- **Share a story or anecdote about the deceased.** The comforter may ask you to talk about your memories of the deceased. If the time is right, share stories with each other. It will help you crystallize the memory of the deceased, not only for you, but for the visitor.

A CAUTION: The temptation to act as host or hostess during the *shiva* may be very strong. We are so conditioned to welcoming guests into our homes, making sure they are comfortable, offering them something to eat or drink. This is not your task during the *shiva*. There will be others worrying about feeding visitors. You do not need to get up from a chair to greet visitors when they arrive, and you do not need to escort each person to the door when he or she leaves. The comforters will understand.

Family Time

As personal as bereavement is, the entire family is affected by the process. Just imagine the impact of a funeral and *shiva* on the normal operation of a family. The house is visited by people on a daily basis, regular routines are disrupted, and the emotional state of the family is characterized by sadness. It is quite easy for the family to be lost in the commotion of the events.

Yet there are things that need to be said, feelings that need to be expressed, and memories that need to be shared just between family members.

In fact, there is an often overlooked, subtle phenomenon that characterizes bereavement within family systems: the person who is both mourner and comforter at the same time. Tamara Greenebaum mourned her mother, but simultaneously spent much of her psychic and emotional energy comforting her father. Sometimes this delays one's own grief-work until a later time. It may also be characteristic of those mourners who have come from out of town to participate in the funeral and *shiva* of a close relative. For the person who is both mourner and comforter, the need for family support is even more acute.

Experts on bereavement suggest families create islands of "family time" during the days surrounding the funeral. The first such time might actually be when the family meets with the rabbi to discuss the funeral and the eulogy. Ideally, this meeting happens on the day or night before the funeral. It is a time to talk about the deceased and what he or she meant to the family, to share feelings and concerns about the funeral and the *shiva*, and to come together as a supportive system at this time of crisis. During the *shiva* week, it is also a good idea to gather the immediate family together once in a while to share how each member is feeling about the experience.

The family times can be especially helpful to children. They often feel the most abandoned during the bereavement experience. Adults are so wrapped up in their own grief that it sometimes becomes difficult to focus on what all this does to a child or teenager. Children need to express their feelings, to hear stories of the deceased, to sense the family is together and will weather the storm.

Even if the family is reluctant at first, find the time to meet together. Late afternoon after the visitors have gone or bedtime are good possibilities. The meeting need not be long; just the opportunity to "check in" will do wonders in keeping the family on course through this trying time.

Another issue facing mourners coming in from out of town is when to leave. Often work and school force out-of-towners to return before a full *shiva* week is over. The decision of when to leave is often quite difficult. Much depends on the overall family dynamic, who in the family is available to be with the primary mourners, and the emotional tone of the *shiva* itself.

Planning for the Future

One of the most important series of discussions to have with the family during *shiva* deals with the many issues caused by the loss of a member of the family system. Disposition of personal effects is, for example, one thing to consider.

Decisions about how to disperse the personal effects of the deceased often can wait until well after the *shiva* or even the *shloshim* period. For some, it is just too painful to face a closet or a drawer. For others, these decisions happen more quickly, especially if family members have gathered from far distances. Still others cannot bear the thought of parting with even one item that belonged to the deceased.

You will know when the time is right for you.

The task itself is one that some people want to do alone, while others welcome the assistance of a close relative or friend. Sometimes, the immediate family participates in a process that, however painful, ultimately stimulates many memories of the deceased. So many items have stories connected to them that can be told by family members. And some family members will ask for items that have special meaning to them.

When my Zayde Louie died, my mother and her sisters faced the job of distributing my grandparents' possessions to various members of the extended family. They gained great comfort in knowing that all of us grandchildren received something of meaning and memory from their home. I chose a silver cigarette lighter. Unfortunately, Zayde was a chain smoker, and his hands were on that lighter nearly every day of his adult life. To this day, when I look at it, I think of him.

A useful approach to this task is to divide items into three categories:

1. Those that the bereaved clearly wishes to keep.
2. Those that the bereaved clearly wishes to give away.
3. Those that the bereaved is not sure about.

Belongings in this third category should be set aside for another sorting a few days or weeks later.

As you make these decisions, talk about the items and tell the stories. Don't be surprised if a particular item elicits crying. The memories these belongings trigger can be quite powerful, although in the end this process is an important step in healing the psyche suffering from grief.

The items to be given away can be divvied up to family members who request them or donated to a charitable institution.

PART 7

"What Can I Write?"

FOR COMFORTERS

MOSHE ROTHBLUM: On one card there was a lovely note from a woman who had been one of my mother's students. When my father died, I received a wonderful letter from a man who had been in a Yiddish-speaking camp with him in the 1930s. He wrote the story of their personal relationship and how encouraging my father was to him. That was very comforting to read.

CAROL STARIN: I got hundreds of letters. I reread them from time to time. It makes me feel good that people loved and appreciated Joel, that his life stood for something, and that he meant a lot to people.

DENNIS GURA: At the funeral, Rabbi Naomi Levy warned everyone how difficult it would be to try to comfort parents who had lost a young child and that some people just would not be able to deal with it. One of the most touching letters we got was from one of Kathy's cousins who wrote, "I'm ashamed to include myself as one of the group of people who 'fell away' from you. The honest truth is that I couldn't deal with it. From the initial diagnosis, I couldn't handle it. Nothing so devastating had ever happened to anyone I have ever known, and I didn't know how to react, what to say to you or what to do. So I said and did nothing. Now I realize what a terrible and costly mistake I made. Costly because it distanced us from you during a period when you needed your family and friends the most. Costly also because it prevented us from really knowing Becca. I don't know quite how to bridge the distance or offer our care and support at this point. I just want you to know that we care …" It was courageous of her to admit that, and it touched us deeply.

How to Write a Condolence Letter

One of the most meaningful acts of kindness you can do for a mourner is to write a letter of condolence. The words of sympathy and memory are comforting to the bereaved. More importantly, mourners are very appreciative that you took the time to sit and compose a personal message to them or share a memory of the deceased. Mourners often save these letters for years.

Yet, the apparently simple act of writing a condolence letter is a lost art. Actually, letter writing itself is a skill in danger of extinction, given the ease of calling on the phone and e-mailing. Of course, you can purchase commercially available condolence cards and add your own brief message, but a well-crafted, personal letter of condolence is a wonderful gift to a mourner.

A good condolence letter has two goals: to offer tribute to the deceased and to be a source of comfort to the survivors. The best letters are like conversations on paper—free flowing as if you were talking during a visit. Most often, they are written to the bereaved person to whom you feel closest, although it could be a general letter to the family. It should be written and sent promptly, generally within two weeks after the death. Use any standard stationery and write it by hand. Some etiquette experts recommend brevity, although if you have particular stories you wish to tell about the deceased, the letter may be lengthy.

Here are some specific guidelines for writing a good condolence letter:

- **Acknowledge the loss and name the deceased.** This sets the purpose and tone of the letter. Let the bereaved know how you learned of the death and how you felt upon hearing the news. Using the name of the deceased is a tribute that comforts most mourners.

- **Express your sympathy.** Let the bereaved know your sadness. Use words of sympathy that share your own sorrow. This will remind the bereaved that they are not alone in their suffering.

- **Note special qualities of the deceased.** Acknowledge those characteristics that you cherished most about the person who has died. These might be qualities of personality (leadership, sensitivity), or attributes (funny, good at sports), or ways the person related to the world (religious, devoted to community welfare). You might write of the special relationship you noted between the deceased and the bereaved.

- **Recall a memory about the deceased.** Tell a brief story or anecdote that features the deceased. Try to capture what it was about the person in the story that you admired, appreciated, or respected. Talk about how the deceased touched your life. Use humor—the funny stories are often the most appreciated by the bereaved.

- **Remind the bereaved of their personal strengths.** Bereavement often brings with it self-doubt and anxiety about one's own personal worth. By reminding the bereaved of the qualities they possess that will help them through this period, you reinforce their ability to cope. Among these qualities might be patience, optimism, religious belief, resilience, competence, and trust. If you can recall something the deceased used to say about the mourner in this regard, you will really be giving your friend a gift.

- **Offer help, but be specific.** "If there is anything I can do, please call" actually puts a burden on those in grief who may be totally at a loss about what needs to be done. A definite offer to help with shopping, the kids, volunteer work, or whatever is more appreciated. Or offer to contact the mourner after the initial *shiva* period when the commotion has subsided. Then, do it—don't make an offer you cannot fulfill.

- **End with a word or phrase of sympathy.** Somehow, "sincerely," "love," or "fondly" don't quite make it. Try one of these:

  "You are in my thoughts and prayers."

"Our love is with you always."

"We share in your grief and send you our love."

"My affectionate respects to you and yours."

Of course, the traditional greeting to mourners is also an excellent close:

"May God comfort you among the other mourners of Zion and Jerusalem."

Let's look at an example of a complete condolence letter written around these eight components:

Dear Aunt Sylvia,

- *Acknowledge the loss and name the deceased.*
  I was shocked when Mom called this morning to tell me the news of Uncle Morton's death. I know he was not feeling well, but the sudden heart attack he suffered brought an end to this wonderful man that was too soon.
- *Express your sympathy.*
  Words really cannot express how sad I feel. My heart is filled with sympathy on the loss of your beloved husband. I loved him too.
- *Note special qualities of the deceased.*
  Uncle Mort was such a colorful man. I have never seen a man so dedicated to his work. He lived for the store. And he was so funny; he loved to kid people, to kibitz, to talk to the customers. Devoted to his beautiful family, especially to you, he loved being surrounded by his children and grandchildren. I know what a source of pride they were to him.
- *Recall a memory about the deceased.*
  It seems like yesterday that I was twelve years old and working during the summer at the market. I'll never forget how Uncle Mort loved to work the aisles. He would get three guys, including me, and we'd stack cases of something on special up to the ceiling. It took hours. Then, when we'd be all done, he'd look at the display and say, "Nope. Let's put it

over here!," and we'd have to take it down and start all over again. But he wanted it to be just right. He'd be all business, but when we were done, he'd take me across the street for lunch.

- *Remind the bereaved of their personal strengths.*
    I know how much you will miss Uncle Mort. We all will. But I know you will remember the many blessings of the beautiful years you shared together. He loved you so and you were always a source of strength to him. I remember his tremendous devotion to you during your illness. The strength and willingness to live you demonstrated then will help you get through the days and months ahead.
- *Offer help, but be specific.*
    You know that Susie, the kids, and I offer our sympathy and love. We hope to be in Omaha soon, and we look forward to being with you.
- *End with a word or phrase of sympathy.*
    Our prayers and thoughts are with you. May God grant you comfort among all the mourners of Zion and Jerusalem.

Ronnie

If you don't have time for a formal condolence letter, you may prefer to send a sympathy note. These are shorter communications that can be written on personal stationery or added to a commercially available card.

As with a condolence letter, the major goal is to offer a tribute to the deceased and to offer comfort to the bereaved:

Dear Moshe,

- *Acknowledge the loss and name the deceased.*
    Our family was deeply saddened today when we learned from Lois that you had lost your mother, Ruth Zahava.
- *Express your sympathy.*
    We are thinking of you and send our heartfelt sympathy.
- *Note special qualities of the deceased and/or bereaved.*

We know that Ruth was a tremendous influence on your interest in drama and the arts, as was your late father. Deep in
their hearts, they were very proud of everything you have
achieved.

- *End with a word or phrase of sympathy.*

With affection and deep sympathy, we pray that God comfort
you among the other mourners of Zion and Jerusalem.

Susie and Ronnie

Carol Starin received this very moving condolence letter from one of
her husband's law partners:

Dear Geoffrey, Rob, and Carol,

Joel's life has filled my thoughts these last days. More than anyone else, he showed me by his example how to live. He showed me
that it is all right to put family and community with or ahead of the
pursuit of one's livelihood, that honor and basic human decency
should hold high places in one's work, that what is best for one's
business is not always what is best. And, perhaps most important,
that nothing is so serious that one should not at least once in a
while joke about it.

I only hope I have learned these lessons well enough to live by
them. Joel has enriched my life in more ways than I can say. I will
be satisfied if I live my life with a small portion of the grace, wisdom, selflessness, honor, and humor with which Joel lived his.

May God comfort you.

Sympathy cards and condolence letters are especially important communication devices for friends and family who live far away from the bereaved. These letters, in addition to phone calls, are a lifeline from you to
the mourner. Just as it is important for local friends to maintain contact
with the bereaved after the *shiva* is over, you might want to send a series of
cards or letters to the mourner, particularly during the *shloshim* period.

FOR MOURNERS

How to Respond to Comforters' Letters

SANDY GOODGLICK: Some people find it painful to answer condolence letters. I found it painful, but healing. I was able to empty the canister of tears when I wrote them, and I was able to express things about my parents that brought me comfort.

After the *shiva* is over, it is appropriate for you to acknowledge the gestures of comfort offered by friends and family. Normally, a simple thank-you note is sufficient. Here are some examples:

Thank you for your kind expression of sympathy. Your thoughtfulness is deeply appreciated.

Commercial thank-you notes are available. It is always nice for you to add a word of thanks in your personal handwriting.

If you have received many gestures of support and letters of condolence, you may wish to have thank-you notes printed with your own message and name. Quick printers can prepare these for you within a day or two. Again, it adds a personal touch for you to write a word or sign such notes.

Moshe Rothblum printed the following message to his friends:

Your expressions of sympathy and generosity are deeply appreciated.

The Family of Ruth Zahava Rothblum

Some families take out ads in a synagogue bulletin or local Jewish press to thank the community for its expressions of condolence. This ad may be in addition to or instead of personal thank-you notes.

Here is an example:

The family of Daniel Schwartz wishes to express our appreciation for the kind words and gestures of condolence from our friends and community. May Daniel's memory continue to be a blessing to all who knew and loved him.

PART **8**

Shloshim to Yizkor

For Mourners

DENNIS GURA: The thirty days of *shloshim* was like a decompression period. I went to *minyan,* which gave each day a structure. The tradition organized our lives so we could go on living.

ALLEN BROWN: I go to *minyan* every morning to say Kaddish. I don't know what I'll do when I have to travel. I'll try to find a *minyan.* I don't understand why I can't say Kaddish to myself if I have to. I know you're supposed to find someone to pay to say Kaddish if you're not able to, but it doesn't feel right. A lot of my friends say, "You know, *minyan* starts at 7:00, and I have to be at work at 7:30," or "I'm on a plane flying from here to there," so they say, "Why can't I pick up the prayer book and do it myself?" I don't know. It will give me peace of mind to know that wherever I am, I can say Kaddish for my dad.

BERNARD LIPNICK: *Shloshim* is the period of transition. Take Linda Katz. Her husband, Saul, was out of it for five years before he died. His darling wife, Linda, visited him every day, spent half the day with him, denied herself every possible joy and diversion out of feelings of grief and guilt that he couldn't enjoy it with her. This had become a way of life for her. The daily visit gave her great purpose in her life, caring for him for five years. At Saul's death, there was a different kind of grief, just as intense but different. Now, two months later, this same lady is able to recognize that she must get on with her life. She can finally begin to branch out and begin to discover new vistas she had no idea existed.

It's Thursday morning. The funeral was last Friday. The final *minyan* has been held, and the last visitor has finished breakfast and left. You have two overwhelming feelings: exhaustion and relief.

It's time to begin the return to normal life. You put on fresh clothes and take off any outward signs of mourning. You uncover the mirrors, pack up the prayer books, and begin to put back in order your home that has been a kind of open house for the past week. Then, you take a walk around the block, a symbolic act that speaks of your "getting up" from *shiva*.

For the next twenty-three days, until thirty days following the burial, you will return to work and your regular routines. Yet, changes remain. You may have decided to say Kaddish every day and find yourself going to the synagogue for the morning and evening services. You know that certain festivities and merriment are not considered appropriate during this month, so you respectfully decline an invitation to a wedding. You're not in the mood to party anyway; in fact, even going to the movies just doesn't feel right yet.

The grief-work you began at the moment of death has proceeded through the most difficult phases, although from time to time, something— a word, a gesture, a letter, a photo, an article of clothing—triggers an episode of weeping and remembering.

When the thirty days are over, normal life returns, but the deep wound of the loss continues to heal. Eventually, there will be a scar on the heart that hurts when occasionally bumped. Friends call or ask about the loss less often now, expecting that the grief has passed. Life continues.

You gather with your closest family and friends to unveil the grave-stone. The rabbi recites some Psalms and offers a few words of tribute. You say Kaddish once more, knowing that from now on, your formal memorials will be at *Yizkor* services and on the *yahrtzeit* anniversary of the loss. The gravestone offers you some comfort, knowing that the final resting place is properly completed.

So, too, the formal Jewish bereavement process has reached its conclusion. You feel a sense of pride at fulfilling the obligations of mourning, including the saying of Kaddish for eleven months. During the process, you have become closer than ever to the synagogue and to Judaism. Through your regular *davening* and classes in Judaica you've taken, your interest and commitment to Jewish continuity has increased. Ironically, through the loss you sustained, you have strengthened the bonds of Jewish life to you and your family. Most importantly of all, your children have witnessed this transformation in you, noting the model of your behavior, a model that will surely influence their own commitments to Jewish life now and in the future.

Shloshim

Shloshim, the period of thirty days from the funeral, is the fourth phase of Jewish bereavement. The *shiva* completed, the mourner begins a slow re-entry to normal life. Most of the prohibitions of *shiva* expire (we can go outside, work, sit in normal chairs, wear leather, have sex), but certain restrictions remain, particularly on those that involve "pleasure."

Since the mourner is still very close to the time of loss and is, in all likelihood, still working through the grieving process, the rabbis restricted the bereaved from a variety of types of merriment during *shloshim*. These include: attending weddings (unless it is the bereaved who is being married and the plans were made before the death), dances and parties, playing or listening to music, and going to movies and the theater. Watching informative as opposed to entertaining television is permitted. In traditional communities, these restrictions are extended to a full twelve months for those mourning the death of a parent.

For most modern Jews, these prohibitions may seem harsh. In fact, they are designed to protect the bereaved from finding themselves in situations that are very difficult to bear psychologically. Mourners who attend parties during the thirty days often find that their hearts are just not in it. As wonderful as the celebration is for everyone else, that's how awful it can feel to the recently bereaved. The rabbis knew this and offered the restrictions to relieve the mourners from facing this situation.

Questions about Shloshim

What if a close relative celebrates an important life-cycle event, say a bat mitzvah, during *shloshim*?

Many mourners find a solution in attending the service, but skipping the party.

Why do we mourn parents for a full year and a child for only thirty days?

Abner Weiss in his book on bereavement, *Death and Bereavement: A Halakhic Guide,* admits that some may think this backwards. After all, parents often die after a long illness, and their demise is somewhat anticipated, while the death of a child is a psychological wound that is difficult to heal. Wouldn't it make more sense to allow extra time for grieving for a child than a parent? Weiss suggests that the tradition in its wisdom recognized that we might find it impossible to terminate mourning for deceased children or of a spouse of many years because such wounds are never fully healed. On the other hand, Judaism considers honor and respect for one's parents to be an ultimate value, codified as one of the Ten Commandments. In order to protect against the tendency to mourn parents too little, the twelve-month period was instituted.

Is *shloshim* ever cancelled by a major holiday?

Yes. Just as *shiva* can be cancelled when a major holiday intervenes, so too the *shloshim* period is cancelled when Rosh Hashanah, Yom Kippur, Sukkot (including Shemini Atzeret and Simhat Torah as one unit), Passover, and Shavuot come within the thirty days, as long as the *shiva* itself has been completed. It is best to consult with your rabbi if you are not sure about your particular case.

Saying Kaddish

SARALIE FOOTE: I was very concerned about who was going to say Kaddish for my father. He was very *frum* about saying *Yizkor* for his family members. I didn't know with my working and a child whether I could get to Temple every night to say Kaddish. What do I do? I call the local *yeshiva* and make a donation and ask them to say Kaddish.

I still and always will have a guilt feeling because I didn't do it.

The most important act associated with *shloshim* and the yearlong period of mourning for a parent is the saying of the Kaddish. We reviewed the meaning of the Kaddish earlier when we discussed the funeral. Recall that the prayer says nothing at all about the deceased. Rather, it is an ancient hymn of praise to God.

Among Jews throughout the centuries, having someone to "say Kaddish for you" was a major reason for parents to have children, particularly boys. In fact, a boy was often referred to lovingly as "my *Kaddishel*." And what about women saying Kaddish?

The issue of women saying Kaddish and otherwise participating in a *shiva minyan* raises the question of the legal status of women in Jewish practice. According to more traditional practice, women are not obligated to perform positive, time-bound *mitzvot*. This includes participating in daily prayer services, and thus, women traditionally are not counted in an Orthodox *minyan*. In practice, this means that if there are only nine men at an Orthodox *shiva minyan,* a woman in the home—including women who are mourners!—are not counted as one of the quorum of ten required for public prayer to take place, including saying Kaddish. In an earlier generation, even when there was a *minyan* of ten men, the female mourners were often escorted to another room while the *davening* took place.

Henrietta Szold, the founder of Hadassah and one of the first Jewish feminists, would have nothing to do with this practice. When her mother died in 1916, a good male friend, Haym Peretz, offered to say Kaddish for the dead woman. In a declaration of Jewish feminism way ahead of its time, Szold refused with these words:

> I believe that the elimination of women from such duties was never intended by our law and custom—women were freed from positive duties when they could not perform them (because of family responsibilities), but not when they could. It was never intended that, if they could perform them, their performance of them should not be considered as valuable and valid as when one of the male sex performed them.
>
> (*Response, Summer,* 1973, p. 76.)

In recent times, Blu Greenberg, a sensitive observer of the Jewish scene, recognizes that Orthodox women normally do not say Kaddish. Yet she reports:

> In the last decade, however, I have known several women who assumed the formidable responsibility of saying Kaddish regularly for a deceased parent. It did not matter to them whether they were or were not counted as part of the *minyan.* In most instances, they gradually came to be warmly accepted as a presence, if not a legal entity in the eyes of Jewish law.
>
> (*How to Run a Traditional Jewish Household,* p. 297.)

With the full equality given to women in most congregations of the non-Orthodox movements, there is no reason why women should not recite Kaddish for parents and other relatives in the same way men are instructed.

Beneath the obvious superstition and uncertainty of the afterlife that motivated a primitive understanding of the efficacy of someone saying Kaddish, a more serious concern for Jewish continuity still resonates in this expectation of parents.

Although the period of mourning for a parent extends a full year, children say Kaddish for only eleven months. An ancient tradition teaches that divine judgment for the deceased takes a full year. Because we are confident that our parents will be judged worthy of God's reward before the end of this period, children stop short of a full year of saying Kaddish.

Unfortunately, many children do not say Kaddish for parents for eleven months, or even the thirty days of *shloshim*. There are several reasons: the demands of modern life, the unease of many in the synagogue service, the absence of a sense of obligation and tradition. Some revert to an old practice of "hiring a Kaddish," literally paying someone to say Kaddish for a parent for the full eleven months. Often, this person is the *shammes,* the leader of the daily service in the synagogue. However, this practice is totally inappropriate. Judaism does not allow prayer by proxy. Just as a rabbi or cantor cannot pray in your place, neither can a stranger "say Kaddish" for a parent or other relative.

On the other hand, those who take on the obligation to recite Kaddish at the daily *minyan* often find themselves reconnected to Jewish life. The supportive community found among other mourners and the regular contact with Jewish practice brings the mourner closer to Jewish issues and traditions. A renewed interest may lead the mourner into classes and experiences that present Judaism in a new and meaningful way.

I understand I need a *minyan* in which to say Kaddish, but if I absolutely cannot get to a service, may I say Kaddish alone?

The *halakhah* is clear: Kaddish is only said when ten adults constitute a community. On the other hand, as with much of Jewish practice, individuals express themselves in a variety of ways. Rabbi Bernard Lipnick recommends that if a *minyan* is not available to you, study the words of the

Kaddish. Rabbi Joseph Brodie suggests reading a psalm instead of Kaddish when finding a *minyan* is impossible.

What if the deceased leave no children?

This is the only acceptable reason someone else may be engaged to say Kaddish for someone.

Gravestones and Unveilings

BEN DWOSKIN: At our cemetery, all the memorial markers are flat. This is another sign of equality in death. It also creates a beautiful setting, a parklike feeling. It invites people to come and visit the gravesite to remember their loved ones, something we encourage people to do.

SARALIE FOOTE: When one of your parents goes, there comes the big discussion: Do you buy a single stone or a double stone? I just didn't want to have to go through it all again, so we got a double stone.

CAROL STARIN: When they asked me if I wanted a double stone, I had no strong feelings about it, but I decided that the kids should be consulted. They felt very strongly that it should be a single stone for Daddy. I think they didn't want to think about the possibility that I would die, too.

MARTHA WHITE: People have no idea that they can visit a grave during the first year. Many think they can only come to the cemetery after the stone is set. It depends a lot on different customs. We try to set the stone as soon as possible. It usually takes a good three months for the family to decide what they want on the inscription, to order the stone, and to have it delivered and set. Most families unveil the stone between the eleventh and twelfth month after the burial.

RICHARD LOPATA: We had no idea what to do about the unveiling. No one really called to tell us what to do. Once we decided to have a service, we didn't know how to invite people. Do you send invitations?

Make phone calls? The service itself called up all the emotions of the funeral. It wasn't easy.

The use of a stone to mark a grave is an ancient custom. One of the most famous graves in Jewish history is that of Rachel who died giving birth to Benjamin along the road to Jerusalem near Bethlehem. "And Jacob set a monument by her grave; that is the monument of Rachel's grave unto this very day" (Genesis 35:20). Traditionally, the *matzei'vah* (monument) is a marker identifying the final resting place, a symbol of respect and a lasting remembrance of the deceased.

In the past, large structures were often built over the grave as a token of respect for the soul of the departed, which was believed to frequent the area. In more recent times, elaborate monuments often are erected more as a sign of wealth and ostentation than anything else. Upright monuments were common in Ashkenazic cemeteries, while the Sephardim required the stones to be flat.

In keeping with the tradition of Rabban Gamliel, whose instruction for burial in shrouds did much to equalize status in death, many modern cemeteries restrict the gravestone to a flat stone, uniform in size for all.

An inscription is either chiseled into the stone or inscribed upon a plaque attached to the marker. The wording of the inscription is left to the family to compose, but most contain one or more of the following:

- The Hebrew name of the deceased. In the Orthodox Ashkenazic tradition, the name includes the name of the deceased's father. In the Sephardic tradition, the name includes the name of the deceased's mother. In non-Orthodox traditions, current practice is to include the names of both of the deceased's parents.
- The Jewish date of death.
- The years spanning birth to death according to the secular calendar.
- Identifying relations, such as "mother and grandmother," "son and father," etc. Often, words of endearment such as *beloved* or *loving* are added.

- Many Jewish gravestones have the Hebrew letters *pei* and *nun* at the top corner. These letters stand for the words *poh nitman*—"here is buried." Sephardic gravestones use the letters *mem* and *kuf,* standing for the words *matzeivet k'vurat*—"the tombstone of the grave of ..."
- Many gravestone inscriptions end with the Hebrew letters *tav, nun, tzadi, bet,* and *hei,* which are the initial letters of the Hebrew words: *t'hei nafsho(ah) tzeruah bitzror ha-hayim*—"may his or her soul be bound up in the bond of life."

It is possible to erect a double marker even if only one grave is presently used.

The setting and unveiling of the gravestone can be done anytime after the conclusion of *shiva.* Most people have the mistaken notion that the unveiling must wait until eleven months or a year after the funeral. This probably originated with the thought that since mourners are keeping the memory of the deceased active through the saying of Kaddish and other acts of bereavement, there was no need to set the stone until the end of this period. Actually, many rabbinic authorities object to waiting this long to unveil the gravestone. The decision of when to set the stone and unveil it is strictly up to the survivors.

The tradition of an "unveiling service" developed as a way for close family and friends to gather once again at the grave to memorialize the deceased. Many families place a notice of the unveiling ceremony in the local Jewish press to invite relatives and friends. Generally, a rabbi officiates, reciting appropriate prayers, psalms, and readings and perhaps offering a short eulogy. Often, the cemetery officials will cover the stone with a veil until the appropriate moment when it is unveiled for all to see. Of course, this normally evokes the anticipated emotions and memories.

Visiting the Grave

SARALIE FOOTE: I try to go several times a year. I go on Father's Day, always before the Jewish holidays. When we go, I bring my son with me and talk to him about Zayde. We put a stone on top of the grave. I always clean it up, take up the weeds, talk to him …

BRUCE WHIZIN: I don't need to visit my mother's grave to talk to her. She's not there; she's in my mind, in my heart. Anytime I want to evoke her, I just say, "Hi, Mom," and I can talk to her. The body is on loan to us from God; it doesn't belong to us. So how can I expect to find her there? Only her bones are in the grave. She was in the bones, but not of the bones. In fact, what I would like on my tombstone is: "Bruce is definitely not here."

JACK RIEMER: There are many superstitions, *bubbemeises,* about unveiling a stone and visiting a grave, but underneath them, there is a real agenda. You've got to forgive the dead, and you've got to get forgiveness from the dead, and your life is not complete until you do. You carry around a big burden until and unless you work that out. If you didn't work it out while they were alive, then you try to work it out after they're dead. That's what unveilings do; that's what cemetery visits do.

One of the problems in delaying the setting and unveiling of the gravestone is that people assume they are not to visit the grave until then or until one cycle of the three pilgrimage festivals (Passover, Sukkot, Shavuot) has passed. In some families and communities, the custom is to wait to visit the grave until the unveiling. Apparently, this was done to prevent excessive grief and an unnatural attachment to the grave.

Kever avot—visiting "the grave of the ancestors"—is allowed from the conclusion of *shiva,* throughout the *shloshim,* and during the twelve months of mourning for a parent. Many survivors visit the grave of a loved one on the conclusion of *shiva,* the conclusion of *shloshim,* at the unveiling service, and on the yearly *yahrtzeit* anniversary of the death. In addition, special community-wide *kever avot* services are usually held in Jewish cemeteries just before the High Holy Days. Graves are not visited on Shabbat or holidays. Local or family custom and tradition may dictate when you make the first visit to the gravesite.

Several traditions have developed for behavior during a visit to a grave. Some touch the gravestone with the left hand and say, "Rest in peace until God who comforts and announces peace comes." Many leave some grass or sod on the grave and a stone on the marker as a sign of reburial. Some visitors to graves are absolutely silent, absorbed in their private memories and thoughts. Others "talk" to the deceased, sharing concerns, hopes, and prayers. Although not required, many visitors bring flowers or plants. Veterans may have small American flags set near the grave. Depending on the rules of the cemetery, benches, gardens, trees, and bouquet holders for flowers might be added to the gravesite, often at extra cost.

One of the problems of our mobility as a people is that often the grave of a loved one is located in a city far away from where we live. Thus, visits to gravesites during vacations and "visits home" are not unusual. For some, that is not enough. My wife, Susie, living in Los Angeles, has a picture of her mother's grave in Omaha that she looks at from time to time, just as her mother had a photograph of her parents' graves in Berlin, Germany. So goes the continuity of memory.

Questions about gravestones

I have seen Jewish gravestones in European cemeteries that have photographs of the deceased. Is that unusual?

Not in Eastern Europe. In fact, many of the immigrants from the former Soviet Union who come to North America request photographs on gravestones. Since this custom is almost universally not recognized in Jewish communities in the United States and Canada, it is not likely to return to Jewish practice.

My father was a *kohen*. Is there a special symbol for his gravestone?

Traditionally, the symbol of the raised hands of the *kohen* offering the Priestly Benediction was etched into the grave marker of a *kohen*. The Levites also had a special symbol—a vessel for washing hands representing one of the functions of the Levites in the Temple. These symbols may or may not be in use in your community.

Memorial Tablets

I never went to a Jewish cemetery as a child, but I was exposed to death in a dramatic way every Yom Kippur. Entering the synagogue for *Kol Nidre,* I was awestruck by the sight of every single light on the memorial tablets lit up, creating an eerie bright glow throughout the sanctuary. On a normal Shabbat during the year, a handful of lights would be on indicating those whose *yahrtzeits* were observed during the coming week. But on *Kol Nidre* night, every light was turned on. In addition, many of those who would remember loved ones during the *Yizkor* service the next day came early to the synagogue to light memorial candles before the service. The flickering flames and electric lights combined to make the back of the sanctuary appear to be on fire. It was as if the *neshamas*—the souls of the departed— were once again in *shul,* their collective glow illuminating the place where they too had come to ask God for *teshuvah* on this, the most mystical, magical night of the year.

All synagogues have large walls of memorial tablets noting the English and Hebrew names of the deceased and the date of death. A light bulb is situated next to each tablet, which is illuminated on the *yahrtzeit* anniversary of the death and when the *Yizkor* memorial service is said.

Yahrtzeit

DENNIS GURA: We had a service at the synagogue on the first *yahrtzeit* of Rebecca's death. Thirty or forty people came. As I looked around the chapel, I realized I knew everyone's sad story: who had lost whom, from what illnesses, who was a Holocaust survivor, who had lost children or siblings. We were a community of pain. It was comforting to know we were not alone in our pain. All these other people were there, too.

Every *yahrtzeit*, every *erev Yizkor*, each of us, Kathy, Ethan, and I, light our own candle in memory of Rebecca, because each of us has our private grief.

At the end of the day, I am compelled to watch the flame sputter and go out. I did the same thing at the end of Rebecca's *shiva*. Somehow, I have to guard the flame at the end. Perhaps it is my own little *Havdalah*, a separation between public and private memory.

DAVID TECHNER: A woman once called me to ask if it was proper for her to light a *yahrtzeit* candle before Yom Kippur, even though the death of her husband had been just seven months earlier. I knew the technical answer: you don't light a *yahrtzeit* candle until after the first year. But this woman had been told by one relative it was okay to light and another that it wasn't okay, and she was filled with anxiety about what to do. So I called my friend Rabbi Irwin Groner and asked him what I should advise this woman. He gave me one of the most wonderful pieces of advice. He said, "Look, Judaism was never meant to be a barrier to healing. It's designed to be helpful to people when they are in pain. If it were me, because I know the law and why the law is the way it is, I wouldn't light the candle. But why shouldn't this lady light a candle if it will help her heal her grief?"

RON WOLFSON: Why don't we say anything when we light the *yahrtzeit* candle? That's so unusual.

JACK RIEMER: It is so unusual. I think there's something missing there. We need a *b'rakhah*. Harold Schulweis has tried to write something. He's right. People feel incomplete—they want to say something.

It Is Less Distant Now

A yahrzeit *Candle Lit At Home*

The yahrzeit *candle is different*

announcing neither Sabbath nor festival.

No benediction recited

No song sung

No psalm mandated.

Before this unlit candle

without a quorum, I stand

unstruck match in my hand.

It is less distant now

the remembrance ritual of parents deceased

I am older now

closer to their age than before.

I am older now

their aches in my body

their white hairs beneath my shaved skin

their wrinkles creased into my face.

It is less distant now

this ritual

once made me think of them

Now makes me think of me.

Once it recalled relationships to them

Now it ponders on my children's relationship to me.

Once I wondered what to remember of them

Now I ask what my children remember of me

what smile, what grimace

What stories they will tell their children of me.

It is less distant now.

How would I be remembered

How would I be mourned

Will they come to synagogue

light a candle

recite the Kaddish.

It is less distant now.

Once Yahrtzeit was about parents deceased

Now it is of children alive

Once it was about a distant past

now it is about tomorrow.

—HAROLD M. SCHULWEIS

Yahrtzeit—a German word meaning, literally, "the time (*tzeit*) of year (*yahr*)"—is the commemoration of the anniversary of a death (Sephardim call the day *Nahalah meldado* or *Annos*). It is observed on the yearly anniversary of the day of death, not the funeral. The day is devoted to reflection and prayers remembering the deceased. *Yahrtzeit* is normally observed for parents, although there is nothing to prevent one from marking the anniversary of other deaths.

Since a Jewish day begins the night before, *yahrtzeit* is observed beginning at sundown. A twenty-four-hour memorial candle is lit and allowed to burn throughout the day. If the *yahrtzeit* falls on Shabbat or a holiday, light the memorial candle first, then the candles for the holiday. There is no blessing recited when lighting the *yahrtzeit* candle, and it may be placed anywhere in the house.

Those observing *yahrtzeit* attend services at the synagogue and recite the Kaddish. They are often offered the opportunity to participate in leading the *davening,* either as the cantor, by having an honor during the Torah service on that day or sometime that week, or reading an English prayer. Most congregations announce the *yahrtzeits* in the coming week during Shabbat services and illuminate a light next to the name of the deceased recorded on a memorial tablet. If you are observing the *yahrtzeit* in the coming week, you may be offered an honor during the Shabbat service, as well.

It is also a custom to visit the grave on the *yahrtzeit* day unless you live in a city other than where the grave is located and such a visit would incur too great an expense.

Giving *tzedakah* is another way to mark the occasion.

Questions about *yahrtzeits*

How will I know the *yahrtzeit* dates?

Many Jewish funeral homes will give the bereaved a list of *yahrtzeit* dates for twenty years following the death. These will be Hebrew dates on the Jewish calendar. Remember, when you look up the date on a Jewish calendar to determine the corresponding secular date, the day begins the night before. Most congregations will send members a reminder card with the date a week or two before the *yahrtzeit.* This reminder may also tell you on which Shabbat the name of the deceased will be announced in the synagogue.

When do I mark the *yahrtzeit* if it falls in *Adar* during a Jewish leap year?

If the date of the *yahrtzeit* falls in *Adar,* it is observed during *Adar I* when a leap year occurs. If the death itself occurred during *Adar I* or *II* during a leap year, the *yahrtzeit* is observed during the same *Adar* in which the death happened.

What do I do if I forgot the date of the *yahrtzeit*?

You should observe the *yahrtzeit* when you remember it.

Yizkor

ALLEN BROWN: I'm superstitious about some things and not others, but on Yom Kippur, because my parents were living, I would leave the service when *Yizkor* started. I knew that in the Conservative movement, it's an option to stay in and say Kaddish, but I never did it—until this year. This past year I stayed, and when Dad passed away, that's the first thing I thought of. I know you might be thinking, "C'mon, give me a break," but I can't help thinking about it.

JACK RIEMER: I'm not sure why people come to *Yizkor*. People who don't keep anything else in Jewish life, keep this. I think there's a hunger for continuity—a desire to feel the presence of one who's absent. Every time I say *Yizkor*, something curious happens that I can't predict. The faces of different people I've lost come into my mind, people I haven't thought of in years. I find myself not only mentioning names and thinking about my parents or my relatives, but my first-grade teacher, or my teachers at the seminary, or my colleagues. People I didn't know I missed as much as I do. And the list is different every time I say it.

As we have seen, Jewish mourning is both private and public. When we visit a grave or observe a *yahrtzeit,* we generally do so in private. *Yizkor* is the public observance for the community of bereaved.

Yizkor means "memorial," from the root word *zakhor*—remember. It is the memorial service, recited four times a year in the synagogue—after the Torah reading on Yom Kippur day, Shemini Atzeret (the last day of Sukkot), the eighth day of Passover, and the second day of Shavuot.

Originally, *Yizkor* was recited only on Yom Kippur. Its primary purpose was to remember the deceased by committing *tzedakah* funds on the theory that the good deeds of the survivors elevate the souls of the departed. It also enhanced the chances for personal atonement by doing a deed of lovingkindness. Since the Torah reading on the last day of the pilgrimage festivals mentions the importance of donations, *Yizkor* was added to these holiday services.

It was originally the custom for each community to read a list of its martyrs at the *Yizkor* service. The practice was eventually expanded to include the names of other members of the community who had died. Today, most synagogues publish lists of those who are remembered by congregants, which are distributed at the *Yizkor* services. In addition, the lights on all the memorial tablets in the synagogue are turned on.

The service itself consists of four parts:

1. A series of readings and prayers, recited and chanted, that sets the mood for the solemn service.
2. Paragraphs that individuals read recalling the deceased. There are paragraphs for a father, mother, husband, wife, son, daughter, other relatives and friends, and Jewish martyrs. During the service, each person reads the appropriate paragraph(s).
3. The memorial prayer for the deceased, the *Eil Malei Rahamim* is chanted by the cantor. This is essentially the same prayer said at Jewish funerals.
4. A special prayer, *Av Ha-Rahamim* (Ancestor of Mercies), probably composed as a eulogy for communities destroyed in the Crusades of 1096, is recited by the congregation as a memorial for all Jewish martyrs. Some also add Psalm 23.

Although in its traditional structure *Yizkor* does not include the recitation of the Mourner's Kaddish, many congregations do add this as the climax of the *Yizkor* service.

When I was a kid in Omaha, *Yizkor* always seemed to be the climax of Yom Kippur day. The *shul* was crowded with people all day long, but it was packed at *Yizkor* time. There was something about this mysterious, awe-inspiring service that drew people. It was the pull of remembrance.

It was also break-time for those of us who were shooed out of the synagogue by our parents. A powerful superstition pervaded the community: If your parents were alive, you didn't stay for *Yizkor.* God forbid, you should tempt the *ayin ha-ra,* the evil eye, by hearing and seeing others mourn for their departed. God forbid, you should sit down while virtually everyone else was standing for the *Yizkor* prayers, somehow making the mourners feel bad. So, during the twenty minutes or so of the *Yizkor,* the "fortunate" people whose parents were alive sat outside kibitzing, while the vast majority of the congregation who had sustained a loss participated in the service.

These superstitions are just that—superstitions, *bubbemeises.* There is no legal requirement for those whose parents are alive to leave the service. In fact, many rabbis today suggest that everyone stay for *Yizkor* so that the entire congregation can offer the prayers for the martyrs of the Jewish people and offer moral support to friends and family who may be deeply touched by the memorial service. But, as with much of the folk religion, this custom is sure to continue in many communities. Ultimately, it is a matter of personal and family decision making as to your practice.

Questions about *Yizkor*

Can I say *Yizkor* privately?

Since the Kaddish is not recited as part of *Yizkor,* there is no technical requirement for a *minyan.* Therefore, the memorial paragraphs can be said privately if you cannot get to the synagogue.

How do I get names listed in the *Yizkor* book?

Most congregations ask their members to list those who are to be remembered in the coming year as part of the yearly membership survey when you join or renew your affiliation. If someone dies during the year, the names are generally added as a matter of course, unless the synagogue publishes one book for use throughout the year. You may want to check this with the synagogue office to spare yourself the unease of the name missing when you expect it to be on the list.

What about donations?

In keeping with the origins of *Yizkor,* it is very appropriate to make a *tzedakah* contribution to honor those you are remembering. Many congregations appeal for funds at *Yizkor* services for the synagogue or for Israel. If you don't belong to a synagogue, consider making a donation to a worthy cause.

Do I light a memorial candle when *Yizkor* is recited?

Yes. The twenty-four-hour memorial candle should be lit in your home before the fast begins on Yom Kippur. On the other festivals, if your custom is to light a *yahrtzeit* candle, use a flame from a preexisting candle or other source to light the candle. These memorial candles are widely available in synagogue gift shops, kosher stores, and often in supermarkets. There is no blessing recited when you light the memorial candle, although it is certainly appropriate to reflect upon the memory of loved ones. The candle may be placed anywhere in the home.

Do I observe *Yizkor* during the first year of mourning

Contrary to popular belief, yes. Clearly, *Yizkor* is observed for a spouse, a child, a sibling, and, according to most authorities, for parents during the first year.

Naming Children

SANDY GOODGLICK: The greatest tribute our kids could give us was to name their children after our parents and my grandmother.

It is a very ancient and powerful tradition in Ashkenazic Jewish practice to name children after deceased relatives (although Sephardim often name children after living people). This is one of the most tangible forms of memorializing the dead and ensuring their spiritual "immortality." Sometimes the child is offered the Hebrew name of the deceased, the English name, both Hebrew and English names, or some variation of either.

Of course, just giving the name of a beloved deceased member of the family is not enough to carry on the memories of that person. When the time comes, a surviving relative should tell the oral history of the honored person to the child who is carrying the name. In this way, the memory of the deceased is truly carried forward.

Excessive Grief

As we have learned, the Jewish mourning cycle allows for a phased recovery from loss. In fact, this cycle continues throughout the life of the mourner through the vehicles of *Yizkor* and *yahrtzeit*. Judaism, however, is a religion focused on the living, not on the deceased. Thus, Jewish tradition cautions the mourner against excessive grief. "Weep not in excess for the dead, neither bemoan him too much" (Jeremiah 22:10).

Exhumation

Judaism abhors the very idea of moving a body from one grave to another. However, there are situations that require exhumation and reburial:

- To transfer the body to a grave in Israel
- To transfer the body to a family plot
- To transfer the body from a non-Jewish cemetery for burial in a Jewish cemeter.
- If the grave is undermined by water, vandals, or other dangers to its stability
- If the body was buried with the intent that it be on a temporary basis
- If civilian authorities must investigate cause of death

The vacated grave may be used for the burial of another person.

Remembering the Deceased

RICHARD LOPATA: It's been a year since Laurie died, and people still don't want to mention her name. They actually avoid saying "Laurie," I suppose because they think I don't want them to bring it up. Nothing could be further from the truth. One friend surprised me at breakfast recently. When we sat down at the table, he said matter-of-factly, "How's Laurie?" I was totally shocked. Then, he continued, "No, in your mind, how is Laurie?" When I realized what he was asking, I replied, "A day doesn't go by when I don't think of her." That was great! Because my friend understood that Laurie is always with me, and he was willing to talk about it.

CAROL STARIN: The worst time of the year for me is around the High Holy Days. It's not only that Joel died at that time of year; it's just so difficult to celebrate the holidays without him.

Any "first" is also very difficult. When my son walked out the door the night of his senior prom wearing a tuxedo for the first time and his father wasn't there to see it, when he graduated high school—all those little momentous occasions.

SAM JOSEPH: Every birthday and anniversary, the deceased is in everybody's mind. I was at a bar mitzvah of a nephew recently, the first life-cycle event in our family since my grandfather died. At the end of the day, my sister came up to me crying. I said, "What's the matter?" She said, "Nobody mentioned Grandpa."

The memory of the deceased is with the survivor always. Beyond the formal sacred times of memory—*Yizkor* and *yahrtzeit*—the "little momentous occasions" when a loved one is missed are perhaps even more difficult to bear. The emptiness, the hole in the heart are palpable.

When a deceased person is recalled in conversation by name, common etiquette suggests adding the words, "may he [she] rest in peace," as in "I've been thinking a lot about Charlie, may he rest in peace." In Jewish tradition, the deceased person may be remembered with these sayings:

"Alav ha-shalom."	"May peace be unto him."
"Aleha ha-shalom."	"May peace be unto her."
"Aleikhem ha-shalom."	"May peace be unto them."

Do try to pronounce the words correctly. Joseph Telushkin, in his remarkable book *Jewish Literacy,* tells of meeting a Jew who suffered from the common affliction of "illiterate" Jews who have picked up Hebrew expressions, but swallow their words. The man told Telushkin that his last religious relative was his great-grandfather, "Oliver Shalom."

Another common saying is:

"Zikhrono liv'rakhah."	"May his memory be a blessing."
"Zikhrona liv'rakhah."	"May her memory be a blessing."
"Zikhronam liv'rakhah."	"May their memories be a blessing."
	or
"Zekher tzadik liv'rakhah."	"May the memory of the righteous be a blessing."

There are, of course, many other ways to remember the deceased. Memorial plaques, donations, scholarships, lectures—all these are common ways to memorialize loved ones.

Starting Over

JACK RIEMER: The real wonder of Adam and Eve is that they lost two children—Cain and Abel—in one fell swoop, and then the Bible says, "And Adam made love to his wife again." It teaches us that when you sustain a loss, you get up off your knees and start all over again. Otherwise, we'd all be descended from a murderer or from a victim. Adam and Eve taught us how to love, and lose, and love again.

Noah gets off the ark and gets drunk. I never understood why he did that until I talked with a Holocaust survivor. He said, "I understand Noah. I did the same thing. I came home and everything was swept away. Every house, every friend, every relative. I got into a drunken stupor too, because I didn't want to live. Eventually, I woke up again, but I understood what Noah did."

Aaron loses two children on the day of his investiture. Moses tries to give him some religious cliché for comfort, and Aaron just looks at him. And the Bible—which doesn't waste words—indicates that Aaron was silent. He could have blasphemed, but he didn't. He could have gone on as if nothing had happened, but God is not so hard up that He needs praise from people who don't mean it. What he did instead was to withdraw, to nurse his wounds, and when he was ready and able to come back, he did.

At the end of the Book of Job, after he has lost everything, it says that he had seven more children. I once heard Archibald MacLeish say that this is the whole point of the book. Having lost seven children,

God planted in Job the courage, the resilience to be willing to risk again and have more children.

The most recent example of this ability to recover from loss is a passage from modern Jewish history. From 1945 to 1948, Jews who survived World War II lived in what is correctly called a "Displaced Persons" camp. They couldn't go back to Poland—it was contaminated. They couldn't go to Palestine—the doors were locked. They couldn't get to America. So they were cooped up for three years in Displaced Persons camps. During those three years, these broken people— shards of people, widows, widowers, mourners—found each other, married, and brought children into the world. There were more children born in those three years than in any other period for which we have Jewish demographic records. You hear a lot of talk from people who aren't sure whether they want to bring children into this world. If our parents had waited until it was a good time to bring children into the world, we'd have a much smaller Jewish community today. They loved, and lost, and risked again—just as Job did. There is no theological justification for evil or suffering—just a response. And the response we learn from Adam, Aaron, Job, and the Holocaust survivors is: Try again.

Being Single Again

CAROL STARIN: It's been three years since Joel's death. It's not comfortable for me to have a social event in my home, except for the holidays. I can't face the idea of having a couple over to my home and having Joel's place empty. To entertain as a single person is something I've never done, and I'll have to grow into it.

It's difficult for my friends who are couples to have me with them. It's awkward to have the fourth chair empty. A few friends do invite me out to do things, but it doesn't happen very often. The people who come forward the most are also single women.

Being single is not easy, not at all. Joel and I were together as friends and partners for thirty years. I've never been single. It's very, very difficult.

Now, this past year, I had essentially my first date in thirty years. It went fine, but I thought I was going to die before it actually happened. A man I knew asked me out to dinner, and I said yes. It snuck up on me. If I had thought about it, I would probably have said no. It was something new for me. I remember hanging up the phone, and my son Geoff was standing there. I was crying, and I put my arms around him, and said, "I'm supposed to be listening to you talk about your dates; you're not supposed to be listening to me talk about mine." He was wonderfully supportive, but it was like a door on part of my past closing.

Thursday nights. Every week. Valley Beth Shalom. Two hundred and fifty people—some young, some middle-aged, some old—walk into the temple for the H.O.P.E. Foundation meeting. One thing characterizes all the people—they are in grief over the death of a loved one.

The facilitator divides the large group into smaller circles based on the number of months since the death occurred. Each circle is led by a professional counselor who gently leads the group into a mutual sharing of concerns, fears, questions, answers. There is crying, but there is also the all-important support that can only come from others who have been there.

No one knows when it will happen, but the time does come when the grief subsides enough to allow those who have lost a spouse to reenter social circles. It's awkward, awkward for you and awkward for your friends. The empty chair, the spirit of the deceased, the memories of good times all conspire to change the social dynamic. Couples who were acquaintances no longer call. Other singles become your circle of friends.

Eventually—it may be months or it may be years—the possibility of meeting someone new, of having a date, of remarriage becomes a reality. It's complicated. What will my children think? What will my single friends think? What do I do with the guilt? For some, being alone is a way of life that suits fine. For others, being alone is a fate worse than death.

With medical miracles lengthening the years of life, it is quite possible that many widows and widowers will seek companionship of another partner. In most cases, when a widow and widower find each other, it is a cause for celebration. The memories of a first marriage do not disappear, and the scars of grief remain forever. New families are formed and combined. Life goes on.

FOR COMFORTERS

Remembering the Living

RICHARD LOPATA: People in general have a tendency to make one *shiva* call and think, "Well, I've done my duty." Then, when they see you a few weeks later, they pretend that nothing ever happened, that the person never lived. I cannot tell you how repelled I feel when someone says, "Hi, Richard, how are you?" and never once say anything about the fact that I've lost a daughter.

SARALIE FOOTE: Stay in touch. Usually, you don't hear from those people who paid a *shiva* call. You may not see them for another year. After the *shiva* is over, nobody is around. Your life has changed drastically, and people go on like nothing's happened. You have to return the *shiva* chairs to the funeral parlor, you've got all this food you've got to dump or freeze, your house is a total shambles. You have to deal with all the thanking, all the paperwork. Your work doesn't stop ... everybody goes back to their place of business, to their own lives. And you, you have this enormous void in your life. I appreciated people calling, "How are you doing?" "How's everything?" It helps when you know people are out there, thinking of you. Stop by, don't ignore the fact that I've changed. Even the temple, the rabbi—they should come after the *shiva,* too.

CAROL STARIN: People wanted to reach out to me after the *shiva.* Usually they invited me out to dinner. Sometimes I didn't feel like going out, but I didn't know how to tell them. So, I went to lots of lunches and dinners with really well-meaning people.

These were social events where I had to act normal. But I didn't feel normal. I quickly learned that there was no way I was going to pick up the check. No one would ever let me pay. It was important to me. I thought, "This is the way it's going to be. I'm alone now. I'm single now. I can't let people pick up bills for me the rest of my life. They should let me carry my own weight." Well, no one wanted to let me.

At none of these luncheons or dinners did we ever talk about Joel. It was a social event in a public place. I guess it would have been uncomfortable if we had talked about him. I wouldn't have wanted to cry in a restaurant, and it would have been really uncomfortable for the hosts. Maybe if we had been in a private home, it would have been easier to talk about him.

Usually, these people took me out once. Since then, they've disappeared.

We often feel the task of comforting the mourner is over when the *shiva* comes to an end. In fact, after the hoopla of the intense *shiva,* the mourner is suddenly left to face life without the community physically surrounding him or her. It is precisely at these moments that the sensitive comforter maintains contact.

There are many ways for family and friends to reach out during the first thirty days of mourning and beyond:

- **Phone calls.** A simple phone call just to see how things are going tells the bereaved that you haven't forgotten about them.
- **Invitations.** Ask the mourner to spend some time with you. An invitation to a Shabbat meal, for tea and conversation, even out to lunch will be welcomed. Do be sensitive to the fact that more traditional friends who are bereaved may not accept invitations to "parties" during the first thirty days or even the first year after burial.
- **Notes.** If your bereaved friend lives far away, drop a note from time to time.
- **Visit the cemetery.** You may want to offer to accompany a close bereaved friend on a visit to the cemetery. Remember, a grave may be visited anytime after the conclusion of *shiva.*
- **Go to *shul.*** If your friend is saying Kaddish on a regular basis or

perhaps expresses a desire to attend a synagogue service to say Kaddish, offer to go along.

- **Be there.** Once again, we return to the basic notion of comforting—being there. Sometimes, it is particularly difficult to be there with those who have sustained a loss, especially at times that would normally be celebrations in the family.

Dennis Gura is the person who organizes and leads the seder for his family. A few weeks before Passover, just after Rebecca died, he called me with a poignant question: "How can we possibly get through the seder when all of us are in such shock and grief? How can we ask the Four Questions, how can we talk about the Four Children with this pain in our hearts?" We talked for a while about the ways the seder ritual could be interpreted in light of this terrible trauma to the family, and I suggested he write a letter to each participant, preparing him or her for what he or she would experience on seder night. Here is his unusually sensitive and powerful statement of personal faith and hope:

Dear Family,

Pesa<u>h</u> and the seder is usually a trying time for all of us. Our different understandings of Judaism and our different Jewish educations stand out in high relief against the backdrop of kosher food, interminable seders, incomprehensible Hebrew and arcane ritual. In the past, all these elements conspired to make much of what we do at the seder only marginally enjoyable. But we persevered, at times together, at times apart, in order to affirm our Jewish identity, maintain our solidarity with the Jewish people, and participate in one of the fundamental acts of the Jewish family.

This year, we will sit and recite the *Haggadah* and sing the songs and chant the blessings and drink the wine.

And remember Rebecca. We cannot avoid remembering Rebecca. Her absence from our table and her presence in our thoughts will dance through the night, from the Four Questions to the closing songs of Praise.

So we will dedicate this seder to Rebecca.

Just as we break the *matzah,* and hide part away, our family has been broken, and part is hid away.

Our children find the *matzah,* the *afikomen,* and let us then complete the seder. So too, many children, all our children, help us complete the order of our healing, of which this seder is a small but important step.

It is not customary among us to discuss what we believe. Certainly we do not try to convert each other to our own private faiths. But I believe, I must share with you, that God is the organizing force Who in some secret way makes the universe sensible. I do not know, particularly in my grief, how the world makes sense. But I believe that it must, or else both Rebecca's death and her life are meaningless.

I hope that we do, in some small, secret way, serve a higher purpose than just to live out our days.

In that spirit, we will start the seder this year with a prayer composed by the Hasidic Master of Berditchev, Rabbi Levi Yitzchak:

"Master of the universe, I do not know what questions to ask. I do not expect You to reveal Your secrets to me. All I ask is that You show me one thing—what this moment means to me and what You demand of me. I do not ask why I suffer. I ask only this: Do I suffer for Your sake?"

It is my sincere hope that this seder will help us heal through our pain.

With love and gratitude to you all.

Dennis

The Community and the Bereaved

BERNARD LIPNICK: The challenge of the Jewish people is to create organic Jewish communities—communities where people feel responsible for other people. If people have meaningful personal relationships with each other, they are going to provide the kind of support that people in bereavement require. The best example of this is the _havurah_. But it's not always easy to get this sort of intimacy in a large congregation.

There can also be a bereavement committee to inform people of the death of an individual, to provide a _minyan_, to prepare a _seudat hahavra'ah_, a meal of condolence. It is even possible to establish a _hevra kadisha_, a group of people willing to prepare the deceased for burial, as Rabbi Arnie Goodman has done in Minneapolis and now Atlanta. The most important role of the congregation is to be there for the member in this time of need.

The role of the synagogue

The synagogue plays a critical role in the bereavement process. Most congregations have mechanisms and professional staff to assist members with the burial of their loved ones. Here are some of the most common:

- **The rabbi.** As we have learned, the rabbi is often among the first people outside the immediate family to be consulted when a death occurs. As a pastoral counselor, the rabbi is trained to assist the bereaved by explaining the Jewish way in dying and death and to offer support during this time of transition in the family.

- **The cantor.** In many congregations, the cantor is also available to the family for support. He or she will co-officiate at the funeral with the rabbi and may offer to lead one or more of the *minyan* services in the *shiva* home.

- **The ritual director.** The ritual director (*shammes*) is the person who organizes and leads the daily *minyan* at the synagogue. This person can often assist the family in setting up the prayer services for the *shiva* by providing books, a Torah scroll, a Torah reader, *kippot, tallitot, tefillin,* and most importantly, people to make up the *minyan* itself.

- **The executive director.** This person is the business manager of the synagogue and is often responsible for any cemetery property owned or supervised by the congregation. He or she can be the liaison between the synagogue, the funeral home, and the family. The executive director can also assist you in arranging memorial tablets and listings in *Yizkor* books.

- **The men's clubs.** Many congregations have chapters of men's clubs or brotherhoods. Often, these men can be called upon to assist in making a *minyan* and other aspects of bereavement support. The Federation of Jewish Men's Clubs, an arm of the Conservative movement, is the co-publisher of this book and will be offering courses and workshops for synagogue members based upon it.

- **The Women's League.** Most congregations have Women's League or sisterhood groups. Many of them offer to arrange the meal of condolence for the family following the funeral. At Valley Beth Shalom in Encino, California, one call to the Women's League produces such a meal for as many people as you specify, plus a team of women to prepare the meal and set up the *shiva* home—at no charge!

- **The educational director.** It is very important for you to contact the educational director to alert her or him that your child or grandchild is experiencing the bereavement process. Children can benefit greatly from the sensitive support of the educational director, the teachers in the religious school, and classmates during this time.

- **The bereavement committee.** Many synagogues have groups of laypeople who constitute a bereavement committee. This group is prepared to support the mourner in whatever way possible. This can include: participating in the preparation of the deceased for burial, assisting in funeral arrangements, providing a meal of condolence, organizing prayer services, and offering a support group. The laypeople who represent the synagogue are a tremendous help to the rabbis and cantors who are often stretched to the limit in their ability to provide the support needed by the bereaved. These laypeople usually have special training from the rabbi for this work and many have years of experience with funerals and *shiva* homes. Welcome them into your family, and let them help you in whatever way you need support.

Future directions in synagogue work with the bereaved

Clearly, the basic requirements for mourning and comforting are presently met by the work of most synagogues. Yet, our research for this volume has unveiled a variety of areas in which synagogues could better serve the needs of the bereaved. Here are some of them:

- **Shiva services.** As it becomes more difficult for individuals to organize a *shiva minyan,* it falls upon the synagogue to ensure that these prayer services are brought to the mourner in the home. Some synagogues have lists of volunteers who can be called at a moment's notice to attend a *shiva minyan,* particularly in the morning.

  It is also extremely important for those who seek to help the mourners with the prayer services and the saying of Kaddish to realize that for most Jews today, the service and the Kaddish prayer may not be familiar to them. It is very helpful to the mourners to point out the page on which the Kaddish is found well before the mourner is called upon to recite it. The leader of the service should recite the Kaddish aloud to provide a model for the mourner to follow; this helps avoid the embarrassing situation of the mourners stumbling through the difficult words all by themselves. It is also good etiquette for the leader to thank people for coming to the service on behalf of the family and to announce the days and times of future services to encourage attendance. It would also be a good idea to have a "transition" *minyan* available to new mourners, a "learner" service during which the prayers are explained and questions answered.

- **Welcoming the bereaved to the synagogue.** When the mourners come to the synagogue for Shabbat services Friday night and Saturday, representatives of the synagogue should be available to welcome the mourners and sit with them during the service. They can help the mourners follow the service and alert them to when the Mourner's Kaddish will be recited.

- **Following-up when the *shiva* is over.** One of the common problems mourners face is the feeling of isolation after the commotion of the funeral and *shiva* are over. Suddenly, no one is around and no one calls. How wonderful it would be for the congregation to provide a regular form of communication with the mourners during the months following the funeral! Perhaps a series of letters can be sent offering information on the healing of grief. Or, perhaps just a reminder notice that the congregation is there for them can be mailed every other month. The Men's Club and Women's League chapters might make it a point to invite the mourner to a meeting or out for coffee. Since many mourners do not regularly attend services, the built-in support group of the daily *minyan* is not available. Many synagogues have filled this need by sponsoring bereavement support groups for mourners, facilitated by trained grief counselors. It is important to remember that while the *shiva* is over for the comforters, the mourning continues for the bereaved. Find ways to be there for them six months after the funeral, and you will be serving your membership well.

Support can also be offered in the form of resources. A number of national organizations have printed and other materials to help those who are grieving and those who seek to comfort. Here are some of the major groups:

> The Compassionate Friends (for bereaved parents)
> P.O.B. 3696
> Oak Brook, IL 60522-3696
> www.compassionatefriends.org

International Association of Widowed People
P.O.B. 3564
Springfield, IL 62708

The National Hospice and Palliative Care Organization
1700 Diagonal Road, Suite 625
Alexandria, Virginia 22314
www.nhpco.org

- **Death education.** Even with the advances in death education over the past twenty years, much work remains to be done in our institutions. Courses, workshops, and seminars in Jewish mourning and comforting can be offered in adult education programs. As shocking as the title may be, "How to Prepare for Your Own Death" is a compelling and important topic for all of us. Especially helpful would be courses on the art of Jewish comforting—what to say, what to write, what to do for our friends and family in mourning.

Historically, when a Jewish community was established in a new place, the first institutions established by the people were a cemetery, a school, and a synagogue. The three meet at the nexus of death and bereavement. It is a major challenge of our generation to create the social and educational support systems for the bereaved that will console them in their grief and bring them—and those of us who comfort—ever closer to the Jewish tradition we love and cherish.

PART 9

How to Prepare for Your Own Death

Before Funeral Arrangements

MARTHA WHITE: I didn't believe in preplanning for death before I began to see what happens in families who suddenly have to decide where to bury somebody. Years ago, when you got married, you bought your property. Or you lived in a small town and really didn't have to worry about whether there would be space for you. Now, in the big cities, it's different.

RON WOLFSON: Why don't people prepare?

MARTHA WHITE: Basically, people just don't want to deal with death. Some are superstitious; they feel if they buy property, something will happen. Some don't think it's their concern. They'll say, "It's too expensive. I don't want to think about it. Let my kids worry about it. I took care of my parents; they can take care of it for me." And almost everyone is afraid of facing mortality. Look, how many people do you know who don't have a will?

RON WOLFSON: Or haven't saved for college, or don't have disaster preparations?

MARTHA WHITE: Right. It's also a generational thing. When our parents had us, they made a will and bought property. But the younger generation today doesn't have that tradition. When I see people coming in to the mortuary at need—bewildered, confused, frightened—having to make these decisions when they're not thinking straight, it's tough. And, then, you have to come up with tremendous sums of money. One of the things we need to do is train people to think about planning for this inevitable event.

ANN MITNICK: One day Marty and I were talking with our friends Tommie and Don Shulman, and we realized that we should get our plots at least so our children would have one less problem to worry about when we die. So, instead of making it a morbid experience, we decided to make a day of it! We went plot shopping! First, we went to Hillside and looked there. Then we had lunch and ended up at Mount Sinai.

Doing this with friends made it so much easier. There was even the inevitable kibitzing and levity about it. The counselor at Mount Sinai told us he thought preneed work was so much better. We called him "our real estate salesman." He took us around the park. He asked whether we wanted curb-side property or underneath a tree or near a waterfall. It made it a light, easy afternoon.

Although the focus of this book has been on how to mourn and how to comfort the mourner, the ultimate goal of death education is to prepare each of us for our ultimate destiny. The experience of caring for the dying, burying the dead, and grieving for a loss does have a major impact on how we think about our own end. How do you want to die? How do you want to be buried? How do you want to be mourned?

With the increased awareness of these questions among the dying, the family, the medical establishment, and the Jewish community, the taboos against discussing issues surrounding death are diminishing. Consumerism—the right to decide what will be done to us and for us—is another force influencing people to consider these questions. Certainly, the often painful experience of being a party to difficult decision-making regarding life and death with loved ones may lead us to take charge of these decisions when it comes to our own death.

You may be someone who still feels the strong taboo against dealing with death before it actually happens. We respect this feeling and want to reassure you that you are in the majority. Less than 25 percent of the Jewish community has made before-need plans for death. If you are in this category, you may want to skip the following section.

But, if you are convinced that by planning ahead, you can do a kindness to yourself and your family, we offer a strategy to do so. With a sincere prayer that the plans we are about to suggest are not needed until you reach *"a hundert und tzvanzig"*—one hundred twenty years of age—here is a comprehensive guide to preparing for your own death.

Think about your own feelings

How do you feel about confronting your own inevitable death? For most of us, dealing with death raises feelings of sadness, fear, and insecurity. While Judaism looks unfavorably on anything that diminishes the hope of a dying person, it makes a specific exception by directing those attending the person to help set her or his financial affairs in order. Moreover, now that the majority of people die of chronic long-term illness, the need to make decisions regarding one's own medical care gives direction to caregivers and relieves the family of agonizing decisions regarding your life and death.

Make before-need funeral arrangements

We've all seen the ads and heard the pitch. But, amazingly, there is great wisdom in making before-need arrangements with a mortuary and cemetery. You can often establish a trust that ensures monies will be available at time of need. Or you may simply want to buy property outright.

By choosing where you wish to be buried, you will save your family the burden of making agonizing choices at a time of tremendous emotional upheaval. As with any other purchase, use your good consumer skills. If you have a choice of mortuary, meet with representatives to discuss the services they provide. If you have a choice of cemetery, think carefully about which one provides easiest access to family members, which one is maintained nicely, and so on.

- **At the cemetery.** Once you have decided on the cemetery, visit the park and select your plot. Discuss with your loved ones the possibility of buying a family plot. Make payment arrangements. You might even select a gravestone: Shall it be single or double? You can compose your epitath: Do you want both English and Hebrew names and dates, other symbols or sayings? How do you wish to be identified?

- **At the mortuary.** You have important choices to make regarding preparation for burial: Which casket? Do you want *tahara?* Do you want a *shomer?* Flowers? Do you have a favorite charity?
- **The funeral.** Perhaps you have definite ideas about what you want said at the funeral. A favorite reading? A poem? Would you want someone close to you to offer a eulogy? Who would you want as pallbearers? Who do you want to officiate? Would you prefer a chapel or graveside service?

  Some Jewish funeral homes can record your vital information and burial preferences in a "memorial record," a copy of which is kept on file and available to your survivors.
- **Second marriage.** The complications of burial and bereavement when a person has been married twice can be very difficult. Are you buried next to your first spouse or second spouse? What would your children want? Where will the *shiva* be held? These questions will undoubtedly present themselves to your survivors and could cause tension at a time of emotional upheaval. It would be helpful to them for you to indicate your desire in the instructions you prepare.

An Ethical Will

JACK RIEMER: I meet with bar and bat mitzvah kids. I ask, "What's your Hebrew name?" They know. I ask, "What's your father's Hebrew name?" Less know. I ask, "What's your mother's Hebrew name?" Even less know. Then I ask, "Who were you named for?" They haven't the foggiest idea. "My Bubbe's cousin." So, I say to them, "If your parents thought this person was important enough that they named you for him or her, then your first assignment is to go to the people who knew that person and find out why you're named for that person."

Now, what if that person had left behind a letter or videotape or cassette for this not-yet-born grandchild to read or to listen to? What a great gift that would have been! That's what an ethical will is—a message to your kids about what you've learned in life, what you want for them and from them after you're gone.

One of the most loving documents you can prepare is known as an "ethical will." This is a statement of your legacy—what you achieved during your lifetime, the values you want to transmit to the next generation, your hopes and dreams for your family in the future. Rabbi Jack Riemer has written extensively on the subject of Jewish ethical wills, compiling a wonderful collection in the book (with Nathaniel Stampfer) *So That Your Values Live On—Ethical Wills and How to Prepare Them*. These statements range from the deeply philosophical reflections of scholars and leaders to the simple statements of wishes from common people. Here is the ethical will of Marcia Lawson, a Jewish communal leader in Chicago, who presents her own powerful feelings about Judaism, but leaves it to her children to find their own path within it:

My Dear Children:

Tradition warns us that one of the signs of a false prophet is his claim to foretell the future. How much care should we ordinary human beings then take in refraining from glib statements regarding what will be in the days to come.

Therefore, I cannot say in what way your lives will differ from the path my life has taken. All I can recount here are my hopes, dreams, and desires for spiritually rich, rewarding and productive lives for you both and for the families you will raise in your turn.

My life was shaped by crashing waves of history: mass emigrations of desperate people, economic depression, war, the decimation of our people, the rebirth of Israel, and the unverbalized response of my family to these momentous occurrences. They were not considered topics to discuss with children, opinions were not asked for, no overt teaching came forth, only background murmur of adult conversations, a sense of uneasiness, of time rushing too quickly forward yet creeping incredibly slowly.

Your life is being formed amidst quieter events on the stage of history. Yet a much more verbal coming-to-grips with the meaning of these events is demanded of you. You must consciously determine how you will internalize them, how you will make the past as well as the present an integral part of yourselves as Jews within the human family.

We, your elders, solicit your perceptions. Perhaps we are too intense and do not leave you time for unfettered dreaming and childish selfishness.

My Jewish identity began as pride in belonging to what seemed an "interesting" and "different" people. Sociologically speaking, I found us a treasure trove of unplumbed depths. At the same time, I shared in Toynbee's misconception of us as "fossils." The inchoate feelings of Jewish affirmation which demanded expression by marriage in the devastated, conquered Germany were many years later to lead us to Masada for your bar mitzvah, Freddy, and God willing, the same for your celebration of bat mitzvah, Dina.

I have attempted to give you a more "normal" Jewish life by living the Jewish calendar as part of our daily life. I hope this steadiness along with the continuous study of our people's history, the shared memories of the Jewish past from biblical times through the rabbinic tradition into the middle ages, Hasidic lore, the *Haskalah,* and the Zionist idea will give you a meaningful understanding of our group personality. Certainly you will be able to bring a measure of spontaneity and authenticity to your own homes that I was unable to reproduce.

You were not born into the world at large, but into a certain family and at a certain time. I would wish for you comfort, love, an "at-homeness" in this family which shares a common historic experience. But I also wish you always a yearning and a seeking for something more for yourselves and the generations to come after you. These generations go back beyond Sinai to a lone wanderer, our father Abraham, and continue into the future. It endures so long as this unbroken chain of generations continues to dare to be a partner with that power that causes us to struggle for justice, peace, love, and beauty.

In conclusion, my dears, care for and protect each other's well-being and share in each other's joys and be an emotional support in times of difficulty.

Your Mother

Leonard Ratner was an immigrant to the United States who became a successful businessman and philanthropist:

To my Family ... and Grandchildren:

This is my last letter and when you will read it, I will only be a memory.

I don't think that I have to write you much as, thank God, you are educated and smart enough to understand that this world is not easy. I am sure you will endure it and will continue to follow in the footsteps of Mother, as she was one of the greatest women who ever lived.

The luckiest thing for me was meeting your mother, and she to some extent was responsible for many of the successes in our life as she was not only looking for herself but what can be done for the family and others. To some extent she copied our grandparents. I am sure you will continue the kind of life and keep close with all our families and try to do as much as you can for each other.

Don't forget your seats at Park Synagogue.

Stay well and keep up your good work.

Your Father, Grandfather

JACK RIEMER: You don't need to be a professional writer to write an ethical will. Words that come from the heart enter the heart. Some of the best wills I've collected are from simple people. One woman wrote, "Daddy and I gave you the best education we could afford. We love you very much. All I want is that you shouldn't fight with each other." I know why she wrote it. Her in-laws had not left a clear will; the kids were in court for years fighting over the estate. She didn't want that. So she told them to be good to each other. Kids who get a letter like that will not end up in court.

BERNARD LIPNICK: On the night before my heart surgery, I made tape recordings for each of my boys, just in case things didn't turn out well. I told them how I saw their lives, their strengths, and the things they needed to work on, what I hoped for them. Years later when we moved to California, I found the tapes. It was an amazing experience to listen to them. Although Daniel had died, may he rest in peace, I sent the tapes to David and Jesse. What was truly remarkable was that so little had changed during the intervening years. And the boys really did appreciate hearing them while I am still alive.

In the section "A Guide to Writing Your Own Ethical Will," the authors of *So That Your Values Live On* suggest six steps:

1. Start by writing sentences on important topics, among them:
   The formative events in my life ...
   The world from which I came ...
   The people who influenced me most ...
   The important lessons I've learned in life ...

My definition of true success ...

The Jewish values I cherish most ...

The things I want to ask your forgiveness for ...

I forgive you for ...

How much I love you ...

2. Organize what you want to say using this format:

Opening

    a. "I write this to you, my ____, in order to _____.

The family

    a. My parents, siblings, antecendents were/are ...

    b. Events that helped shape our family ...

Personal history

    a. People who strongly influenced my life ...

    b. Event(s) that helped shape my life ...

Religious observances, insights

    a. The ritual(s) of most meaning to me ...

    b. Specific teachings from Jewish source(s) that moved me most ...

Ethical ideals and practices

    a. Ideals that found expression in my life ...

    b. I would like to suggest to you the following ...

Closing

    a. My ardent wishes for you ...

    b. May the Almighty ...

3. Personalize and strengthen the links with words that have special meaning to you and your family, favorite sayings, anecdotes, and stories that help crystallize the memories of your life.

4. Write the will on acid-free paper with fountain pen, or use modern technologies of communication, including audio- and videotape.

5. Decide when to present the ethical will—before your death, leave it as a spiritual legacy after your death, or both.

6. Attach the ethical will as a codicil to other wills, estate plans, or living wills.

You may want the rabbi to read portions of your ethical will as part of the eulogy.

A Living Will

We have already discussed the importance of this document designed to make known your desire to die with dignity.

A living will tells doctors, hospital staff, or nursing-home employees whether you want to be kept alive on artificial life-support systems if you are in a coma beyond all reasonable hope of recovery. You also need a durable power of attorney that names someone to carry out your wishes.

Rabbi Elliot Dorff and Rabbi Avram Reisner have both written extensively on the Jewish approach to dying and modern medical ethics. Both have written Jewish living wills that have been accepted by the Committee on Jewish Law and Standards of the Rabbinical Assembly as recommended procedures for rabbis within the Conservative movement. Here is Rabbi Dorff's:

Your advanced directive for health care

States differ in their laws concerning advanced directives for health care. They even differ in what they call such documents. Some state laws provide for a living will, others for a durable power of attorney for health care, and others for both. In an effort to encourage people to fill out such documents, many states have deliberately tried to make it as easy as possible to do that. Thus, if your state has a particular approved form, it is often possible to procure that in a stationery store, and you may not need a lawyer to fill it out or to make it legally effective. It may nevertheless be advisable, however, to discuss the form with your attorney and, in any case, to file a copy of it with him or her.

It is strongly recommended that you talk over these matters with your physician. He or she can explain relevant facts and alternative treatments so that you make your decisions knowing the medical realities. Moreover, your physician, after all, is not your enemy but your ally in your health care, and so you should make these plans together.

In order to avoid conflict among the members of your family as to how to care for you, it is also advisable to give a copy of your document appointing a proxy to the close members of your family. A clear-cut specification of who has the authority to decide can go a long way in averting guilt and bad feelings among the ones you care about most.

Recent articles have pointed out that if a person specifies certain kinds of treatment and also appoints someone to make medical decisions when he or she can no longer do so (a proxy), there may be a conflict between what the proxy says and what the document says, or difference of opinion as to how to interpret the document. Consequently, recent legal opinion has suggested giving your primary-care physician only the document that appoints a particular person to act as proxy and to give any specific written instructions only to the proxy. This makes it clear that the proxy, and the proxy alone, has the authority to interpret the document and to make decisions for you. We will follow that advice in the form below.

That will mean that the only legally binding act you will be doing in filling out this form is to appoint a proxy. It is nevertheless important to fill out the entire advance directive for three reasons. First of all, it will help you think about at least some of the various choices people must make about their medical care. The document will thus help to educate you to this area of life.

Second, it will give your proxy concrete evidence of your choices. Even if the proxy knows you well—and the proxy is typically someone who knows you well—you probably have not discussed such matters very much, for few people like to talk about their death. It is therefore often helpful for your proxy to have a written expression of your desires on these matters so that he or she can know what you want in the situations this form specifically mentions and what you would most likely want in the situations it does not.

And, finally, this form was prepared in accordance with a rabbinic responsum approved by the Conservative movement's Committee on Jewish

Law and Standards. As such, you can be assured that the options it mentions are in accord with Jewish law and tradition.

In sum, then, give a copy of your appointment of proxy to your physician, proxy, and family, and a copy of your full advance directive to your proxy. Be sure to have two witnesses who will not inherit any of your property sign the document in the presence of a notary who signs and seals it. In addition, you might want to carry a card in your wallet indicating that you have appointed a proxy and how that person can be reached.

Filling out this form will undoubtedly not be pleasant. Aside from the sheer time and effort involved, it will require you to think of things you would rather not imagine. Remember, though, that in completing this form you are enabling yourself to have a say in your health care when you are no longer mentally competent to decide; that you are helping your family to make what may be extremely difficult decisions with a minimum of guilt and rancor; and that you are doing what your Jewish tradition would have you do.

DURABLE POWER OF ATTORNEY FOR HEALTH CARE APPOINTMENT OF PROXY.

My name: _____

I am over eighteen years of age and of sound mind. Should I become medically incompetent to make health-care decisions for myself, I name

_____,

my _____, (relationship) as my representative to make medical decisions for me. He or she currently resides at _____ where the telephone number is (____)_____.

First Alternative Agent:

Should the person appointed above as my proxy be unavailable, unable, or unwilling for any reason to serve in that capacity, I would have

_____, (name)

my _____, (relationship) serve instead.

He or she currently resides at _____

where the telephone number is (____)_____.

Second Alternative Agent:

Should both the person appointed above as my proxy and the person appointed as my first alternative agent be unavailable, unable, or unwilling for any reason to serve in that capacity, I would have

_____, (name)

my _____ (relationship) serve instead.

He or she currently resides at _____

where the telephone number is (____)_____.

I make these instructions, being of sound mind and more than eighteen years of age, and understanding fully the consequences of these appointments.

Signed: _____

Date: _____

Address: _____

_____

Signature of designated proxy: _____

Signature of first designated
alternate: _____

Signature of second designated
alternate: _____

Witness: _____

Witness: _____

NOTARY'S SEAL AND SIGNATURE

Dated: _____

Renewed: _____

Renewed: _____

Renewed: _____

"A Time to Be Born and a Time to Die"— A Jewish Medical Directive for Health Care

Rabbi Elliot N. Dorff

Name: _____

> A season is set for everything, a time for every experience under heaven: A time to be born and a time to die ... (Ecclesiastes 3:1–2)

I am a Jew. I express that affiliation in a variety of ways in my life, and I want Jewish perceptions and values to inform the way in which I live through the final stages of my life. I know that at some point I may not be able to make decisions about my health care, and so I have completed this form to make my wishes known. Let me say in advance that I fully appreciate the loving care given to me by my family and friends and by members of the health-care professions in my last period of life. If I cannot thank you personally at that time, I wish to do so now from the depths of my heart.

You are truly performing what the Rabbis called a _hesed shel emet_, an act of devotion that, since I cannot possibly repay you, comes from pure fidelity and love. If the pain I suffer at that time makes me cranky and hard to tolerate, please forgive me. Please understand that I may not be in control of my reactions at that time and that, no matter what I say or do, I deeply appreciate the many kindnesses you have bestowed upon me throughout life and especially at that critical stage.

In the instructions below, I have indicated the types of care I wish and/or the person or people whom I would like to make health-care decisions for me if I am unable to do so on my own. I have made these decisions with full mind and heart, and I take comfort in knowing that they comply with the options open to me according to Jewish law as affirmed by the Committee on Jewish Law and Standards of the Conservative movement.

Part of my intention in filling out this form is to relieve any family member or health-care professional who decides in accordance with these instructions of any residual guilt feelings. Please rest assured that I know the moral ambiguity and emotional distress inherent in making such decisions; we do not, after all, possess God's omniscience, and so we cannot always know unequivocally what is the proper choice. Anyone determining the course of my health in accordance with the instructions below, however, has my endorsement and my appreciation. Moreover, my compliance with Jewish law as interpreted by the Conservative movement's Committee on Jewish Law and Standards makes me satisfied that I am doing what God and the Jewish tradition would have me do, and as a result I bear no feelings of guilt in making these decisions and neither should anyone deciding according to the instructions below on my behalf.

Because I cannot possibly anticipate what will happen to me in years to come and the health-care decisions which will have to be made, I want to say at the outset that I wish those making decisions for me to act for my benefit. I have tried to spell out below what I understand that to mean in the circumstances I can envision, but I recognize full well that I may not have foreseen the specific circumstances of the last stages of my life or the complications that may arise. Therefore, I declare now that, more than any specific instruction below, I want those caring for me to act for my benefit, interpreting that in light of the choices I have made below and any other knowledge you have of me.

I understand that Jewish law permits me to ask you to act for my benefit within the parameters indicated below. Judaism values life and demands we seek medical care. I share Judaism's respect for my body, the creation and possession of God, and I consequently wish that all prudent medical treatment be extended to me with the aim of effecting my recovery. I recognize, however that, like all human beings, I will not live forever, that there is "a time to be born and a time to die." My tradition, therefore, gives me some choices in determining the course of my medical care, especially as my time to die approaches, and I have made my choices on these matters below.

In accordance with the Jewish tradition's respect for the life God has given us and its consequent bans on murder and suicide, however, I unequivocally reject any form of active euthanasia ("mercy killing") or assisted suicide. I recognize that in a number of situations no one choice of medical therapy is indisputably better for me than another.

Judgments must be made, and they inevitably involve the values, commitments, beliefs, and feelings of the one making the decision. In the event that I cannot make such a decision for myself at some future time, I shall now indicate my choices in some instances of that type. I trust that my physician and/or family member(s) and/or designated surrogate will use these instructions to guide any decisions they must make, not only in the circumstances described below, but also in those not explicitly covered.

Specifically, then, I am making one choice in each of the following areas to express my wishes:

1. **Diagnostic tests:**
   ___ I wish to have available all possible information concerning my condition. I consent to all diagnostic tests as ordered by my physician. Even if my situation is medically hopeless, I am interested in knowing all I can about it, and so the information gleaned from such tests will help me psychologically. I also hope that further analysis of my disease may someday help doctors help someone else.
   ___ I do not wish to have diagnostic tests performed on me unless they are clearly related to my own treatment.
2. **Knowledge of my condition:**
   ___ I wish to know all relevant facts of my disease, even if the news is bad. I can cope better with a known threat than with the unknown.

___ I do not wish to know all the gruesome details of my disease, especially if the news is bad. I fear that such knowledge will diminish my will to live and will cast a shadow over the time left to me.

3. **Surgery:**

___ I would consent to reasonable surgery as proposed by my physicians.

___ All surgery carries an implicit risk through anesthesia, the increased possibility of infection, and through trauma to the body. I do not consent to such risk except if it is required to restore me to health or to free me from unbearable pain.

4. **Amputation:**

___ I am prepared to lose a limb if, in the best medical judgment of my physician(s), this is necessary in order to prolong my life.

___ There may come a time when my physicians feel that my life is threatened by infection and that the most effective defense lies in amputation of the affected limb. I find the notion of amputation unbearable and am convinced that I will not survive the loss of a limb. I prefer all other treatments to fight the infection save where the limb has already been substantially severed.

5. **Nasogastric feeding:**

___ I will accept the advice of my physicians to provide me with nutrition and hydration through a nasogastric tube, when and if that becomes necessary. I understand that this procedure may at some point require restraint so that I do not dislodge the tubes.

___ I find reliance on nutrition provided through tubes emplaced in my nose to be abhorrent. I fear the pain and the risk of aspiration. If I cannot feed myself, I prefer to be fed intravenously or gastrointestinally. I have discussed the relative risks of these procedures with my physician.

6. **Surgically emplaced feeding tubes:**

___ If I cannot feed myself, and if the less invasive procedures of nasogastric tubes and intravenous feeding are no longer possible, I will accept the advice of my physicians to surgically emplace feeding tubes in my stomach or intestines to provide me with nutrition and hydration. I understand the risks involved in this type of surgery.

___ I find reliance on nutrition provided through tubes emplaced surgically in my stomach or intestines to be abhorrent. I fear the risks of surgery, infection, and aspiration. I prefer to feed myself for as long as I can, and when I can no longer do that, to let nature take its course.

7. **Persistent vegetative state:**

___ If I am in a persistent vegetative state, I nevertheless want to be maintained on artificial nutrition and hydration and, if necessary, heart, lung, and/or kidney dialysis machines until I die from other natural causes. While I wish this, I recognize that there may be limits to the time my relatives or surrogate can maintain such treatment. Restrictions imposed by the state, our insurance company, or the personal finances available for my medical care, and/or the need for the use of the machines to help people with a better chance of recovery may singly or together force my removal from an aggressive regimen of treatment. If that occurs, I want to relieve those making health-care decisions for me from any sense of guilt; you did all you could to fulfill my wishes.

___ If I am in a persistent vegetative state—a diagnosis tested over a reasonable period of time and confirmed by more than one physician—I prefer to forego artifical provision of nutrition and hydration, since I consider them to be medications. Even if artificial nutrition and hydration are used during the period in which my diagnosis is being formed and tested, I hereby give permission to remove the feeding tubes (wherever they are attached to my body) once the diagnosis is confirmed, just as other medications that have proven to be ineffective in effecting my cure may be removed.

8. **Irreversible, terminal illness:**

___ I wish above all to live. To that end I would undertake any regimen, however difficult, that, in the eyes of my physicians, stands even the slightest of chances of helping me to extend my life. While I wish this, I recognize that there may be limits to the time my relatives or surrogate can maintain such treatment. Restrictions imposed by the state, our insurance company, or the personal finances available for my medical care, and/or the need for the use of the machines to help people with a better chance of recovery may singly or together force my removal from an aggressive regimen of treatment. If that occurs, I want to relieve those making health-care decisions for me from any sense of guilt; you did all you could to fulfill my wishes.

____ Aggressive medical or surgical procedures can be most debilitating and destructive. While I desire to fight my disease with all effective tools, I do not wish to undertake treatments that are futile, untested, or unlikely to offer meaningful, measurable results. If my physician determines that a given mode of therapy will probably not produce remission or recovery, I prefer to engage in hospice care, accepting the inevitability of my impending death, curbing pain as much as possible, and living out the remainder of my life to the fullest.

9. **Mechanical life support:**

____ I consider that as long as my brain is still active, even if I must breathe with the aid of life-support equipment, my God-given life has not yet been called back. These technologies should therefore be maintained. I recognize, however, that if the total absence of brain activity can be verified, I will be considered dead despite mechanically induced respiration and heartbeat.

____ I consider mechanical means of life support to be impediments to my death at God's behest, even though they may prolong biological functions, if they cannot contribute to my recovery. Therefore, I instruct that they be forgone or withdrawn when my physician and designated representative jointly conclude that they offer no reasonable chance of return to unaided functioning.

10. **Cardiopulmonary resuscitation:**

____ Should my cardio-pulmonary system fail for any reason, in every case I would like the utmost done in my behalf.

____ If my heart has stopped beating and my condition is such that there is no reasonable expectation of my recovery, I would consider cardiopulmonary resuscitation, by whatever means, to be contrary to God's will, and therefore ask that my body not be subjected to such handling. In such a case I would consider a Do Not Resuscitate order to be in order.

11. Pain relief:

____ I trust that all possible pain relief will be provided to me, save that I do not wish my death to be hastened thereby. I will accept considerable periods of sedation to avoid pain.

____ I trust that all possible pain relief will be provided to me, save that I do not wish my death to be hastened thereby. If I remain alert, however, I am prepared to accept a reasonable amount of pain to maintain my awareness.

____ I trust that all possible pain relief will be provided to me, even if it may have the secondary, unintended effect of hastening my death.

12. Hospital or home care:

____ I prefer to be supported by the best medical technology. To that end, if my death is not sudden, I wish that it will occur in the confines of a hospital.

____ To the extent that it is practicable and not an undue hardship upon my family, I would prefer to die at home or in a congenial supportive-care facility such as a hospice rather than in a hospital. When hospital care is no longer able with confidence to effect my recovery, I would prefer such comfort-oriented care, with the clear understanding that all essential palliative medical care will be continued.

13. Organ donation:

____ When I die, I hereby empower my representative to effect the donation of any or all of my body parts for the purpose of transplant. I want the following person or institution to be the recipient of my bodily parts: _____, whose current address is _____.
The rest of my remains should then be buried in a Jewish cemetery in accordance with Jewish law and custom.

____ I hereby empower my representative to effect the donation of only the following body parts for the purposes of transplant into another human being: Kidneys____ Heart____ Skin____ Corneas____ Liver____ Pancreas____ Other_____

I want the following person or institution to be the recipient of my bodily parts: _____, whose current address is _____.

The rest of my remains should then be buried in a Jewish cemetery in accordance with Jewish law and custom.

____ I do not wish that any of my body be used for purposes of transplant.

14. Autopsy:

____ I understand that governmental authorities may require an autopsy if there is suspicion of foul play in my death. If my physician requests an autopsy to learn more about the disease from which I died, I hereby grant _____ to withhold _____ such permission.

RABBINIC CONSULTATION

____ If I can make my own decisions about my health care when my physical situation becomes critical, I intend to consult my rabbi for further advice about the specific issues that arise in the medical situation in which I actually find myself. If I cannot make my own decisions regarding my care, I would ask that those making decisions for me likewise review them with my rabbi,_____

of the synagogue _____,

whose address is _____.

Should he or she be unavailable, it is my wish that some other rabbi be consulted and that he or she consider my situation in light of the guidance offered by the responsum by Rabbi Elliot N. Dorff, entitled "A Jewish Response to End-Stage Medical Care," *Conservative Judaism* 43:3 (Spring, 1991), pp. 3–51.

As God is my rock and my fortress and my deliverer, so may God be my refuge, my shield, and my salvation, forever.

Signed: _____

Date: _____ Address: _____

Signature of designated proxy: _____

Signature of first designated alternate: _____

Signature of second designated alternate: _____

Witness: _____

Witness: _____

NOTARY'S SEAL AND SIGNATURE

Dated: _____

Renewed: _____

Renewed: _____

Renewed: _____

Estate Instructions

SANDY GOODGLICK: I remember going into my mother's room after she died, rummaging through her desk, thinking she must have left me something written. "It must be here." But there was nothing.

One Thanksgiving, Bill and I were on a trip to visit our son Todd in Washington, D.C. The night before we left, we realized that if something happened to both of us, if the plane went down, the kids would have to be detectives to come up with everything they would need. I made up my mind that I would put together all the information the kids would need concerning our estate: where to find bank accounts, life insurance policies, health insurance, where to turn off the water to the house, letters of instruction about our wills and personal matters, how to handle Bill's business—all in one loose-leaf binder that can be kept current. It will be a real help to the kids, and it is a tremendous comfort for us.

CAROL STARIN: When I rewrote my will after Joel's death, I needed input from my kids about certain issues. For example, when they were younger, Joel and I wrote instructions about who would be their guardians should both of us die. Now, I asked them what they would want to happen should I die. They felt very strongly that they would want to live in their own home and not go to live with someone else. At their ages, that's a possibility.

Many people die without leaving any instructions about what is to be done with their estate. This is unfortunate for all parties concerned. First, without an estate plan or legal will, the probate court makes decisions about your estate instead of you. Second, your survivors are placed in a very awkward and potentially distressful situation when your desires are not formally expressed in a written document. Third, your family stands to lose significant sums of money to estate taxes without the guidance of a will prepared with the help of an estate planner.

Sandy Goodglick thinks most survivors must scramble to collect the vital information necessary to complete the affairs of the deceased. In her work, she offers guidance in organizing estate matters into an always current matrix:

- **Bank accounts.** Bank addresses, account numbers, how title is held, current balances, location of check ledgers, passbooks, monthly statements, cancelled checks.
- **General instructions.** Names and addresses of attorneys, accountants, professional advisors, directions concerning funeral arrangements.
- **Health insurance.** Location of policies, policy numbers, summary of benefits and restrictions, customer service phone numbers.
- **Household information.** Gas and water turnoffs, location of utility meters, drain and sewer cleanouts, location of keys (cars, security alarm box).
- **Life insurance.** Location of policies, policy numbers, summary of benefits, current values, agent's name, address, phone number.
- **Insurance policies.** Homeowner's, automobile, liability, disability.
- **Miscellaneous information.** Vital statistics, Social Security numbers, birth dates, place of birth, driver's license numbers, mother's maiden name, Hebrew names, credit card account numbers, safe combination.
- **Real estate.** Addresses, legal descriptions, vesting of title, property taxes, insurance policies, tenant rent roll, partnership agreements, income tax returns, property manager, homeowner's association covenants and restrictions.
- **Safety deposit box.** Address, location of key, list of contents (birth

certificates, marriage certificate, deeds, wills, trust documents, promissory notes, military papers).

- **Securities.** Stocks, bonds, municipals, mutual funds, brokers' and/or agents' names and addresses.
- **Service and repair.** Names and phone numbers of service people (gardener, electrician, auto mechanic, piano tuner, plumber).
- **Tickler.** Important date reminders for making payments (loans, insurance premiums, income taxes and estimates, real estate taxes, special assessments), for receiving payments (rent, interest income, stock dividends), and for action (renew appliance service contract, update records, review estate planning).

Although this information can be stored and kept current on a computer, Sandy suggests that her clients prepare a loose-leaf notebook with sections for each of these headings. A hard-copy list of the important information can then be placed into the binder. A letter written to the surviving spouse/children detailing what should be done in the case of death is placed at the front of the binder. (See Appendices for example.) The binder is then placed in a safe and accessible place known to the children.

Sandy reports that her clients, many of them widows, are tremendously comforted that the deceased has left these business affairs in good order, saving them the anguish and trouble of collecting this information in the difficult days following a death.

Distribution of Personal Items

Sandy Goodglick recommends that people make an inventory of important personal property and decide to whom they wish to bequeath the item. She suggests creating a file of three-by-five-inch index cards on which each item is described in clear detail ("men's 14-carat gold ring with diamond"), along with who is to receive it. Jewelry, clothes, autos, property, books, furniture, art, electronic equipment—even photo albums can be listed. Again, this will save the survivors the agony and sometimes the arguments that often accompany this difficult task.

PART 10

Afterlife

Talking to My Grandfather

I was trying to reach my grandfather this morning.

I needed to talk to him.

He would have been 99 on September 12th.

Nothing was working.

I thought I could do it

by remembering the arrangement of his kitchen

and putting him across from me at the table

where he used to read his racing forms

for the harmless two-dollar bets

he liked to place now and again,

but I had no luck.

After I failed with that trick,

all I could come up with, by way of comparison, was:

it was like fiddling with the TV antenna

and still not getting a picture without shadows

no matter which way you turned it or angled the rabbit ears.

Then I tried to remember

the smell of the work boots and gloves in his store,

hoping from there I would see him standing at the

> *cash register*

and slipping me a quarter to play the pinball machines down

> *the block,*

but that didn't happen either.

I needed to talk to him.

and tell him I missed him,

and how was business?

and did he still have a cold?

and did the optometrist get him his new glasses yet?

and did he want me to come over

to watch the wrestling matches with him
so we could cheer or boo when the champ—
Gorgeous George in those days—
threw the other guy half-way across the ring
or got all bent up in a vicious hammer lock?
I even tried imagining how huge and quiet his
    old Hudson was,
(picturing the old cars was always a sure stimulus in
    the past,)
and I would be sitting as straight as I could in the back
so I could reach the windows to see outside
while he got behind the wheel
to take me up the hill to the nice fish place
where, in my mother's absence,
(she had stayed behind for some reason or another,)
he would let me use as much ketchup as I wanted
on the french fries
because that was one of the ways he spoiled me.
But, for the third time, I had no luck,
which, as I write this, seems so wrong,
because I just wanted to talk to him
and see how he was doing.
But, as the writing of poems has its way
of sometimes resembling love,
which, in this case at least,
is also exactly the way life operates—
at the beginning, in the middle,
and sometimes even toward the end of love and of life,
you still might not know how it's going to turn out—
I see just at this moment I had this need to stay in touch

because there were two questions I had to ask,

maybe during the commercials between the wrestling matches:

Is there some form of happiness after you die?

and Was the Talmud right when it said dying

is as simple and painless as pulling a hair out of

a cup of milk?

—DANNY SIEGEL, *A HEARING HEART*

What Happens after We Die?

No one knows. No one has ever been beyond the grave and come back to tell about it. All we know is what we think about, dream of, and hope for when we move on to the Great Unknown.

Every generation has speculated on what it will be like on the Other Side. Common opinion holds that Judaism downplays afterlife in favor of an emphasis on the way one leads a life in this world. Yet, Jewish sources do reveal an ongoing fascination with the world to come.

In a superb article entitled "Afterlife," Rabbi Jack Riemer outlines the Jewish view of what happens after we die by looking at history, law, and legend. The Bible records a simple, yet profound instruction to the Jewish people vis-à-vis death and its aftermath, "In the ways of the land of Egypt, you shall not go" (Leviticus 18:3). Riemer recalls the elaborate exhibit of magnificent objects that adorned the burial place of the nineteen-year-old King Tut, an opulence created only for the grave. The pyramids were mausoleums, and the treasures were bribes into the world to come. The Israelites, who perhaps built those pyramids, totally rejected the cult of death central to Egyptian religion. The Bible speaks only of *this* life, not of afterlife. As Riemer puts it, "The silence of the Torah is no accident; it is an eloquent response to Egypt." In a fundamental sense, many of the cautions against elaborate funerals, coffins, and signs of ostentatiousness in mourning can be traced to the simple instruction not to go "in the ways of the land of Egypt."

A law of mourning that, on the surface, appears quite strange informs the rabbinic view of life after death. The law is this: If a person is in the *shiva* mourning period and a festival is to be celebrated, the mourning must stop. The *halakhic* principle underlying this law is, "A positive commandment which is addressed to the entire community, such as the commandment to rejoice on a festival, has priority over a positive commandment which is addressed to an individual, such as mourning."

Riemer understands this explanation as evidence that Judaism is not an I–Thou religion; rather, it is a We–Thou religion. "We come before God, and we understand ourselves and our identity, not only, and not even primarily, as individuals, but as members of a people, an eternal people, a covenanted people … What the law seems to be saying is that although we as individuals are all destined to die, we have the power to make ourselves part of something that will not die. We have the power, and with it, the obligation, to make ourselves a part of the destiny of the Jewish people, and then in its life we too shall have life and continuity and fulfillment." This interpretation sees afterlife not in heaven, and not in resurrection, but in the life of the Jewish people here on earth.

Throughout the ages, Jewish thinkers have speculated on the question of what happens after we die. The Bible has no clear idea of heaven and certainly not of its opposite, hell. It does talk about a place called *sheol*, a kind of murky underground. However, it is not clear that those who go "down" there are punished, as happens in most other conceptions of hell. Some believed the Valley of Gehinnom, a place near Jerusalem where heathens sacrificed children, was the earthly embodiment of a place of punishment for the dead.

Rabbinic Judaism included belief in a concept of resurrection, both of body and soul. The rabbis called the world we live in *ha-olam ha-zeh*, "this world," and the hereafter *ha-olam ha-bah*, "the world to come." The notion of the *mashiaḥ*—the anointed one, a descendant of David who would bring the messianic times—developed throughout rabbinic literature. A Day of Judgment would await all who died, and on it God would decide who would earn a portion in the world-to-come. Much of the High Holy Day liturgy centers on this idea of ultimate judgment and those things that can avert an evil decree—namely, *t'shuvah* (repentance), *tefilla* (prayer), and *tzedakah* (righteousness).

In modern times, the idea of immortality has been expanded to include concepts of living beyond one's physical existence on earth. A popular notion is that while the body decomposes upon death, the soul remains immortal. The great medieval philosopher Maimonides seems to emphasize the immortality of the soul or intellect over the notion of bodily resurrection. The idea of reincarnation also has its proponents within Jewish historical thought, primarily among those of the mystical bent. Most modern non-Orthodox thinkers have argued that it is our spirit, our intellect, our soul that survives the body's decay.

There are other ways to interpret immortality. Three modern views, informed by the Jewish predisposition to practice and deeds over dogma and creed, are these:

1. **We live on through our descendants.** The idea that we are a link in the chain of human experience gives our lives meaning after death. Specifically, our children and grandchildren and those that come after them are direct descendants of our lives. Some will carry on our names, remind others of how we looked and our personalities, and tell the stories of our lives from generation to generation.

2. **We live on through our deeds.** Our achievements, our contributions, our work can be our legacy. We think of famous people—artists, musicians, politicians, authors, philosophers—whose thinking and acts have influenced us in our generation and whose works will likely continue to be studied in decades to come. But we need not be famous for each of us, in our own way, to contribute to the lives around us, to influence them through our thoughts, our actions, our decisions, our beliefs. This, too, is part of our immortality.

3. **We live on through our common destiny with the Jewish people.** Every Jew is thought of as a partner with God in the creation of the world. A famous statement from our literature says: Keep two pieces of paper with you at all times. On one inscribe, "I am nothing but dust and to dust shall I return." On the other inscribe, "For my sake was the world created."

When we have a sense of belonging to an historical people, when we believe ourselves to be links in the chain of tradition dating back thousands of years, we understand that our time on earth is a fulfillment of the immortality of the Jewish people. Whatever may happen to my body and soul upon my death, the people of Israel live.

As Riemer puts it, Judaism walks a thin line between saying that this is the only life there is and saying that the world-to-come is the only real world. It insists on holding both these views rather than choosing between them. "For to affirm only this life is to end up in despair and disillusionment; this life, taken in its own terms, is too brief and too incomplete. But to affirm only the life to come is to diminish the importance and sacredness of this world. Somehow we must learn to balance both truths ..."

Our friend Maynard Bernstein, *alav ha-shalom*, understood the wisdom of Jewish tradition in valuing both this life and the next. On a plane to Scranton, Pennsylvania, to attend the funeral of his mother, Maynard wrote the following words to his family. His wife, Sylvia, discovered the letter in an envelope marked "Do Not Open Until My Death" among his papers after his untimely death:

May 29, 1971

SORROW FADES—LOVE LINGERS

Death is a transition, not a tragedy—the soul simply moves in its immortal way to a new home, a new life. Our souls are linked; I feel and experience the presence of my parents though I cannot touch them. We cannot touch them because our bodies are finite and souls eternal.

My mother once said, "You will survive my death just as I survived my mother's death."

My father once said, "Prepare yourself for life, not death."

I tell you, we will meet again.

I love you.

Epilogue

A time to mourn. A time to comfort.

We end where we began this journey through the experience of mourning and comforting—by reiterating the fundamental truths Judaism incorporated in its approach to bereavement.

We are not alone.

Can there be any doubt of the intention of the laws and customs of Jewish bereavement? It is simply, profoundly, to accompany the bereaved, to dispel the loneliness, to surround those who are dying and those who grieve for the dead with community.

We will all die.

Yes, as difficult as it is to confront, we will all die. Although we have seen that there are views of an afterlife within Judaism, the overwhelming emphasis is on this life. Death is a part of this life, and how we die is in large measure a reflection of how we live.

We will all mourn.

Judaism understands that we are a community of mourners. At a certain point in our lives, we all become bereaved. Think of the great power and emotion that envelopes a congregation of hundreds, perhaps thousands, at a *Yizkor* service on Yom Kippur. By preparing ourselves for the inevitable bereavements in our lives, we learn to face our own mortality.

We must all comfort the mourners.

We have learned that comforting the mourners is among the most valued of all Jewish imperatives. It is a *mitzvah* in transition, an obligation that is often ignored or mishandled. If this volume has called attention to new strategies and approaches to reinvigorating and transforming the way we comfort the mourners in our midst, then we will have re-empowered our community to engage in this most important task.

May God comfort us all who are among the mourners of Zion and Jerusalem.

Appendices

Estate Instructions

This is a sample of estate instructions left by parents for children:

August 12, 1992

Dear Daniel, Marc, and Debbie.

We have written of our love for you and our wishes for your future in the document entitled "Ethical Will." Now, we want to help you with the difficult task of settling our estate. In the event of our simultaneous deaths, the work of settling the estate will fall upon your combined shoulders. In this notebook is recorded some of the most pertinent information you will need to know. Backup data is on the files referred to throughout this material. The key to the file cabinet is located in the top drawer of John's desk in the library.

Life insurance policies are in the larger gray metal box in the closet. These are owned by the three of you AND ARE NOT PART OF OUR ESTATE. Please be reminded, the John Doe Company Profit Sharing Plan closed September 30, 1989. Jane Doe's and John Doe's holdings have been transferred to separate individual IRA accounts at Paine Webber. Our account executive at Paine Webber is Bob Bach. Bob is not very attentive and will have to be pushed repeatedly to accomplish anything in a timely matter.

The property taxes for the Kenter and Carmelina properties must be paid (post-marked) NO LATER THAN DECEMBER 10TH (1ST INSTALLMENT) AND APRIL 10TH (SECOND INSTALLMENT). The tax bills, which are mailed out in the early part of October, are kept in the flat gray metal box in the closet, prior to payment. Once they are paid, the tax bills are filed under "Taxes" in the main filing cabinet. Note: Sometimes it is advantageous to pay all annual real estate taxes (1st and 2nd installments) by December 31st. Check with our accountant on this.

The combination for the wall safe can be found in the "S" file in the main file cabinet. Stocks (other than those in John's IRA account at Paine Webber) are held by Alex Brown and Sons (601 Figueroa St.,

Suite 3650, L.A. 90017, phone: 213-892-0500). Our broker there is Bob Ready, a young man recommended to us by Jess Bain. Like all stockbrokers, Bob is anxious to have one buy and sell on his recommendation. We do not find him any more gifted or informed than other brokers. Our best advice is to do your own "research." The stock dividends are recorded in the Reference Book. Monthly statements are located in the file "Stocks" in the main filing cabinet.

Municipal bonds are held by Stonway Investments (152 Ventura Boulevard, Sherman Oaks 91403). Don Moodman is our contact person there. Municipal bond interest payments are recorded in the Reference Book. The funds are deposited directly into the Dreyfus Fund Account. Monthly statements are located in the file "Municipal Bonds" in the main filing cabinet.

Our accountant should be able to give you sound advice regarding all financial matters; our attorney will guide you through legal procedures. DO NOT hesitate, however, to question anything you are told or to ask for further explanations until you fully understand all aspects. Many times, additional inquiry will spark more expedient and/or wiser decisions or plans of action.

The original copies of our wills are on file at Hoffman, Sabban, & Brucker (Nina Sabban, 10880 Wilshire Blvd., Suite 1200, L.A. 90024, 213-470-6735). Duplicate copies are in the "Wills" file in the main filing cabinet.

Note: All title in our real estate, bank accounts, stocks, municipal bonds, etc. is held as "Jane Doe and John Doe, Trustees of The Doe Family Trust of November 25, 1980." The only exception to this is the interest-earning checking account at City National Bank which was opened because the IRS recently ruled that gifts cannot be given from a living trust; so we use this vehicle for making cash gifts to the three of you. The estate planning has been done by Nina Sabban. She is extremely astute and thorough and works closely with our accountant. Caution: When working with attorneys, accountants, or any professionals, DO NOT HESITATE TO CHALLENGE ANYONE until you have an answer that seems logical and sensible to you.

Sidney Canton can handle all life insurance matters. House insurance is managed by Milo Firestone of ABC Associates. (See "Insurance" file in main cabinet.)

By way of reference, these are the approximate sales values and existing loan balances on the following properties:

Kenter Residence $ 250,000   ($70,000 loan)

Carmelina Residence $ 125,000   (-0- loan)

Upon our deaths, funds remaining in the IRA accounts are so heavily taxed that at this date we have been advised that such monies should not be bequeathed to the three of you. Instead, the funds will go to a Jane and John Doe Philanthropic Fund and you will have the discretion of deciding to which charity or charities they should be distributed.

In the safety deposit box you will find a card file marked "Daniel, Marc, and Debbie." This contains an inventory of our personal items and how we suggest they be divided among the three of you.

Above all, throughout your lives, care for each other and your grandmother. You can pay your parents no greater tribute than to love and respect each other and maintain close family ties.

Love,

Mom and Dad

Estate Planning Checklist

A good estate planner will need a detailed list of information in order to organize and write a will. Here are some of the major categories:

- **Family data.** Name, address, phone, date and place of birth, name of spouse, date and place of spouse's birth, date and place of marriage, prior marriages (if any), children's dates of birth, children's spouses, grandchildren, parents, brothers and sisters, employer's name and address, Social Security number, veteran's benefits, location of safety deposit box and important papers, prior wills.
- **Annual income.** Salary, other income.
- **Total assets:** Real property, cash, securities, tangible personal property, life insurance, death and retirement benefits, debts, business interests, copyrights, patents and royalties.
- **Other interests.** Beneficial interests in trusts, expected inheritances or gifts, annuities.
- **Total liabilities.** Secured obligations, pending lawsuits or claims, unsecured obligations, other liabilities.
- **Past gifts.** Outright, in trust.
- **Will provisions.** Testamentary gifts, household effects, personal property, residential property, other real property, gifts of money, gifts of specific items, residue, trust provisions, marital deduction, manner of apportioning death taxes, executor and alternates, guardian, trustee, funeral or burial instructions, charitable gifts.
- **Important documents** (to be brought to the estate planner). Deeds, life insurance policies, contracts, last federal income tax returns, trust agreements where you or your spouse are listed as donor or beneficiary.

Glossary

Aliyah. Ascend. The honor of ascending the pulpit and reciting a blessing before and after the reading of the Torah.

Aninut. The time between death and burial, the first phase of mourning.

Ashkenazim. Jews of Eastern European descent.

B'rakha. A blessing.

Daven, davening. Pray, praying.

Eil Malei Rahamim. "God, the merciful ruler." The memorial prayer.

Halakha. Jewish law.

Hashkava. Laying out the dead.

Hesped. A eulogy.

Hevra Kadisha. Holy society. Those who prepare the dead for burial and provide services to the mourners.

Hol Ha-Moed. The intermediate days of the festivals of Passover and Sukkot.

K'riah. The ritual tearing of garments as a sign of bereavement.

Kever avot. "Ancestral graves." Visiting a grave.

Kippah (pl. *kippot*). Head covering.

Kohen. Descendant of Aaron, the priestly tribe.

Ma'ariv. The evening prayer service.

Maimonides. Medieval philosopher, physician, and codifier of Jewish law (1035–1104).

Matzeivah. Gravestone.

Minha. The afternoon prayer service.

Minyan. A quorum of ten Jewish adults, required for a communal prayer service.

Mitzvah. Commandment. An act required by Jewish law. A good deed.

Mourner's Kaddish. A prayer of praise for God, recited by the bereaved.

Onen (m.)/Onennet(f.). From *aninut.* A bereaved person in the period between death and burial.

Passover. The spring festival celebrating freedom from Egyptian slavery.

Pidyon ha-ben. Redemption of the firstborn on the thirty-first day of life.

Po nitman. "Here lies buried."

Rosh Hashanah. The Jewish new year.

Sephardim. Jews of Spanish/North African ancestry.

Se'udat Ha-Havra'ah. (Common usage is *Se'udat Havra'ah.*) Meal of condolence. The meal served to mourners upon returning home from the burial.

Shabbat. The Jewish Sabbath, beginning at sunset Friday night and ending Saturday night.

Shaḥarit. The morning prayer service.

Shalom. Hello, peace, goodbye. An all-purpose Hebrew greeting.

Shavuot. Festival celebrating the giving of the Torah fifty days after Passover.

Shloshim. Thirty. The thirty-day period of mourning for close relatives, beginning on the day of burial.

Shomer. A guard. A person who attends the body of the deceased from the time of death until burial.

Shiva. Seven. The seven-day period of intense mourning beginning on the day of burial.

Shemini Atzeret. "The eighth day of solemn assembly" following Sukkot.

Shulḥan Arukh. The Code of Jewish Law.

Siddur. A prayer book.

Sukkot. The fall festival of Tabernacles celebrating the autumn harvest.

Tahara. Ritual preparation of the body of the deceased for burial.

Takhrikhin. Burial shrouds.

Tallit. Prayer shawl.

Tefilla. Prayer.

Tefillin. Phylacteries. Leather boxes containing verses of the Torah, wrapped on the arm and around the head with leather straps during the morning prayer.

Torah. The Five Books of Moses, the Hebrew Bible.

Tzidduk ha-din. A prayer said at interment.

Tzitzit. The fringes of the *tallit.*

Yahrtzeit. Anniversary of the day of death.

Yizkor. Memorial service held on Yom Kippur, Shemini Atzeret, Passover, and Shavuot.

Yom Kippur. The Day of Atonement.

Selected Bibliography

General Bibliography

Angel, Marc D. *The Orphaned Adult: Confronting the Death of a Parent.* Northvale, N.J.: Jason Aronson, 1997.
Fine book about confronting the death of a parent from a Jewish perspective.

Borg, Susan, and Judith Lasker. *When Pregnancy Fails: Families Coping with Miscarriage, Stillbirth, and Infant Death.* New York: Bantam, 1988.
A helpful guide for dealing with the aftermath of miscarriage and neonatal death.

Brener, Anne. *Mourning & Mitzvah: A Guided Journal for Walking the Mourner's Path Through Grief to Healing.* 2nd ed. Woodstock, Vt.: Jewish Lights Publishing, 2001.
A wonderful journal for those in mourning.

Buckman, Robert. *I Don't Know What to Say: How to Help and Support Someone Who Is Dying.* New York: Vintage Books, 1992.
An excellent book of advice for supporting someone who is dying.

Cardin, Nina Beth. *Tears of Sorrow, Seeds of Hope: A Jewish Spiritual Companion for Infertility and Pregnancy Loss.* 2nd Ed. Woodstock, Vt.: Jewish Lights Publishing, 2007.
Infertility and miscarriage are devastating losses requiring a unique approach to grieving. This is a phenomenal resource for anyone experiencing this kind of loss.

Chance, Sue. *Stronger Than Death: When Suicide Touches Your Life—A Mother's Story.* New York: W. W. Norton, 2004.
A moving account of a parent's reaction to a child's suicide—and more.

Cole, Diane. *After Great Pain: A New Life Emerges.* Houston: Winedale Publishing, 2002.
A sensitive look at healing the pain of loss.

Colgrove, Melba, Harold H. Bloomfield, and Peter McWilliams. *How to Survive the Loss of a Love.* Los Angeles: Prelude Press, 1993.
A grief-recovery manual. An interactive journal-workbook is also available.

Committee on Jewish Law and Standards. Responsa. New York: The Rabbinical Assembly. www.rabbinicalassembly.org/law/teshuvot_public.html.
A review of the findings of the Conservative movement's Law Committee on mourning and funeral practices.

Cutter, William. *The Jewish Mourner's Handbook*. West Orange, N.J.: Behrman House, Inc., 1992.
A fine, brief guide to the basic rituals of Jewish mourning, written with the assistance of a trans-ideological editorial committee.

Elkins, Joshua C. "An Exploration of Alternatives for Educating Jewish Adolescents to Dying, Death and Bereavement." Unpublished Ph.D. dissertation, Teachers College, Columbia University, 1979.
Excellent review of Jewish bereavement with specific suggestions for death education.

Feifel, Herman. *New Meanings of Death*. New York: McGraw-Hill, 1977.
Explorations of the meanings of death by some of the best thinkers in the field.

Fein, Leonard. *Against the Dying of the Light: A Parent's Story of Love, Loss and Hope*. Woodstock, Vt.: Jewish Lights Publishing, 2001.
How one father's grief over his daughter's sudden death offers a philosophy of abundant living.

Friedman, Dayle, ed. *Jewish Pastoral Care: A Practical Handbook from Traditional and Contemporary Sources*. 2nd Ed. Woodstock, Vt.: Jewish Lights Publishing, 2005.
A handbook of comfort for comforters.

Ganzfried, Solomon. *Code of Jewish Law (Kitzur Shulhan Arukh)*. Translated by Hyman E.Goldin. New York: Hebrew Publishing Company, 1991.
The abridged code of Jewish law. See the section on laws of mourning.

Goldman, Ari. *Living a Year of Kaddish: A Memoir*. New York: Schocken, 2003.
A detailed description of what it's like to say Kaddish for a year.

Goodman, Arnold M. *A Plain Pine Box: A Return to Simple Jewish Funerals and Eternal Traditions*. Hoboken, N.J.: KTAV, 2003.
The interesting story of how a rabbi and his congregation took on the tasks of burying their own.

Greenberg, Blu. *How to Run a Traditional Jewish Household*. New York: Fireside, 1985.
An excellent overview by a modern Orthodox feminist rebbetzin.

Greenberg, Sidney. *A Treasury of Comfort*. North Hollywood, Calif.: Wilshire Book Company, 1978.
A collection of poems, essays, and sayings about death and grief.

Grollman, Earl A. *Explaining Death to Children*. Boston: Beacon Press, 1987.
An anthology of writings about children and death from a variety of religious ideologies and academic disciplines.

———. *What Helped Me When My Loved One Died*. Boston: Beacon Press, 1982.
A personal account of dealing with grief.

Harlow, Jules, ed. *The Bond of Life*. New York: The Rabbinical Assembly, 1975.
A Conservative movement prayer book for use in a house of mourning, with a brief guide to bereavement and readings of comfort.

Heilman, Samuel. *When a Jew Dies: The Ethnography of a Bereaved Son*. Berkeley: University of California Press, 2001.
Another informative story of a year of mourning.

Ilse, Sherokee, and Linda Hammer Burns. *Miscarriage: A Shattered Dream*. Minneapolis, Minn.: Wintergreen Press, 1992.
A guide for dealing with miscarriage, written by the founders of "Resolve," a support network.

James, John W., and Frank Cherry. *The Grief Recovery Handbook*. New York: Perennial Currents, 1998.
A step-by-step program for moving beyond loss.

Kay, Alan A. *A Jewish Book of Comfort*. Northvale, N.J.: Jason Aronson, 1997.
A moving personal story of coping with death, plus a superb anthology of readings of comfort.

Kelman, Stuart. *Chesed Shel Emet: Guidelines for Tahara*. Berkeley, Calif.: EKS Publishing, 2003.
A practical and sensitive guide for those who perform the mitzvah of ritual cleansing of the deceased.

Klein, Isaac. *A Guide to Jewish Religious Practice*. New York: The Jewish Theological Seminary of America, 1979.
A code of Jewish law for the Conservative movement. The sections on the laws of mourning are found on pages 269–302.

Kübler-Ross, Elisabeth. *On Death and Dying*. New York: Scribner, 1997.
The book that popularized the idea of stages of death and dying.

Kushner, Harold S. *When Bad Things Happen to Good People*. Landover Hills, Md.: Anchor, 2004.

Lamm, Maurice. *The Jewish Way in Death and Mourning*. New York: Jonathan David Publishers, 2000.
A comprehensive guide to Jewish bereavement written by a modern Orthodox rabbi.

Le Shan, Eda. *Learning to Say Good-bye When a Parent Dies*. New York: Avon Books, 1988.
The stages of grief presented in a written-to-the-mourner fashion by a popular psychologist.

Lightner, Candy, and Nancy Hathaway. *Giving Sorrow Words: How to Cope with Grief and Get On with Your Life*. New York: Warner Books, 1991.

Candid and comprehensive look at grief written by the founder of Mothers Against Drunk Driving.

Maimonides. *Mishneh Torah.*
The laws of mourning are clearly outlined.

Manning, Doug. *Comforting Those Who Grieve: A Guide to Helping Others.* Collingdale, Pa.: Diane Publishing, 1985.
A sensitive guide for comforters who wish to console the bereaved.

———. *Don't Take My Grief Away: What to Do When You Lose a Loved One.* New York: Harper & Row, 1984.
One of the first guidebooks written directly to mourners.

Meszler, Joseph B. *Facing Illness, Finding God: How Judaism Can Help You and Caregivers Cope When Body or Spirit Fails.* Woodstock, Vt.: Jewish Lights Publishing, 2010.
Focuses on spiritual well-being as an essential aspect of physical healing and wholeness.

Mykoff, Moshe. *The Empty Chair: Finding Hope and Joy—Timeless Wisdom from a Hasidic Master, Rebbe Nachman of Breslov.* Woodstock, Vt.: Jewish Lights Publishing, 1996.
A treasury of insights from one of the great Hasidic masters, Rabbi Nachman of Breslov.

———. *The Gentle Weapon: Prayers for Everyday and Not-So-Everyday Moments—Timeless Wisdom from a Hasidic Master, Rebbe Nachman of Breslov.* Woodstock, Vt.: Jewish Lights Publishing, 1999.
More insights from Rabbi Nachman of Breslov.

Olitzky, Kerry. *Grief in Our Seasons: A Mourner's Kaddish Companion.* Woodstock, Vt.: Jewish Lights Publishing, 1998.
Readings of comfort for those in mourning.

———. *Jewish Paths toward Healing and Wholeness: A Personal Guide to Dealing with Suffering.* Woodstock, Vt.: Jewish Lights Publishing, 2000.
Why do the righteous suffer? Words of healing from Jewish tradition.

Peppers, Larry G., and Ronald J. Knapp. *Motherhood and Mourning: Perinatal Death.* New York: Praeger Publishers, 1980.
A psychological exploration of mothers whose children die.

Rabinowicz, Tzvi. *A Guide to Life: Jewish Laws and Customs of Mourning.* Northvale, N.J.: Jason Aronson, 1989.
Well-written narrative from an English Orthodox rabbi detailing major customs of Jewish mourning.

Rabow, Jerome A. *A Guide to Jewish Mourning and Condolence.* Encino, Calif.: Valley Beth Shalom, 1982.
An excellent guide to Jewish mourning written by a pararabbinic for the members of Valley Beth Shalom, 15739 Ventura Boulevard, Encino, CA, 91436.

Rando, Therese A. *Grieving: How to Go on Living When Someone You Love Dies.* Lanham, Md.: Lexington Books, 1995.
One of the best sources on healing grief from one of the leading experts.

Riemer, Jack. "Afterlife." New York: The Rabbinical Assembly of America, 1992.
A monograph reflecting on the Jewish view of life after death.

———. *Jewish Reflections on Death.* New York: Schocken Books, 1987.
Outstanding collection of essays on Jewish bereavement by leading thinkers.

Riemer, Jack and Nathaniel Stampfer. *So That Your Values Live On: Ethical Wills and How to Prepare Them.* Woodstock, Vt.: Jewish Lights Publishing, 1991.
Wonderful collection of ethical wills with a primer on how to write one.

Schulweis, Harold M. *In God's Mirror.* Hoboken, N.J.: KTAV Publishing House, 1990.
In addition to his penetrating essays on American Jewish life, Rabbi Schulweis shares his moving poetry on Kaddish, *Yizkor,* and *yahrtzeit.*

Siegel, Danny. *A Hearing Heart.* Pittsboro, N.C.: The Town House Press, 1992.
Inspirational poems by Danny Siegel, *tzedakah*-maven and poet laureate of the American Jewish community.

Sonsino, Rifat, and Daniel B. Syme. *What Happens after I Die?* New York: URJ Press, 1990.
Jewish views of life after death across the spectrum of ideologies written by two Reform movement educators.

Spiro, Jack D. *A Time to Mourn: Judaism and the Psychology of Bereavement.* New York: Bloch Publishing Company, 1985.
A brilliant analysis of the psychology of Jewish bereavement.

Spitz, Elie Kaplan. *Does the Soul Survive?: A Jewish Journey to Belief in Afterlife, Past Lives, and Living with Purpose.* Woodstock, Vt.: Jewish Lights Publishing, 2001.
A deeply felt study of Judaism's view of afterlife and the experiences of congregants who come to believe in one.

Viorst, Judith. *Necessary Losses.* New York: Free Press, 1998.
A penetrating and moving exploration of the many losses we all endure, including a chapter on love and mourning.

Weintraub, Simkha Y., ed. *Healing of Soul, Healing of Body: Spiritual Leaders Unfold the Strength and Solace in Psalms.* Woodstock, Vt.: Jewish Lights Publishing
Reading the Psalms as a source of comfort.

Weiss, Abner. *Death and Bereavement: A Halakhic Guide.* Brooklyn, N.Y.: Mesorah Publications, 2001.
An encyclopedic volume of Jewish law on death and mourning, compiled by a modern Orthodox rabbi. The *midrashim* for study at a house of mourning are superb.

Weizman, Savine Gross, and Phyllis Kamm. *About Mourning: Support and Guidance for the Bereaved.* Delaware Water Gap, Pa.: Shawnee Press, 1986.
A book of support and guidance for the bereaved.

Wieseltier, Leon. *Kaddish.* New York: Vintage, 2000.
A moving account of a year of saying Kaddish by one of the finest writers of our time.

Wolpe, David J. *The Healer of Shattered Hearts: A Jewish View of God.* New York: Penguin Books, 1991.
An exploration of God's power to heal, beautifully written by a bright young rabbi.

Wolpe, David J. *In Speech and in Silence: The Jewish Quest for God.* New York: Henry Holt, 1992.
An eloquent celebration of the power of speech and silence in Jewish tradition.

Zunin, Leonard M. and Hillary Stanton Zunin. *The Art of Condolence: What to Write, What to Say, What to Do at a Time of Loss.* New York: Perennial, 1992.
Outstanding guide for those seeking to offer condolence.

BOOKS FOR CHILDREN

Death of a Sibling

Sims, Alicia. *Am I Still a Sister?* Albuquerque, N.M.: Big A NM Publishers, 1988.

Death of a Parent

Byars, Betsy. *Good-bye, Chicken Little.* New York: HarperTrophy, 1990.

Krementz, Jill. *How It Feels When a Parent Dies.* Magnolia, Mass.: Peter Smith Publishers, 1993.

Lanton, Sandy. *Daddy's Chair.* Harrington, Wa.: Lanton Haas Press, 2001.

Death of Grandparent

Liss-Levinson, Nechama. *When a Grandparent Dies: A Kid's Own Remembering Workbook for Dealing with Shiva and the Year Beyond.* Woodstock, Vt.: Jewish Lights Publishing, 1995.
A terrific way for kid's to deal with *shiva* and the year beyond.

Pomerantz, Barbara. *Bubbie, Me and Memories*. New York: URJ Press, 1983.

Techner, David, and Judith Hirt-Manheimer. *A Candle for Grandpa: A Guide to the Jewish Funeral for Children and Parents*. New York: URJ Press, 1993.

Zolotow, Charlotte. *My Grandson Lew*. New York: HarperCollins, 2005.

On Dying

Brown, Margaret. *The Dead Bird*. New York: William Morrow, 2005.

Paterson, Katherine. *The Bridge to Terabithia*. New York: HarperTrophy, 1987.

Rofes, Eric, ed. *The Kid's Book about Death and Dying*. New York: Little, Brown, 1985.

Sanford, Doris. *It Must Hurt a Lot: A Child's Book about Death*. Portland, Ore.: Miltnomah Press, 1985.

Smith, Doris B. *The Taste of Blackberries*. New York: HarperTrophy, 1992.

Stein, Sara. *About Dying: An Open Family Book for Parents and Children Together*. New York: Walker, 1984.

Viorst, Judith. *The Tenth Good Thing about Barney*. New York: Aladin, 1987.

About the Federation of Jewish Men's Clubs

The Federation of Jewish Men's Clubs is the male volunteer arm of Conservative/Masorti Judaism.

Designed to "involve Jewish men in Jewish life," the FJMC has been enriching the quality of Jewish life since 1929. Most recent efforts have resulted in *The Ties That Bind,* a dynamic film teaching the mitzvah of tefillin and its programmatic component; The World Wide Wrap; and the Hearing Men's Voices Initiative, which consists of a series of books devoted to men's issues. *Building the Faith: A Book of Inclusion for Dual Faith Families* is one of our most far-reaching publications.

For a complete list of our publications, films, and services visit our webpage at www.fjmc.org.

About American Jewish University
(formerly the University of Judaism)

American Jewish University (formerly the University of Judaism) in Los Angeles is a fully accredited institution of higher Jewish learning that includes a four year undergraduate College of Arts and Sciences, the Ziegler School of Rabbinic Studies, graduate professional schools in Jewish education and business administration, an extensive Department of Continuing Education, as well as a variety of cultural arts programs and academic think tanks. The Whizin Center for the Jewish Future hosts the Whizin Institute for Jewish Family Life, a leading resource for Jewish family education, and Synagogue 3000, a transdenominational institute for the synagogue of the 21st century.

Pastoral Care Resources
LifeLights/™החיים אורות

LifeLights/™ **החיים אורות** are inspirational, informational booklets about challenges to our emotional and spiritual lives and how to deal with them. Offering help for wholeness and healing, each *LifeLight* is written from a uniquely Jewish spiritual perspective by a wise and caring soul—someone who knows the inner territory of grief, doubt, confusion and longing.

In addition to providing wise words to light a difficult path, each *LifeLight* booklet provides suggestions for additional resources for reading. Many list organizations, Jewish and secular, that can provide help, along with information on how to contact them.

Categories/Sample Topics:

Health & Healing
Caring for Yourself/When Someone Is Ill
Facing Cancer as a Family
Recognizing a Loved One's Addiction, and Providing Help

Loss / Grief / Death & Dying
Coping with the Death of a Spouse
From Death through Shiva: A Guide to Jewish Grieving Practices
Taking the Time You Need to Mourn Your Loss
Talking to Children about Death

Judaism / Living a Jewish Life
Bar and Bat Mitzvah's Meaning: Preparing Spiritually with Your Child
Yearning for God

Family Issues
Grandparenting Interfaith Grandchildren
Talking to Your Children about God

Spiritual Care / Personal Growth
Easing the Burden of Stress
Finding a Way to Forgive
Praying in Hard Times

Now available in hundreds of congregations, health-care facilities, funeral homes, colleges and military installations, these helpful, comforting resources can be uniquely presented in *LifeLights* display racks, available from Jewish Lights. **Each *LifeLight* topic is sold in packs of twelve for $9.95.** General discounts are available for quantity purchases.

Visit us online at **www.jewishlights.com** for a complete list of titles, authors, prices and ordering information.

About Jewish Lights

People of all faiths and backgrounds yearn for books that attract, engage, educate, and spiritually inspire.

Our principal goal is to stimulate thought and help all people learn about who the Jewish People are, where they come from, and what the future can be made to hold. While people of our diverse Jewish heritage are the primary audience, our books speak to people in the Christian world as well and will broaden their understanding of Judaism and the roots of their own faith.

We bring to you authors who are at the forefront of spiritual thought and experience. While each has something different to say, they all say it in a voice that you can hear.

Our books are designed to welcome you and then to engage, stimulate, and inspire. We judge our success not only by whether or not our books are beautiful and commercially successful, but by whether or not they make a difference in your life.

For your information and convenience, at the back of this book we have provided a list of other Jewish Lights books you might find interesting and useful. They cover all the categories of your life:

Bar/Bat Mitzvah	Life Cycle
Bible Study / Midrash	Meditation
Children's Books	Parenting
Congregation Resources	Prayer
Current Events / History	Ritual / Sacred Practice
Ecology/ Environment	Spirituality
Fiction: Mystery, Science Fiction	Theology / Philosophy
Grief / Healing	Travel
Holidays / Holy Days	12-Step
Inspiration	Women's Interest
Kabbalah / Mysticism / Enneagram	